With the Guns
of the B.E.F., 1914

With the Guns
of the B.E.F., 1914

A Personal History & Recollections by an
Officer of the Royal Horse Artillery

The Retreat From Mons

and

The Marne—and After

Arthur Corbett-Smith

LEONAUR

With the Guns of the B.E.F., 1914
A Personal History & Recollections by an Officer of the Royal Horse Artillery
The Retreat From Mons
and
The Marne—and After
by Arthur Corbett-Smith

FIRST EDITION

First published under the titles
The Retreat From Mons
and
The Marne—and After

Leonaur is an imprint
of Oakpast Ltd

ISBN: 978-1-78282-201-1 (hardcover)
ISBN: 978-1-78282-202-8 (softcover)

http://www.leonaur.com

Publisher's Notes

Contents

GENERAL SIR H. SMITH-DORRIEN

The Retreat From Mons

Contents

For who is he, whose chin is but enrich'd
With one appearing hair, that will not follow
These cull'd and choice-drawn cavaliers to France?

General Sir H. L. Smith-Dorrien, G.C.M.G., G.C.B., D.S.O., etc.

Dear General Smith-Dorrien,

When, some few months ago, you honoured me by your acceptance of this dedication I had in mind to make a single volume which should trace the course of the war during the period of your command of the Second Army, the unforgettable days from Mons to Ypres.

Since then I have found that there is one phase of the operations which has gripped the imagination of the public more than any other event of the past two years: the "Retreat from Mons." It is, indeed, almost incredible how little the people know of this, and how splendidly they respond to the telling of the story.

But it seems to me that the story can never be told as it should be. Only those who actually experienced the horror and the splendour of those ten days could hope to tell it, and for them the facts are blurred and distorted by the nightmare through which they passed.

Still, I am rashly making the attempt, and in doing so I try to write of the big, human side of things. For it is the trivial, homely incidents in the daily life of the British soldier, and the stories of noble devotion and chivalry of gallant gentlemen like Francis Grenfell and Bradbury, which fire the imagination. I know that you will understand and appreciate my motives.

For the rest, should the public be kind to this trivial volume I shall hope later to continue the narrative as I had originally intended.

Will you, then, accept my book, not in tribute of a command

which must remain indelibly scored in letters of gold on the page of our country's history so long as Britain endures, but as a memory of the two or three years of peace when I was privileged to work with you and of the year of war when I had the honour of serving, one of that "band of brothers," in your command?

I am.

Very faithfully yours,

A. Corbett-Smith.

The Middle Temple, London.

Author's Acknowledgment

I tender my very grateful thanks to General Sir Horace Smith-Dorrien for his kindness in reading the proof-sheets of the book and for several most valuable items of information.

My thanks are also due to Captain C. T. Atkinson, of the Historical Section, Committee of Imperial Defence, for his courteous help in the task of compiling the Roll of Honour. Also to the Secretary, R.A. Institution, for the loan of material for the same purpose.

I have availed myself to some extent of the researches of Mr. Hilaire Belloc in my estimates in Chapter 5; while my details of the German Army are taken from German sources, *Deutsche Landund Seemacht*, by Rabenau, and other volumes.

To my comrades-in-arms (few, alas! remain), whose deeds and experiences have contributed to the writing of the story, I hold out a hand of greeting. I salute in reverence the immortal souls of the gallant dead.

A. C.-S.

The Roll of Honour of the First Expeditionary Force

General Officer Commanding-in-Chief the British Forces:
Field-Marshal Sir J. D. P. French.
Chief of the General Staff:
Lieutenant-General Sir A. J. Murray.
Adjutant-General:
Major-General Sir C. F. N. Macready.
Quartermaste-General:
Major-General Sir W. R. Robertson.

FIRST ARMY CORPS

General Officer Commanding-in-Chief—Lieutenant-General Sir Douglas Haig,

1ST DIVISION

General Officer Commanding—Major-General S. H. Lomax.

1ST INFANTRY BRIGADE

Brigade Commander—Brigadier-General F. I. Maxse.

1st Batt. Coldstream Guards.	1st Batt. R. Highlanders.
1st Batt. Scots Guards.	2nd Batt. R. Munster Fusiliers.

2ND INFANTRY BRIGADE

Brigade Commander—Brigadier-General E. S. Bulfin.

2nd Batt. R. Sussex Regt.	1st Batt. Northampton Regt.
1st Batt. N. Lancs. Regt.	2nd Batt. K. R. Rifle Corps,

3RD INFANTRY BRIGADE

Brigade Commander—Brigadier-General H. J. S. Landon.

1st Batt. R. W. Surrey Regt.	1st Batt. Gloucester Regt.
1st Batt. S. Wales Borderers.	2nd Batt. Welsh Regt.

Cavalry (attached)
C Squadron 15th Hussars.

ROYAL ENGINEERS

23rd and 26th Field Companies.

ROYAL ARTILLERY

R.F.A. Batteries—113, 114, 115, 116, 117, 118, 46, 51, 54;
(Howitzer) 30, 40, 57.
Heavy Battery R.G.A.—26.
An Ammunition Column and an Ammunition Park.

2ND DIVISION

General Officer Commanding—Major-General C. C. Monro.

4TH INFANTRY BRIGADE

Brigade-Commander—Brigadier-General R. Scott-Kerr.
2nd Batt. Grenadier Guards.   3rd Batt. Coldstream Guards,
2nd Batt. Coldstream Guards. 1st Batt. Irish Guards.

5TH INFANTRY BRIGADE

Brigade Commander—Brigadier-General R. C. B. Haking.
2nd Batt. Worcester Regt.   2nd Batt. Highland L.I.
2nd Batt. Oxford and Bucks   2nd Batt. Connaught Rangers.
    L.I.

6TH INFANTRY BRIGADE

Brigade Commander—Brigadier-General R. H. Davies.
1st Batt. Liverpool Regt.   1st Batt. R. Berks Regt.
2nd Batt. S. Staffs. Regt.   1st Batt. K. R. Rifle Corps.
Cavalry (attached)
B Squadron 15th Hussars.
Royal Engineers
5th and 11th Field Companies.
Royal Artillery
R.F.A. Batteries—22, 50, 70, 15, 48, 71, 9, 16, 17;
(Howitzer) 47, 56, 60.
Heavy Battery R.G.A.—35.
An Ammunition Column and an Ammunition Park.

★★★★★★

CAVALRY

A Division (Four Brigades)
General Officer Commanding—Maj.-Gen. E. H. H. Allenby.

1st Brigade

Brigade Commander—Brigadier-General C. J. Briggs.

2nd Dragoon Guards.   5th Dragoon Guards.

11th Hussars.

2nd Brigade

Brigade Commander—Brigadier-General H. de B. De Lisle,

4th Dragoon Guards.   9th Lancers.

18th Hussars.

3rd Brigade

Brigade Commander—Brigadier-General H. de la Poer Gough.

4th Hussars.   5th Lancers.

16th Lancers.

4th Brigade

Brigade Commander—Brigadier-General Hon. C. E. Bingham.

Household Cavalry (composite regiment).

6th Dragoon Guards.   3rd Hussars.

And—

5th Brigade

Brigade Commander—Brigadier-General Sir P. W. Chetwode.

12th Lancers.   20th Hussars.

2nd Dragoons.

Royal Horse Artillery

Batteries "D," "E," "I," "J," "L."

Second Army Corps

General Officer Commanding-in-Chief—General Sir H. L. Smith-Dorrien.

3rd Division

General Officer Commanding—Maj.-Gen. H. I. W. Hamilton.

7th Infantry Brigade

Brigade Commander—Brig.-General F. W. N. McCrachen.

3rd Batt. Worcester Regt.   1st Batt. Wilts Regt.

2nd Batt. S. Lancs. Regt.   2nd Batt. R. Irish Rifles.

8th Infantry Brigade

Brigade Commander—Brigadier-General B. J. C. Doran.

2nd Batt. R. Scots.   4th Batt. Middlesex Regt.

2nd Batt. R. Irish Regt.   1st Batt. Gordon Highlanders.

9TH INFANTRY BRIGADE

Brigade Commander—Brigadier-General F. C. Shaw.

1st Batt. Northumberland Fusiliers.

1st Batt. Lincolnshire Regt.

1st Batt. R. Scots Fusiliers.

4th Batt. R. Fusiliers.

Cavalry (attached)

A Squadron 15th Hussars.

Royal Engineers

56th and 57th Field Companies.

Royal Artillery

R.F.A. Batteries—107, 108, 109, 6, 23, 49, 29, 41, 45; (Howitzer) 128, 129, 130.

Heavy Battery R.G.A.—48.

An Ammunition Column and an Ammunition Park.

5TH DIVISION

General Officer Commanding—Maj.-Gen. Sir C. Fergusson.

13TH INFANTRY BRIGADE

Brigade Commander—Brigadier-General G. J. Cuthbert.

2nd Batt. K. O. Scottish Borderers.

1st Batt. R. W. Kent Regt.

2nd Batt. Yorks L.I.

2nd Batt. W. Riding Regt.

14TH INFANTRY BRIGADE

Brigade Commander—Brigadier-General S. P. Rolt.

2nd Batt. Suffolk Regt.

1st Batt. Duke of Cornwall's L.I.

1st Batt. East Surrey Regt.

2nd Batt. Manchester Regt.

15TH INFANTRY BRIGADE

Brigade Commander—Brig.-Gen. Count A. E. W. Gleichen.

1st Batt. Norfolk Regt.

1st Batt. Cheshire Regt.

1st Batt. Bedford Regt.

1st Batt. Dorset Regt.

Cavalry (attached)

A Squadron 19th Hussars.

Royal Engineers

17th and 59th Field Companies.

Royal Artillery

R.F.A. Batteries—11, 52, 80, 119, 120, 121, 122, 123, 124; (Howitzer) 37, 61, 65.

Heavy Battery R.G.A.—108.

An Ammunition Column and an Ammunition Park.

19th Infantry Brigade

Brigade Commander—Major-General L. G. Drummond.
2nd Batt. R. Welsh Fusiliers. 1st Batt. Middlesex Regt.
1st Batt. Scottish Rifles. 2nd Batt. Argyll and Sutherland
Highlanders.

★★★★★★

Royal Flying Corps

Aeroplane Squadrons Nos. 2, 3, 4 and 5.

Army Service Corps

Horsed and Mechanical Transport.

Royal Army Medical Corps

★★★★★★

There came into line at Le Cateau on August 25th the—

4th Division

General Officer Commanding—Major-General T. D. O. Snow.

10th Infantry Brigade

Brigade Commander—Brigadier-General J. A. L. Haldane.
1st Batt. R. Warwickshire Regt. 1st Batt. R. Irish Fusiliers.
2nd Batt. Seaforth Highlanders. 2nd Batt. R. Dublin Fusiliers.

11th Infantry Brigade

Brigade Commander—Brig.-General A. G. Hunter-Weston.
1st Batt. Somersetshire L.I. 1st Batt. Hampshire Regt.
1st Batt. E. Lanes. Regt. 1st Batt. Rifle Brigade.

12th Infantry Brigade

Brigade Commander—Brigadier-General H. F. M. Wilson.
1st Batt. R. Lanes. Regt. 2nd Batt. R. Inniskilling
Fusiliers.
2nd Batt. Lancashire Fusiliers. 2nd Batt. Essex Regt.
Cavalry (attached)
B Squadron 19th Hussars.
Royal Engineers
7th and 9th Field Companies.
Royal Artillery
R.F.A. Batteries— 39, 68, 88 (xiv. Brigade); 125, 126, 127 (xxix.
Brigade); 27, 134, 135 (xxxii. Brigade); 31, 35, 55 (xxxvii. Brigade).
Heavy Battery R.G.A.—31.

★★★★★★

Lines of Communication and Army Troops
1st Batt. Devonshire Regt.   1st Batt. Cameron Highlanders.

CHAPTER 1

Mobilisation

Now all the youth of England are on fire.
And silken dalliance in the wardrobe lies;
Now thrive the armourers, and honour's thought
Reigns solely in the breast of every man.

August 5th, 1914! "Who would have dreamed of such a thing!" exclaimed the big majority. "So it has come at last," said the small minority.

Broadly speaking, there you have the country's opinion during those now dimly remembered days which followed immediately upon Germany's throwing down of the gauntlet.

Officers and men of our once-upon-a-time professional Army did not bother very much about it either way. War was their job. Active service was to be welcomed as a picnic change from the monotony of soldiering in England. Also, to the man keen on his profession (and since the Boer War such men have been steadily increasing in numbers) it meant the chance of promotion and of showing what he was made of.

A war, even long foreseen, must inevitably come as a surprise when it does actually break out, and this one was no exception. During the last week of that July there were very, very few in Aldershot who felt certain that the hour was at last striking.

But Aldershot was ready for it. For many a long year past Aldershot had existed for the army. Latterly it had been the forge where Britain's little striking force, the spear-head of her armies, had been welded, sharpened and tested, made ready for instant launching. So, with the fleet, were we prepared to fulfil our pact with France; or, if the summons came, to stand by Belgium.

Aldershot existed for war, and the comings and goings of troops passed almost unnoticed. True, it now became increasingly difficult to find rooms in the town, and the local outfitters promptly set to work to reap a golden harvest from the fantastic prices which they put upon war gear of all kinds, but that was all—at least to the eye of a casual observer.

There was Fritz, the doyen of Aldershot hairdressers. I wonder how much he learned in those days of the movements of units. Fritz had been an institution in the camps when present-day G.O.C.'s, grizzled and weather-beaten, had, as junior subalterns, sought his advice upon the training of incipient moustaches. Fritz remembered them all, could instantly reel off details of their careers, their regiments or stations, from the time they had left Aldershot until they had returned in senior commands. All duly pigeonholed in Berlin together with seemingly trivial incidents in their private lives.

Later on, sometime at the Aisne, rumour came round that Herr Fritz had been up to mischief of a more serious nature and that he had been duly lodged in prison, or shot, or something equally suitable.

Those were happy if very strenuous days at Aldershot that week or so before the embarkation. Men talked very little about the future, everyone was really too busy. Thoughts naturally flew back to the South African War when they did talk.

"Nobody was particularly keen on that," was the generally expressed opinion; "nobody wanted to kill the Boers; too one-sided. This—oh! this is the real thing. We've got our work cut out."

The very day after the mobilisation the Officers' Mess showed signs of packing up. It reminded one so much of the third act in *The Second in Command*. Two notices in the hall brought things home:—

"Officers may wear Service dress or blue undress jackets in Mess."

"Officers are particularly requested to pay their mess bills before leaving."

Packing-cases and parcels began to drift in and lie about: dozens of telegrams passed in and out: a smaller variety of dishes appeared at luncheon and dinner: the regimental band came and played to us every night (the cheerier spirits all took a hand at conducting, especially rag-time).

Everybody had his job, and nobody knew what anyone else was doing. Right at the beginning we experienced a curious feeling of secrecy. You would see an officer at lunch and miss him at dinner.

"Oh yes! I believe he has gone this afternoon," someone remarks.

"When are you off?" Colonel X. would say to an officer in a moment of forgetfulness, hastily adding, "No, I don't want to know—but, mind you pay your mess bill before you go."

This secrecy of movement was certainly the most striking feature of those early days: that, and the splendid organisation. We have got accustomed to it since, but at the time, and to men used to the happy-go-lucky methods of this dear, lovable, muddle-headed old country of ours, that organisation struck one as amazing.

On August 5th every C.O. was handed a file of documents. In these were given the most precise directions as to times, places and dates when his unit was to leave Aldershot. For instance:

Train No. 463Y will arrive at siding B at 12.35 a.m., August 10th.
You will complete loading by 3.40 a.m.
This train will leave siding C at 9.45 a.m., August 10th.
You will march on to the platform at 9.30 a.m. and complete your entraining by 9.40.

And I believe it is a fact that every train left five minutes ahead of its scheduled time. The London and South Western Railway was given sixty hours in which to send to Southampton 350 troop-trains. They did it in forty-five hours. "Some" hustle! The astonishing efficiency of it all, and the admirable cooperation between military and civil authorities.

I very much doubt if there were more than two officers of the staff at Aldershot H.Q. who knew details of the intended movements. Fritz must have been annoyed. C.O.'s, and other individual officers, who knew when their own unit was timed for departure, entered splendidly into the spirit of the game and loyally kept the information to themselves; would not even tell their people, nor their best girls.

One day the king came down. The visit was as secret as everything else. Each unit received about a quarter of an hour's warning of His Majesty's approach, and the men turned out of their tents or broke off their work to line up by the road. A few words of "goodbye, and good luck" to the men, a warm hand-clasp to the officers, three cheers, and the royal car slipped forward to the next unit. One could hear the ripple of cheering flow round the camps as His Majesty passed.

By the way, it is a little curious how, from the very beginning, there have been just three words used by everyone in bidding "goodbye." "Goodbye, and good luck." A kind of spontaneous, universal formula.

Officers used it, the men, mothers, wives and sweethearts.

> *Goodbye, and good luck" to our sailors*
> *(It's a big debt we owe you today),*
> *"Goodbye, and good luck "to our soldiers*
> *(Some day we shall hope to repay).*
> *Though anxious the hearts left behind you,*
> *And a tear from the eye seems to fall,*
> *Yet— "goodbye"—God be with you, "good luck" attend you,*
> *"Goodbye, and good luck to you all"—*

—as the refrain of a popular song had it later.

Impressions of those few hurried days are blurred. In a sense one had been through it all many times before. It differed but little from moving station or preparing for manoeuvres. And yet there was something of the glamour of an unknown future before one: an instinctive feeling that this was the end of soldiering as we had known it. Not that anyone dreamed of the war lasting beyond Christmas; there are no pessimists in the Army. We were all at school breaking up for the holidays, and I think that just about sums up the situation as we saw it at Aldershot. The unknown future was more on the lines of "Shall we get any skating?" "Will there be some good shows at the theatres?" "What sort of fun will the Pytchley give us?" "Shall I be able to get in the Hunt Ball?"

And so one has little enough to say about the days of mobilisation and packing up. Besides, quite enough has already been written to satisfy an interested public. One little adventure, however, seems worth recording. It befell a certain Gunner captain who was detailed to conduct a draft of men from one unit to another. The yarn has the merit of being true in every particular. It may form a small chapter to itself.

A TOURING COMPANY

"Putting two and two together," said the A.S.C. major, "I imagine that you're to take this draft on to Portsmouth and hand over to the O.C. of the company down there."

Why a gunner captain should have to conduct a draft of field gunners to a place like Portsmouth and hand them over to the tender mercies of an A.S.C. company commander, I couldn't imagine. Nor indeed why a gunner should take his instructions from an A.S.C. major at all. But the divisional C.R.A. had sent me up to him with the remark, "It looks as though you ought to report there," and that was all about it.

Mobilisation is responsible for a good many queer happenings, and here at Aldershot on the third day of it most men were rather at sea.

Even in those few hours one had learned not to ask questions. There was no objection to the asking, but the answer was usually a vacant, far-away look over the shoulder and "Eenteenth Brigade Office? Oh, it's over there"; and a wave of the arm would comprehensively include Farnborough, Deepcut and the Town Station.

And that was how the trouble began. If only the A.S.C. major had exercised a little imagination and made five out of his addition sum: if only he had read his own instructions a little more carefully (although we didn't know that till afterwards), a draft of tired gunners would not have spent the next week trailing about the South of England looking for an A.S.C. company which didn't want them, and their officer would not have received a black mark which nearly damned his future chances at the very outset. But that by the way.

"The men had their breakfast at three this morning," and the cheery little subaltern, who had brought the draft down from Newcastle, saluted and discreetly made himself still smaller by vanishing hastily round the nearest corner.

I took my railway warrant and went out to have a look at the draft.

A fresh-looking lot they were; young, most of them, averaging about twenty-three years old; special reservists the senior sergeant told me. The few old hands, who sadly needed a shave and a wash, showed how young the rest of them were. I didn't take much stock of them, then. One doesn't when it's just a conducting job of a few hours, handing over, and back to Headquarters right away.

The men stood to attention, picked up their kits, and, with a "Fours left," we were off to the station down the shimmering, dancing, sandy roads of the Aldershot camps. The A.S.C. major returned to his ledgers and more arithmetic, and the cheery subaltern reclined at lordly ease in a Gunner Mess armchair, with a tinkling glass of gin and ginger beer at his elbow, and discussed the striking results of the previous day's battle in the North Sea—which had not taken place.

The station-master, who didn't look as worried as he felt, touched his cap.

"A local to ——, then change and go on to Reigate" (was it Reigate? I forget now, one visited so many out-of-the-way places), "and from there you'll probably get a through train to Portsmouth. If there

27

isn't room in the train you can always turn people out."

Visions of burly, homespun-clad farmers and comfortable market-women being turned out, protesting, by a mere gunner captain danced through my brain. Actions for assault and battery, damages, bail, prison.

"How an if they will not turn out?" said I.

And then I realised. This was war, red war; and Great Britain was mobilising. The needs of the State were paramount.

"You shall bid them turn out in the prince's name," and, unlike Dogberry, shall see that you are obeyed.

And I made myself two inches taller because after all a gunner captain was somebody in the world now. And people looked with a new interest at the lads in khaki and began to realise, perhaps for the first time, that they would have to count on the British Army even though it were "such a little one."

To do the good folk justice there was never a word of protest at the idea of having to turn out. And we had to invite them to do so a good many times before the company finished its tour of the Southern ports. Really it might have been a railway in Germany from the way the civilians gave road to the uniform. This change of attitude was certainly a vivid contrast to the days—last week was it?—when a man in His Majesty's uniform was looked at askance in crowded street and bar.

At Reigate, where we had to wait an hour, a bombardier, one of the old hands, begged leave to visit a certain hotel outside the station to buy some bread and cheese.

He was a man who hardly gave the appearance of being bread-and-cheese hungry, if you quite take my meaning, and the glassy stare with which this ancient tried to fix me augured ill for discipline if there were many others in the draft like him. Permission was refused. It was a trivial point gained but it had its consequences.

Portsmouth was reached in some five hours; and twenty minutes' march brought us to the A.S.C. barracks where a hot dinner would cheer us all; for I had remembered to send a telegram *en route* to tell them to expect us.

We were received with cordiality by a decrepit old store-keeper, and the stables' cat. Otherwise the barracks looked as though an army had lately sacked the place from floor to basement.

The men looked glum, and there was more than a hint of a move to a near-by hotel for "bread and cheese." Well, they were only young reservists and discipline was an almost unknown quantity.

But dinner had to materialise somehow. So, demanding the keys of the castle from the unwilling seneschal, the senior sergeant, the bombardier, the stables' cat and myself started on a tour of inspection.

Good! The kitchen contained a sack of flour and most of a sheep. Apparently the sheep was intended to last the decrepit servitor and his struggling family for the rest of the week. But we paid no heed to tearful entreaties and ruthlessly tore the meat away from their very mouths.

"This is war," said I.

Soon dinner was well on the way, blankets were found for the men, and off I went to report to Headquarters.

H.Q. *"received me most politely,"* as Harry Fragson used to sing, and didn't think they wanted me nor my company for any performance in Portsmouth.

"Come back tomorrow morning," said H.Q., "and we'll tell you."

The next day. "Oh, yes!" said H.Q., "you're field gunners, you're evidently sent here for Hilsea (two miles out): you'd better move on at once."

"Parade with kits in half an hour," I ordered.

Merrily we marched forth from the castle gates. Were we not wanted at Hilsea?

A cyclist orderly threw himself, panting, from his machine.

"H.Q.'s compliments and will you please report there at once."

"Halt! Fours about! Quick march!"

H.Q. again received me most politely.

"No, you're not to go to Hilsea. You've evidently got to join the Eenty-eenth A.S.C. Company which has gone on to Bristol. You'll just catch the 5.0 train if you're sharp."

"We're to go to Bristol," said I to the senior sergeant, "and you've got to get a move on or we'll miss the train."

"I've heard tell of Bristol," he ruminated; "nice place, so my wife's cousin's husband used to say. He did tell as how—"

But I cut the soliloquy short and got the draft out of the castle again.

A few minutes later peaceable citizens fled into doorways and up courts, electric cars pulled up short with a grinding of brakes, policemen held up traffic. The R.F.A. draft approached at a steady double.

"Where's the fire?" yelled some.

"The Germans have captured the 'Hampshire Arms,'" said others.

"It's for a cinema show," screamed a ragged urchin. Everyone gave us kindly encouragement, and girls waved merrily as we flew past. The bombardier, who was on the pavement side, threw an arm gallantly round the waist of a stout matron of some forty summers and dragged her, not unwillingly, half a dozen yards before he could get home with a kiss on the cheek.

But we caught that train with five minutes to spare. The men were now beginning to see the joke. As yet it had escaped me. Of course it was not the first time I had seen "Tommy "at his cheeriest under misadventures; but this cheeriness now struck me vividly for the first time. Today it is world-famous.

They certainly made that journey a lively one. Six hours in a slow train across country—it is apt to become somewhat tedious. I tried to look like the man who owns a dog which persists in nibbling the trousers of total strangers—to pretend they (the men, not the trousers) didn't belong to me. It was no good. They might have been Lancashire lads off to Blackpool for the "wakes."

So with imitations of Harry Tate, George Robey and other well-known favourites of the music-halls, the railway officials at the various stations being made the butt of the jokes; with a weird medley of harmony and melody, from "Hallo, hallo, who's your lady friend?" to "Sun of my Soul," the journey passed happily enough until the first of the Bristol stations was reached about 11.45 p.m.

As no one knew where the A.S.C. barracks were I got through on the telephone to H.Q.

"This is Captain Estcourt, R.F.A., speaking. I've got—"

The orderly evidently went to fetch someone else. It turned out to be an adjutant, who listened to me most politely.

"No, we've got no A.S.C. here. I don't think there are any in Bristol. But you might ring up —— Barracks and see." *Prrr.*

"Hallo! Is that —— Barracks? I'm Captain ——"

The orderly went to fetch someone. This time, after a long wait, it was evidently an irascible senior officer.

"No. No A.S.C. here. Try Avonmouth." *Prrr.*

This looked like bedding down in the station waiting-rooms. Still we would try Avonmouth.

Avonmouth Headquarters received me over the telephone most politely, considering the time of night.

"No, we've got no A.S.C. here; but you might ring up the Embarkation Office." *Prrr.*

"Hallo! Embarkation Office? I'm ——, etc."

The Embarkation Office was not quite so polite in its reception. It sounded very worried.

"No. We've got no A.S.C. here. You can come along down if you like in case the company should turn up."

Luckily the last train had not gone. When it drew up in the station the men greeted it as a long-lost friend. To the strains of "All aboard for Dixie" they clambered in, more cheery than ever.

At Avonmouth we came out into a wilderness of mighty sheds. The night breeze from the Bristol Channel carried with it the pungent, cleanly smell of tarred rope.

"This is Avonmouth," said I to the senior sergeant, "and we can't go any farther unless a ship is waiting for us. I'm going to see where we can bed down."

The Embarkation Office had had time to recover from its worries and received me very politely.

Eventually we got the men into one of the sheds where hundreds of sacks of oats lay about. In ten minutes they had made themselves amazingly comfortable and peace reigned.

But I'm glad we went to Avonmouth. It gave me my first real glimpse of the astonishing organisation under which the Expeditionary Force was to take the field; and also of the methods of supply.

Outside the dock gates, by all the approach roads into the little town, there were streaming in hundreds upon hundreds of great motor lorries, the majority of them built to carry three tons.

From all parts of England and Scotland dozens were arriving every hour. The organisation of it! Here was the third or fourth day from mobilisation and there were a couple of thousand ready for transportation.

You picture a vividly green lorry of a big whisky distillery up North axle to axle with the scarlet of a Brixton firm with its blatant advertisement of somebody's corsets. The cockney driver from a London furnishing house exchanged honeyed words with a colleague from "'twixt Trent and Tweed" in a polite inquiry as to why the hell he couldn't let his tail-board down without using his (the Londoner's) radiator to scrape his boots on.

"Can't you imagine Tommy's comments when he finds a 'Johnny Walker' van bringing up his ammunition in the wilds of Belgium," was the general remark, "but I suppose they'll give them a coat of paint first."

They didn't, as a matter of fact; at least not for several months, so that Tommy was able to indulge his gift of language to the full.

And so nearly two days passed. The men amused themselves by wandering about the docks, wondering at the shipping, and making sarcastic remarks about the lorry drivers who were being taught how to handle a rifle.

Then came a telegram from H.Q., Aldershot.

Return and report here immediately.

"Good," said the senior sergeant to me, "I always did like Aldershot. But we've had quite a pleasant holiday seeing the country."

The draft duly paraded again, and when they learned their next destination their remarks were a joy to listen to.

We caught a 9.0 train in the evening into Bristol. Then we marched across the city, a matter of, say, three miles. It was a Sunday night, the good citizens were abed. But my lads were determined to show that they were by no means downhearted.

The march across was one long pageant of melody. "I'm going home to Dixie" was prime favourite, and splendidly they sang it in harmony. Then some evening hymns, then more rag-time—they were really excellent exponents of that difficult art—then "Onward, Christian Soldiers"; but never a note of "Tipperary." That immortal chorus had not yet "arrived."

The midnight train from Bristol to Reading. A wait of three hours. Finally, Aldershot (the wrong station) at 6.30 a.m. A march of four miles into camp somewhat took the spirit out of the men, breakfastless and carrying heavy kits. But we rallied them at the last post and came in singing "Somewhere the sun is shining," like a choir of Welsh colliers. We certainly looked the part.

"We've been looking for you for a week; where on earth have you been?" was hurled at us as we marched in.

The bombardier started upon a story which would have made that intrepid explorer Captain de Rougemont green with envy. I left him to his astonished audience and went off for a bath and shave before attending my own funeral at H.Q.

It will have been observed that there were varying degrees in the politeness with which successive H.Q.s greeted my touring company. The politeness with which Aldershot Headquarters now greeted me was well below freezing-point.

"I received your telegrams from Portsmouth and various other places," was the chief's opening. "You appear to have been taking your men upon an extended holiday round the southern coast health resorts. May I inquire, without appearing too inquisitive, your authority for this expenditure of public money?"

"Will you allow me to explain, sir?"

"I am waiting for your explanation."

I began. When I had recounted the story of the A.S.C. major's arithmetical problem I saw that I had the Great Man's attention. As soon as I had caught the 5 p.m. train from Portsmouth——

"Sit down, won't you," said the Great Man; "cigarette?"

I took one from his proffered case and lit it carefully.

"If only I can hold him," thought I, "I shall pull through."

I did hold him, and I did pull through.

"I don't know that I can compliment you on your perspicacity," said the Great Man, "but I can see now where the blame lies. I had intended to withdraw your name from the Expeditionary Force, but——"

I got up, mouth open.

"Expeditionary Force?" It can only have been a feeble gasp which the Great Man heard.

"Am I going out with the Force?"

The Great Man smiled and put his hand on my shoulder.

"We'll overlook it this time. Let's see how well you can do your job. And if you send in your claim for travelling expenses, send it to me and I'll countersign it."

I suppose I must have said something by way of thanks. I suppose I must have saluted, and closed the door behind me. I know that I cleared half a dozen or so of the stairs down at a bound and fell over an astonished sentry at the bottom. It must have looked most undignified in a gunner captain, but—I had actually been selected to join the British Expeditionary Force with a command of my own and—

I leaped into the waiting taxicab in a state of delirium.

The driver touched his cap.

"Where to, sir?" said he.

"Where to? Where to? Oh! Brussels; anywhere."

The driver grinned in sympathetic understanding and got on to third speed in as many seconds.

And that is how I very nearly missed the most gorgeous adventure of my life.

Chapter 2

The Sailing of the Force

Follow, follow!
 Grapple your minds to sternage of this navy;
And leave your England as dead midnight still.

For who is he, whose chin is but enrich'd
With one appearing hair, that will not follow
These cull'd and choice-drawn cavaliers to France?

I consider that I have command of the sea when I am able to tell my
Government that they can move an expedition to any point without
fear of interference from an enemy's fleet.—Sir Geoffrey Hornby.

Train No. B46 had slipped unostentatiously into its appointed siding precisely on its scheduled time. For a couple of hours the men
had been working like galley-slaves to get the ammunition on board
in time. The C.O. and two other officers with their coats off were
working as hard as the rest. And it is no joke heaving up and packing
neatly cases of 18-pr. and howitzer shell, especially when you are not
used to it.

Finished at last, and with half an hour to the good. Another four
hours and they will be on the road themselves, the first step into the
unknown.

A couple of hours' sleep, a shave and a bath, a final look round the
battery office, a last hurried breakfast in the mess, and a last handshake
with the colonel.

"You off? Well, goodbye, and good luck to you. We shall meet over
the other side, I expect."

The battery parades. "Battery all present, sir," reports the sergeant-
major. The report runs through until it reaches the C.O. A few minutes to ride round the teams and then:

"Column o' route from the right. Walk—march!" and the battery is off through the early morning quiet of the Aldershot streets, bound for the port of embarkation.

Thus the mounted units, or most of them. Others by train. A few lines will serve as description for all these.

A Railway Transport Officer meets the C.O. on the platform as the men march in.

"Get your men in as quickly as you can, please; we always get off five minutes ahead of time."

"What's our port?" asks the C.O.

"No idea. Push on, please."

The C.O. "pushes on."

"All in," he reports to the R.T.O., and turns for a final shake of the hand.

"Well, goodbye, and good luck" (always that phrase); "wish I was coming with you."

The R.T.O. gives the signal and looks wistfully for a moment after the train before he clambers across the metals to dispatch another dozen or so units from other sidings.

"Where are we embarking?" asks everyone. Not a soul knows. I don't believe the engine-driver himself knew. He just went gaily forward following the points or stopping for signals.

"Through Winchester! Why, it must be Southampton. Wonder what our port will be the other side?"

Detraining and embarkation at Southampton were carried out under the same admirable conditions of efficiency and speed, and with never a single hitch. It seems little enough to read the sentence in cold print, but the more one thinks about it the more wonderful appears the organisation. Had it been the German War Staff directing movements the affair would have seemed no more than an ordinary episode. But with memories of the South African War, and a hundred everyday incidents constantly revealing muddling, red-tape methods, one can find no words in which to express adequately one's admiration for this astonishing volte-face.

One single incident, one of fifty like it, will show to what excellent purpose the Authorities had profited by experience, even in those early days.

An A.S.C. motor transport unit was detailed to embark upon a certain ship. Nearly a day's warning had been given to the O.C. The lorries were driven to the dock-side and were just being got on board.

The embarkation officer, who was standing quietly by, suddenly informed the C.O. that his ship was not that one but another due to sail from another dock some distance away.

The C.O. had barely time in which to get his lorries across, and the ship sailed the moment all was reported clear.

An incident trivial enough, and how unEnglish it seemed at the time. But after the secret landing of the 9th Army Corps at Suvla, and the subsequent evacuation of Gallipoli, it would appear that we have nothing to learn in the art of ruse.

The weather in those early days of August was perfect: the sea so calm that there was no discomfort even with the men and horses packed on board like sardines in a tin. If it was a night crossing, the men bedded down in rows out on the decks just as they had filed on board. The transports were of all kinds, from an Atlantic liner to a coasting tramp.

The ship's officers did more than their best for everybody's comfort, giving up their cabins to the officers, sharing their meals and refusing to accept any payment for food and drinks. If the skipper of a certain ship of the Royal Mail Company, which sailed on the early morning of August 16th from Southampton, chances to see these lines I would tell him how gratefully his kindness is remembered, and how the little mascot, in the shape of a tiny teapot from the steward's pantry, brought the best of luck through ten months' hard service, always made excellent tea whenever called upon, and now occupies a place of honour in my china cabinet. Here's wishing everything of the best to those who carry on the fine traditions of the blue or red ensign!

"Well, where are we bound for?" This to the first officer.

"Don't know a bit," he replies. "The skipper *may* know, but I'm not sure. Anyway he's as close as a barnacle about it."

We steamed across Channel with all lights on. It was another of those astonishing facts which didn't strike one until later. We were off the mouth of the Seine exactly twelve hours after sailing. And all that time we only once sighted anything in the shape of a convoy, and that was a T.B.D. for about twenty minutes a couple of miles to starboard.

At this stage it seems almost invidious to say anything more about the work of the Grand Fleet during that first fortnight. And yet, even now, the public is amazingly ignorant of what the navy has accomplished, or, indeed is still accomplishing. Ignorant, not through indifference, but because the authorities still steadily refuse to take seriously in hand the work of education in war facts and ideas.

How the navy succeeded in sweeping the enemy flag from the North Sea and the Channel in a couple of days, apparently without firing a shot, we cannot pretend to guess. Some day the story will be told. But the result was the most astonishing manifestation of the real meaning of naval supremacy that the world has ever seen, or is ever likely to see. And Germany, by her naval inaction, lost for ever her great chance of the War, and so, in failing to intercept or damage the British Expeditionary Force, failed also to enter Paris and to end the war upon her own terms within the period she had intended. The British Army may have saved Paris, but the British Navy enabled it to do so.

Entering the Seine the skipper revealed the name of our destination, Rouen. Another instance of organisation and forethought on the part of the authorities in using small ships so as to get right up the river and disembark troops and stores well inland.

Again, this has become a matter of everyday routine, but in those days each such new manoeuvre was sufficiently remarkable for admiring comment.

Here the pilot came on board. A typical old son of Normandy he was, grizzled and weather-beaten, clambering aboard with stiff heavy gait.

On to the bridge he climbed: saw our lads clustered thick as bees in the fo'c'sle and lower deck. Up went his cap into the air, tears sprang to his eyes.

"*Vivent les Anglais!*" he shouted, "*vive l'Angleterre! A—ah*" (with an instinct of triumph), "*ça va bien. Ils arrivent.*"

How the lads yelled in answer.

"Cheer-o, moossoo. *Veeve* France!" 'Who's your lady friend?' 'For he's a jolly good fellow,'"—and other pertinent observations.

Then, to my astonishment, they burst into the "*Marseillaise.*" How and where they had learned it I have no idea. But sing it they did, and very well too. They took that little curly bit in the middle, where a B flat comes when you least expect it, just like an old hunter clearing a stiff post-and-rails. And that old chap stood on the bridge and mopped his eyes, and didn't care who saw him do it. The English had really come to stand by his beloved France. *Comme ça va bien!*

That was the first hint we had of the reception which awaited us.

You picture the transport steaming slowly up river between the high, wooded banks. Little houses, such as Peter Pan might have built for Wendy, seem to sway dizzily in the tree-tops. Out on to the verandas, down to the river path run the women and children, and the few old men who remain. Everyone carries a little flag; not the French tricolour, but the British Jack—or rather an excellent substitute.

Dimly one can see the waving hands, faintly across the water echo the treble voices. But we know now what it means, and gallantly our lads respond to this welcome of our future hosts, who, with true French courtesy, have met their guests at the very entrance gates.

Far up the hill-side, close under the ridge, there nestles a tiny cottage. A blot of deep crimson staining the deeper green of the trees makes me take out my binoculars. The good house-wife, with no British flag available, yet determined to do honour to her country's allies, has taken the red tablecloth, has stitched long bands of white across it to form a St. Andrew's Cross, and flung it proudly across the balustrade. What monarch ever had truer-hearted welcome from his own people? Well, the sight brought a lump to the throat of at least one Englishman.

And so slowly we steamed up the historic river. France had indeed flung wide her gates in welcome. Here we found ourselves moving in a small procession of transports. Greetings swung across from one ship to the next, to combine and roar out a British answer to our French friends on shore.

Ah! but it was good to feel that Britain had not failed France, though the obligation were no more than a moral one. It was good to be an Englishman that day; good to feel that Englishmen then in France could now look Frenchmen squarely in the face and say:

"You thought we were going to stand aside, didn't you? Well, you see we are coming in with you and you can bet that means that we intend to see it through."

Yes, one felt proud as never before.

CHAPTER 3

The Landing of the Force

*Shall not thou and I, between Saint Dennis and Saint George, com-
pound a boy, half French, half English, that shall go to Constantinople,
and take the Turk by the beard?*

The dominant note in the reception which the French gave to the
Force on landing was undoubtedly that of *relief*, Happy in showering
little courtesies, surprised and delighted with everything British—all
these, but it was relief which came uppermost in their minds. The
feeling which the old pilot had expressed in his "*comme ça va bien,
maintenant.*"

And as transport after transport slid quietly to her berth alongside
the broad Rouen quays, discharged her freight of men, horses, guns,
stores, lorries, and the countless trappings of a modern army, and then
as quickly and noiselessly vacated the berth for her successor, so increased the wonder and delight of the good Normandy folk.

That *les anglais* should really have arrived was splendid enough, but
that they should also bring with them their own food and cooking
arrangements—"*mais c'est étonnant! et quelle organisation!*"

Everyone spoke in admiring comment about it. And how Rouen
crowded down to the quays or out to the rest camps to watch *les
anglais* cooking their dinners! Army stores those few days were sadly
depleted of tins of jam, biscuits and "grocery ration." How could one
refuse the hungry look in the eye of a motherly matron as she espied
a packet of the famous English tea?

And the children! We learned for the first time how hungry children could be when they saw biscuits and jam.

Make a fuss of the kiddies and you have won the mothers! And if
you have won the mothers and women of France you have conquered

39

"*la belle France*" herself. And *les anglais* conquered France in those few days at the French ports. The happiest of victories, and one which augured well for the future.

Nothing pleased the French more than British courtesy and gentleness to women and children; and their kindness to and care of their horses. British love of personal cleanliness, and the unfailing cheeriness of the men, these have, of course, long since become proverbial. But then it was all new to France, almost to the world, and so one records these things as first impressions.

And the Scotties. Everyone knows how the lads from north of the Tweed made sad havoc among French hearts. Have they not always done so since Frenchmen and Scotsmen first clasped hands in alliance?

If a Scotsman was asked once a day whether he wore anything under his kilt he was asked a hundred times. And truth compels me to add that it was generally the ladies who put the question. What the answer was I never found out. I imagine that our lads were not sorry to hide their blushes in the troop trains which carried them forward to the frontier.

But all these little details have been so admirably recorded by Philip Gibbs in his masterly book, *The Soul of the War*, that there is really not much more to tell. I shall have still a little to add in the next chapter, when it comes to trekking upcountry.

I had some little cause on the first day of landing to regret the exuberance of French hospitality. Half my men, they were mostly Special Reservists, suddenly disappeared into the unknown directly they set foot on shore. And they hadn't a week's pay in their pockets either.

Eventually I got them rounded up and next morning there were twenty-five prisoners, "caps off," for "office." To say they were surprised is to give a very poor indication of their feelings when they found varying degrees of punishment awarded to them.

But this was nothing to the ludicrous expressions of the men when all the remainder were paraded and informed what they had to expect on active service. It ran somewhat as follows:

When a sentry, sleeping upon his post. Punishment—DEATH.
Leaving his C.O. to go in search of plunder. Punishment—DEATH.
Forcing a safeguard.—DEATH.
Quitting his guard without leave.—DEATH.

Disobeying the lawful command of his superior officer.—
DEATH.

And so on, the lightest punishment being about fourteen years'
rigorous imprisonment.

Their faces got longer and longer as the list proceeded, and it was
a very meek detachment who turned to their dinners on the quay-
side. And that was the beginning and end of any trouble with those
good lads until the day when they, or the poor remnant who pulled
through, crowded round to sing "Auld lang syne" and give me a fare-
well cheer. Fine work they did, and always as cheery and lovable as
any unit in the Force.

Disembarkation was carried on with the same admirable efficiency
which had characterised embarkation. A large number of British Staff
officers had, I believe, crossed to France immediately upon mobilisation. There, in collaboration with French colleagues, every possible
arrangement was made for the reception of the Force.

Rest camps were pitched or billets were allotted, branches of the
Army Post Office were established, a field cashier was installed at the
Banque de France and imprests in French notes for the men's pay could
be obtained on demand.

Of course everybody had seized the few hours' holiday on board
ship to write more or less lengthy letters home, hoping, in their in-
nocence, that the ship's officers would post them on returning to England.

Alas! before ever the ship was berthed, an all-powerful bogy
swarmed up the companion way and greedily snatched away the ship's
correspondence. Calling for a brush and a barrel of black fluid, he
gleefully set to work upon the letters and postcards. When he had finished with them (and it took him a good couple of hours on our ship)
they looked like the slips of paper you use in the parlour round-game
where the first player writes a line and leaves the next to continue the
sentence.

We had all given the most vivid description of our adventures, filling page after page. When the precious documents ultimately reached
their destination, our fond parents, or best girls, must have been grati-
fied to find that their four-page letter had dwindled down to:

My dear Father,—
(Four pages of brush and fluid work.)
Well, I think I have told you all the news now. My love to the

Mater and, cheer-oh, we shall soon be home again.

  Your affect, son,

    ————

It was very interesting to compare the way in which French and British temperaments expressed themselves; intensely interesting to note how each so quickly became the complement of the other.

One knew so well the attitude of disdain of anything foreign which invariably characterises the Briton abroad; an unfortunate attitude which has been encouraged, or so it would almost seem, by the invariable courtesy, under the most irritating conditions, of men and women of the Latin races.

Here were some seventy or eighty thousand men thrust headlong into a strange country. Probably at least two-thirds of that number had never been out of England before. Everyone knows the impression which your average Englishman of the middle and lower classes has of French men and French women. Certainly it has not been very complimentary. How would our men now bear themselves?

And if our attitude to the French has for the most part been one of cold disdain and amusement, the French would seem to have regarded us, as a race, with incredulity, tempered by such a degree of irritation as their native courtesy would permit. This, together with an under-current of admiration.

"*Que j'aime la hardiesse anglaise!*" says Voltaire, "*que j'aime les gens qui disent ce qu'ils pensent.*"

During those early August days before the Retreat there was little real opportunity to modify racial opinions. But if British disdain was not yet effaced, the overwhelming reception by the French went far to break it down. Soon it was to be washed clean away in the blood sacrament which united French and English in a closer tie than that of brothers-in-arms.

French methods and customs still amused our men, but the amusement became that light-hearted gaiety, in tackling and surmounting trifling difficulties in a foreign country, which is quite irresistible. Here the British soldier or sailor is always at his very best, and the anecdotes of his adventures in French villages and towns would fill a volume.

Wiseacres who try to invent some universal language should certainly base it upon that of Thomas A. in a strange country. He is equally at home in China, Peru, the wilds of Africa or Spain.

The fact which astonished him more than anything else about the

French language was that all the children spoke it. He could understand grown-ups learning it in time; but how the kiddies were able to talk it with such amazing fluency, that was quite beyond him.

As for the French attitude of mind, I am inclined to think that their incredulity, admiration and irritation were all intensified; the last named, however, being even less in evidence than before.

The attitude of the French women is easier to define. It is literally true to remark that, from highest to lowest in the land, there were no half measures in their welcome. One can say this now because the fact has long since been recognised and openly discussed in France. This, however, is not the place in which to make more than passing reference to a subject which, apart from the purely human aspect, is more a matter for the student of physiology or psychology.

"*Combien de coeurs vous avez ravagé dans un si petit délai que vous avez stationné ici,*" a French girl once remarked, "*et cependant on ne devrait pas refuser aux anglais les baisers qu'ils nous demandent puisqu'ils se donnent pour nous.*"

And the last half of the sentence admirably sums up the French woman's point of view.

This landing of the portion of the Force at Rouen was typical of what happened at Boulogne or Havre. John Buchan,[1] in his first volume of the *History of the War*, has given a most interesting glimpse of incidents at the former port.

In no case did the troops remain at these bases for more than a couple of days. Nobody appeared to have the least idea of what was going on up at the frontiers, but time was obviously of importance.

No one knew where they were bound for; no one appeared to have the slightest presentiment of the tragedy, and the magnificence of the days which were so soon to crowd upon them. Still the cheery, light-hearted, end-of-term spirit. A summer holiday on the Continong! Cheer-oh!

And so they were merry parties of men which boarded the funny French trains; where you had to clamber up the sides of the carriages from platforms which didn't really exist, and where you were packed in like a Cup Tie crowd returning from the Crystal Palace.

How the horses hated those French trucks. Never before had they suffered such indignity. I would not have been a stableman on duty in one of those trucks for many a month's pay.

"*Mais, quelles bêtes!*" said the railway officials. And the porters would

---

1. Also soon to be republished by Leonaur.

run and fetch the stationmaster and gesticulate at the Compagnie's trucks, which had begun to look like bundles of firewood long before the frontier was reached.

"Third return Clapham Junction, please," said the company wag.

"Wotto! Berlin! Not 'arf," shouted the rest. . . .

And off the trains would steam, every compartment labelled "Berlin." It's rather pathetic how history repeats itself. This time the French were silent. They *knew*.

So, forward into the unknown!

CHAPTER 4

Up Country

So be there 'twixt your kingdoms such a spousal.
That never may ill office, or fell jealousy,

Thrust in between the paction of these kingdoms,
To make divorce of their incorporate league:
That English may as French, French Englishmen,
Receive each other!

Patience, still a little patience! The stage is not yet set. The actors have not yet reached the theatre. Very soon now shall you see unfolded the opening scenes of the Great Drama, and hear the first clash of the armies. Soon shall you have your fill of the horror and splendour of modern warfare.

We have seen the Force into the French troop trains, horse, guns and foot. But not all journeyed thus to the frontier. Some of the units, the most mobile, went by road. Units which were intended to take their places in the reserve lines, and especially the A.S.C. motor transport, ammunition or supplies. Let us move forward with one of these and see a little of the France through which so soon the armies will come rolling back.

Out from Rouen and across the lovely Normandy country. You picture the excitement and amusement of the country folk as a great procession of those motor lorries, which we have seen coming into Avonmouth, pants heavily through the towns and villages.

Here is a part of a letter, from an officer in one of those units, which appeared in the *Times* towards the end of August.

It seems to give a very happy picture of the French reception of our men.

I can, of course, tell you nothing of our movements, nor where we are. I can, however, say something of the reception we have met with moving across country. It has been simply wonderful and most affecting. We travel entirely by motor transport (if the censor will allow that), and it has been flowers all the way. One long procession of acclamation. By the wayside and through the villages men, women, and children cheer us on with the greatest enthusiasm, and everyone wants to give us something. Even the babies in arms have been taught to wave their little hands.

They strip their flower gardens, and the cars look like carnival carriages. They pelt us with fruit, cigarettes, chocolate, bread, anything, and everything. It is simply impossible to convey an impression of it all. One village had stretched across the road a big banner, "Honour to the British Army." Always cries of "*Vivent les anglais, vive l'Angleterre,*" etc., and often they would make the sign of hanging, and cutting the throat (the *Kaiser*), pointing forward along the road. This always struck me as so curious.

Yesterday, my own car had to stop in a town for petrol. In a moment there must have been a couple of hundred people round, clamouring. Autograph albums were thrust in front of me; a perfect delirium. A tray of wine and biscuits appeared, and before we started again the car had come to look like a grocery delivery van with a florist's window display in front.

In another town I had to stop for an hour and took the opportunity to do some shopping. I wanted some motor goggles, an eye bath, some boracic, provisions, etc. They would not let me pay for a single thing, and there was lunch and drinks as well.

The farther we go the more enthusiastic is the greeting. What it will be like at the end of the war one cannot attempt to guess. This all sounds like a picnic, but the work is hard and continuous. One eats and sleeps just when one can. There is no division between night and day. But we are all very fit and well, and the men, who have an easy time compared to the officers, look upon it as a huge joke—at present.

My French is, of course, simply invaluable, and each day I can understand and talk better and better. It is extraordinary that I am absolutely the only officer I have come across (except one or two staff men) who can speak it with any fluency. Well, this will surely be the last of war amongst civilised peoples, and the dreams of the idealists will be fulfilled. The French seem to think that it will all be over certainly by Christmas. I wonder?

Thus the men came to see something of French life away from the beaten track of the tourist, and, needless to say, they made friends at every stopping-place.

"*Mais, si polis, ces messieurs anglais,*" everyone remarks. And how could "*ces messieurs*" refuse some little trifles in return for such hospitality? The word "souvenir" soon became a nightmare in their dreams. There was a peculiar bleat in the intonation of the word which was, after a time, positively hateful. But during the first few days the men gave readily enough all sorts of little articles for which they had no immediate use, and others for which they had.

Before a week had elapsed very few had any buttons left. It was a mystery how they kept their trousers up. Regimental badges on caps and shoulder-straps were much appreciated, especially the gunners' letters. It did not take long for the quick-witted French girl to discover that R.F.A. was obviously intended to represent the Triple Entente—*Russie*, France, *Angleterre*.

When these units eventually rolled up at their destination it was found that about half the men had lost not only all their buttons and badges but their caps as well, getting in exchange some horrible provincial product in the shape of a rakish tweed cap. Bits of tape and string held coats and trousers together.

But long ere this Thomas Atkins was fed up with souvenir-hunters, and one recalls a *Punch* picture which showed a weary and wounded soldier sitting by the roadside with what remained of his kit and arms.

"'Souvenir' is it you want?" he remarks in reply to a little urchin who is bleating the hateful word at him. "Here, you can take the —— lot." And he pitches his rifle and kit at the youngster's head.

The officers and men who came up by road must have had a very cheery time in the various towns where they were billeted. The route lay, I believe, by way of Amiens, and so up through St. Quentin and Bohain to Le Cateau.

Hardly was there a hint of war in all that lovely countryside. What war could ever touch those glowing cornfields, those orchards heavy with plum and apple, the stately chateaux or dim cloisters of mediaeval church or convent? As little can we conceive our fragrant villages of Kent or Surrey blasted and devastated by poisonous shells.

Very, very few men were to be seen anywhere; only Government officials and others over military age. Such guards or sentries as were posted were somewhat decrepit-looking Territorials, with arms and accoutrements which looked as if they had done good service in 1870. But they made up for their deficiencies in other respects by an excess of zeal in carrying out imaginary orders.

Their method of challenging, in particular, had the merit of simplicity and, at the same time, involved no undue straining of the vocal powers. It was merely the thrusting of a rifle-barrel into the face or chest of the passer-by. And when there is a very shaky hand on the trigger you don't lose much time in getting out your credentials.

One of these men caused much excitement one evening by holding up and clapping into the guardroom every single individual who attempted to pass him. He was performing sentry duty across a certain main road.

This went on for a couple of hours, and the guardroom was becoming uncomfortably crowded with a very miscellaneous assortment of travellers. In fact, when a particularly plump matron, carrying a basket of particularly evil-smelling cheeses, was incontinently thrust in, to fall heavily across the toes of an already irate railway porter, there was very nearly a riot.

At length a gilded staff officer came along. He too was held up. But this time the sentry met his match. The officer demanded to see the N.C.O. of the guard. Whereupon the sentry, who was really somewhat the worse for drink, fell down upon his knees in the road, and with salty tears coursing down his cheeks piteously besought the officer to allow him to go home and get his supper.

But French Territorials did their "bit" gallantly enough a few days later, away on the British left. Old reservists as they were, they hung on splendidly at Tournai, and, led by de Villaret, fought gallantly against overwhelming numbers until they were surrounded, killed, or captured.

So, on through the golden August sunshine or beneath the heavy harvest moon. Interminable processions of columns, horsed and petrol-driven, threading their way along the endless, poplar-lined roads of France; the white dust churned up and drifting over men and vehicles until they look like Arctic adventurers.

No one knows what is happening in the great "beyond." No one very much cares. "Let's get on and have it over," is the philosophy of the hour. "Expect those Germans are being held up a bit in Belgium; wonder where we shall come in?"

The enemy had marched in triumph through Brussels on August 20th. The British Force was not actually in position until two days later: and Brussels is only 30 odd miles from Mons.

After it was all over; after the tide of war had crashed forward almost to the gates of Paris and then rolled sullenly back, one saw a little of the devastation it had left behind. Here are two pictures.

★★★★★★

August 20th. Can you, too, see that little vicarage hard by the tiny church? (Think, it might have been plucked from a Surrey hamlet.) The cool, veranda-shaded rooms filled with a hundred homely treasures; the tiled kitchen with its winking copper pots and pans. Out through the flagged yard, where pigeons coo in gentle defiance of predatory sparrows, and down to a miniature farmstead. The pretty alleyed garden of roses, hollyhocks and the flowers and sweet herbs of English garden-lovers.

Can you see the old *curé* as he browses over a volume of Renan? He has tended his flock in that village for a quarter of a century. A pretty niece keeps house for him; and her dainty herb-potions and unwearied nursing have saved many a life in the little community. They think of her as of an angel from heaven.

September 7th. A fortnight later! The village street has disappeared beneath the debris of what was once the village. One cowshed is still miraculously intact, and from it creeps a gaunt, haggard old crone. *They* have not touched her. She was too old and infirm to make good fun, even for the rank and file.

She points with shaking finger to the wayside crucifix from which the Christ looks down with infinite patience. He also has been miraculously preserved. He gazes still over His tiny sanctuary, now but two blackened, battered walls. The vicarage has disappeared as though in an earthquake. The incendiary tablets have done their work well. The little garden with its pretty rose trees has been ploughed up, it would seem, by giant shares.

Stay, in one corner, down by the brook, there is planted a rough wooden cross.

The old *curé* had refused to leave his post when the stream of refugees had passed through. They told him of the horror behind them.

He stood firm. Jeannette, too, would stay with her uncle.

They came. The *curé*, they said, must be a spy left behind by the French troops. Besides, he had carrier-pigeons. "What need have we of further witnesses?"

And so they tied him against the stem of his pigeon-cote. He met his death as a gallant gentleman of France.

The girl. Ah, young and tender! Good sport for the plucking! First let her bury the old man. "Rather hard work using a spade when you're not used to it, isn't it."—Done? Good, now get us dinner."

After dinner, a dance—Eastern slave fashion. First, good sport for the officers. "When we have finished throw her to the men."

What need to tell the horrors of it? The village marked the ebb of the tide. The French and British had turned at last. Hurried orders came to retire at dawn. The girl had not been such good sport after all—fainted too easily. A leering, drunken satyr slashes at her naked breasts with his bayonet and Jeannette falls dead over the threshold. The house is fired, the body is pitched on to the pyre.

One village in France? No, one of a hundred where such things were done. And this is almost as nothing beside such as this England of ours has, by God's gracious mercy, been spared. What does England know of this war?

★★★★★★

Now the various units begin to converge and concentrate on the French frontier. "Each unit," says the G.O.C.-in-Chief in his first dispatch, "arrived at its destination in this country well within the scheduled time."

For some days past the French troop trains have been disgorging their living freight at a number of stations and sidings, most of them hastily improvised, within a few miles' radius on a line Valenciennes-Maubeuge.

The columns which came by road halted in various little villages about the town of Le Cateau. You will get the general lie of the land and the principal points of interest from the picture-map.

Now to set the stage.

CHAPTER 5

The Marshalling of the Armies

Now entertain conjecture of a time,
When creeping murmur, and the poring dark,
Fills the wide vessel of the universe.
From camp to camp, through the foul womb of night.
The hum of either army stilly sounds,

> *and from the tents,*
The armourers, accomplishing the knights,
With busy hammers closing rivets up,
Give dreadful note of preparation.

A well-known American, it was probably Roosevelt, remarked *à propos* of the outbreak of the war that Germany's readiness would redound to her eternal dishonour, while Britain's unreadiness would be to her eternal honour.

The term "unready" applies to the nation as a whole. Fortunately for civilisation the British Navy and the little striking Force were, as we have seen, kept trained to an hour. And so it was that, upon a single word, the whole machine moved precisely as the admirable organisation had planned for it.

It must also be remembered that for some years past everybody who had studied international affairs with any intelligence knew precisely how and where Germany would attack; that even in 1908 it was possible to give the approximate date of such attack; and that when the attack came the position of the British Expeditionary Force would be in the post of honour upon the left of the French line in, approximately, the district in which it actually deployed.

Thus, up to a certain point, events fell out as anticipated. But one or two big factors were not foreseen, or, at least, not sufficiently appreciated. These were the amazing speed and mobility with which the German initial attack was destined to develop; the overwhelming numbers of the enemy; and, lastly, the astonishing effect of big gun fire, as instanced at Liége and other fortresses. This lack of foresight came within an ace of losing the war for the Entente Powers.

It was not until Saturday, August 15th, that the gates into Belgium by way of Liége were fully opened for the German armies, although Liége itself had been entered on the 7th.

The immediate effect, apart from the great moral value, of Belgium's heroic and successful resistance of those two or three days was to give to the British Force at least a sporting chance. The Force was late; those three days allowed it to get into position. It needs no great effort to imagine what would otherwise inevitably have happened.

Now let me at this point disclaim any intention of giving details of strategy and tactics, even were I sufficiently competent to do so. So far as I can I shall try to tell the story as simply as possible, omitting everything which may tend to confusion or which may render necessary continuous reference to maps. In a word, I am making this record of facts and impressions for the public, not for the experts. It is the human side and not the military which I would emphasise.

It is, however, necessary at the outset to get a good general idea of numbers, and the disposition of the armies on August 22nd in the particular area, if we wish fully to appreciate the events, and their significance, of the succeeding ten days. For the sake of convenience I will make sub-headings:

THE GERMAN FORCES

The total strength, all ranks, of a German *Army Corps* is, roughly, 45,000; of a *division*, roughly, 17,500. We may take this as a minimum.

Each corps and each division has, respectively, about 160 and 72 field-guns, and 48 and 24 machine-guns. The numbers of the latter arm were materially increased during 1913-14.

The German forces which concentrated on this far Western front, from Namur to about Tournai, consisted of no fewer than 13 Army Corps, *each corps being augmented by an extra division*. These Reserve Divisions were, I believe, combined into separate "Reserve Corps."

The corps were divided up:—

5 under von Kluck (First German Army), attacking British.

4 under von Buelow (Second German Army), attacking 5th French Army.

4 under von Hansen (Third German Army), attacking 4th French Army.

The general lines of advance will be seen in plan A and plan B., (on the next pages.)

Thus, the total German force concentrated on or about this immediate front must have numbered at least 812,500, with, say, 3,016 field-guns and 936 machine-guns.

It is not unreasonable to add to this total the not inconsiderable number of cavalry which operated, more or less independently, on the extreme flanks, and particularly from Tournai down through Amiens towards Le Havre.

THE FRENCH FORCES

The total strength, all ranks, of a French Army Corps is, roughly, 40,000, with, say, 160 field- and 48 machine-guns.

In this area there were present 3 corps under Lanrezac (5th French Army) holding the line Charleroi—Namur, and 3 corps under de Langle de Gary (4th French Army) holding a line west of the River Meuse south-west from Namur.

Away on the left flank of the British was another corps, of Territorials, under d'Amade; and near Maubeuge, in reserve, were two or three cavalry divisions. These last did not, I believe, operate; and the Territorials were also fully occupied in their own area.

Reckoning up, then, we get an approximate total of, say, 240,000 men, 960 field- and 288 machine-guns.

THE BRITISH FORCES

A British Army Corps, of two divisions, contains about 36,145, all ranks, with 152 field- and 48 machine-guns.

A cavalry division contains about 9,270, all ranks, with 24 field- and 24 machine-guns; a cavalry brigade about 2,285, all ranks, 6 field- and 6 machine-guns.

This is not revealing State secrets, because the numbers may be obtained from any military reference books.

Now it was, I believe, originally intended that the Expeditionary Force should be about 120,000 strong, or half the strength of the army with the colours.

The force actually present at Mons on August 22nd consisted, nominally, of two army corps, a cavalry division and a cavalry brigade. But several authorities, including Mr. Hilaire Belloc, assert that one

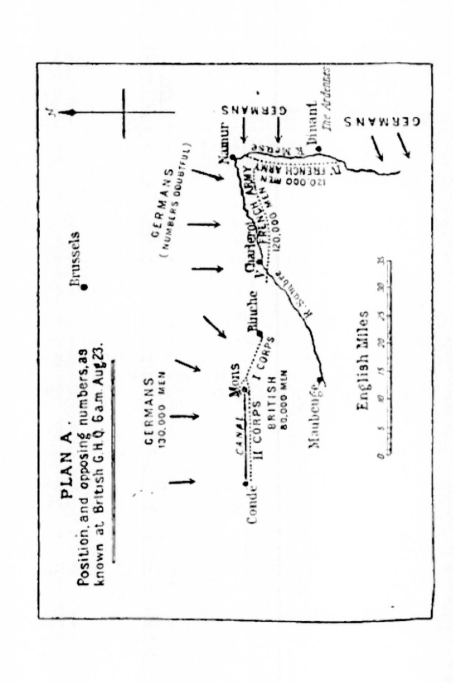

PLAN A.

Position, and opposing numbers, as
known at British G.H.Q. 6 a.m. Aug. 23.

N

Brussels

GERMANS
130,000 MEN

GERMANS
(NUMBERS DOUBTFUL)

Condé

CANAL

Mons

II CORPS

I CORPS

Binche

BRITISH
80,000 MEN

R. Sambre

Charleroi

FRENCH ARMY

120,000 MEN

120,000

Maubeuge

Namur

R. Meuse

IV. FRENCH ARMY

Dinant

The Ardennes

GERMANS

GERMANS

GERMANS

English Miles

0   5   10   15   20   30   25

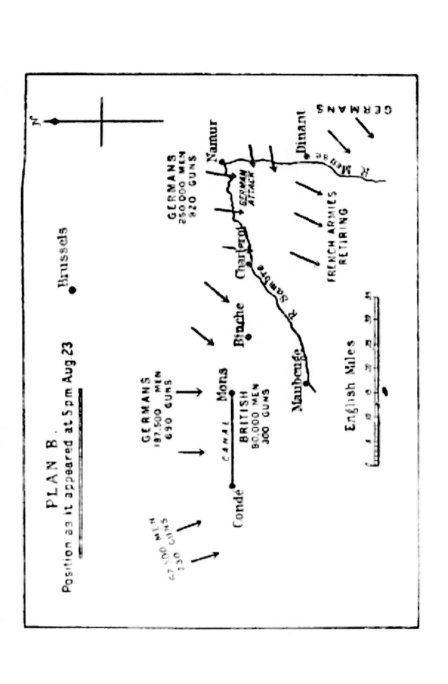

PLAN B.

Position as it appeared at 5 pm Aug. 23

N

Brussels

GERMANS
187,500 MEN
690 GUNS

GERMANS
250,000 MEN
820 GUNS

Namur

GERMAN ATTACK

Binche

Mons
CANAL

BRITISH
80,000 MEN
300 GUNS

Condé

67,500 MEN
230 GUNS

Charleroi

R. Sambre

Maubeuge

Dinant

R. Meuse

FRENCH ARMIES RETIRING

GERMANS

English Miles

of these corps was considerably below strength, and that, in round numbers, the strength of the Force was no more than 75,000, with 250 guns.

If we calculate up the *official* strength the numbers should work out at 83,845 all ranks, 334 field- and 126 machine-guns.

Another infantry brigade came up on the 23rd and joined the Second Corps, and another division (the 4th) also arrived.[1]

Taking everything into account it is, I think, reasonable to put the British strength at about 80,000 men, 300 field- and 100 machine-guns when battle was first joined.

Let me put these figures in tabular form so that we can get a comparison at a glance.

Actual Approximate Numbers on August 22nd

	All ranks.	Field-guns.	Machine-guns.
British	80,000	300	100
French	240,000	960	288
German	812,500	3,016	936
Excess German strength over Franco-British	492,500	1,756	548

It is always rather difficult to grasp the *meaning* of big numbers like these, so let me put it another way.

Place one German against each man in the Franco-British Force, and one German field-gun against each field-gun on our side. Now take all the German soldiers and guns still remaining over and imagine that you are watching them march past you down Whitehall, the men in fours all doing their "goose" parade step and the guns going by at a trot.

The army, marching night and day, without a moment's halt, would take just about three days to pass you.

Such then was the enemy superiority; about four or five times as great as the most pessimistic prophets had anticipated. We shall see shortly what this superiority developed into against the British Force.

---

1. Until Wednesday the 26th, the 19th Brigade was acting directly under orders from G.H.Q. On that date, being isolated, it was appropriated by the Second Corps. The 4th Division detrained at Le Cateau and took up position In and about Solesmes to cover the retirement.

British.—The general position of the opposing forces before battle was joined, at least for the British, will be realised from plan A, and there is little need to add anything by way of explanation.

It will be noted that the British line extended along a front of about 25 miles, with Mons near the centre of the line. On Saturday, August 22nd, Sir John French disposed the Force into its positions. The Second Corps, under Sir Horace Smith-Dorrien, held the canal line from Condé, on the west, to Mons, on the east. The First Corps, under Sir Douglas Haig, extended from Mons, on the west, to Binche, on the east.

As there were no British reserves, the cavalry division, under General Allenby, was detailed to act as such and to be ready to move forward where and as required.

The 5th Cavalry Brigade, under Sir Philip Chetwode, was posted in and around Binche.

French.—I have indicated the composition of the French force, and plan A will show how it was disposed on the morning of the 22nd; i.e. 5th French Army from Charleroi to just south of Namur, and 4th Army down the River Meuse to south of Dinant.

Similarly, there is nothing further to add about the German dispositions if the general lines of the enemy advance be noted: an attempted out-flanking movement on the extreme west, and the driving in of a wedge in the neighbourhood of Namur. These, together with heavy frontal attacks.

★★★★★★

In all that follows it is necessary to add in, by way of reinforcements on the German side, the very great moral encouragement which the enemy had received by their triumphal passage through Belgium. They were in overwhelming strength; their heavy guns had crushed the fortresses in a few hours like so many egg-shells; they had, for many a long year, believed themselves invincible as against the world; and now they were marching directly upon Paris with the confident hope that within three months France would have ceased to exist as a nation, and that by the end of the year the war would be finished, with terms of peace dictated by their all-highest and supremely-powerful deity, the *Kaiser*.

It was, too, not merely an army disciplined and trained in the minutest details of war which was thus bludgeoning forward into France; it was, in effect, a nation in arms. A nation which, for many a long year past, had been educated to regard war as the greatest of all earthly things—a supreme issue to which all the sciences and arts of the preliminary years of peace were to be directed.

It was a nation which regarded as fully legitimate any means whatever to the supreme end desired.

I recall a remark made to me during the South African War by a Prussian naval officer.

You English do not know the rudiments of war. When the day comes for us to go to war you shall see how we deal with the men, women and children. With us terror is our greatest weapon.

Today the world knows how that weapon has been mercilessly wielded; and how impotent it has been.

On her side Britain was equally united, but in a different sense. She had taken up the gauntlet because her people were assured that the cause was a just one. In those early days the Expeditionary Force was not concerned one way or the other with the reasons for its presence in France. The men were, for the most part, quite ignorant of the facts; they were there as a professional army to do their "bit," as they had often had to do it before, and I cannot recall a single instance during the first month where the men spoke of the meaning of the war.

In numbers they were hopelessly insignificant beside the enormous masses ranged against them, but, for its size, the army with the colours has always been recognised the world over as without a peer.

There was, however, one factor which in no small degree tended to level the balance. Discipline in the Germany Army meant discipline in the mass, by regiments or companies, under constant supervision of officers and N.C.O.'s. In the British Army it meant discipline of the individual. In a word, if a British soldier finds himself alone in a tight corner he generally knows how to get out, if it is humanly possible. The German, accustomed from his childhood to be dry-nursed in every trivial detail of his everyday life, would be hopelessly at sea when forced to act on his own initiative. When properly led the German is splendidly courageous, and in this respect, quite apart from numbers and moral, it was an exceedingly tough proposition which French and British were up against at Mons.

As regards the French it is rather more difficult to estimate their outlook in the early days. From their experience in 1870 they knew what war with Germany meant, both in the actual fighting and in the nameless atrocities which the enemy committed on the civil population. Thus they wanted their revenge.

But France had not yet suffered in this war. She had not yet seen her borough officials taken as hostages and murdered in cold blood; her older men sold into slavery; her women raped and mutilated; her infant children impaled upon the bayonet and thrown into the fire; her Cathedral of Rheims tortured and desecrated. All this was yet to come.

At the beginning they fought valiantly but blindly. The shock was too sudden and overwhelming. Mistakes were made in the higher commands.

But within the month France awoke. The Soul of her still lived; and it was the Soul of a nation which was mighty many a generation before ever Germanic tribes had banded together in primitive community.

The Soul of France awoke in every one of her children. Not one, man, woman or child, but saw the way clear before him, but felt the grip of steel-cold determination to follow that path straight to the end.

Such was the France which turned at bay before the very gates of her capital, to show the world that the doom of civilisation's enemy was irrevocably sealed.

CHAPTER 6

Mons

If the English had any apprehension they would run away.
That island of England breeds very valiant creatures: their mastiffs are
of unmatchable courage.

The dawn of Sunday, the 23rd, broke dim and misty, giving promise of heat. From the late afternoon of the previous day squadrons and reconnaissance patrols from Chetwode's Cavalry Brigade had been pushing well forward on the flanks and front of the British line. They were regiments with names "familiar in our mouths as household words": 12th Lancers, 20th Hussars and Scots Greys.

It was pretty though delicate work this feeling forward to get into touch with enemy outposts and patrols. Nor was there a troop which did not have some story to tell that evening of a tussle with enemy cavalry, with its ending, happy or otherwise, determined by the more wide-awake patrol.

In one place an officer's patrol, moving quietly out from a grassy forest track, stumbled straight upon a dozen Uhlans having a meal. The British had no time to draw swords, and certainly the Uhlans hadn't, it was just a question of riding them down, and swords and pistols out when you could.

In another place a German and a British patrol entered a village simultaneously from either end, unbeknown to each other. The turn of a corner and they were face to face. Our men were the more wide-awake, and they got spurs to their horses and swords out before the enemy grasped the situation. The little affair was over in five minutes.

But as our cavalry pushed farther and farther northwards they found themselves confronting ever-increasing numbers, and retirement became necessary.

Thus were the first shots fired.

At six in the morning of this Sunday, Sir John French held a "*pow-wow*" with the three G.O.C.'s, Generals Haig, Smith-Dorrien and Allenby, and discussed the situation, somewhat in these terms:[1]

So far as I can see from the messages I've had from French H.Q. I don't think we've got more than a couple of corps in front of us, perhaps a cavalry division as well.[2] And it doesn't look as though they are trying to outflank, because the cavalry have been right out there and didn't meet with much opposition; nor do the aircraft appear to have noticed anything unusual going on. It'll be a big enemy superiority, but I don't think too big if we've got dug in properly and the lines are all right. We ought to hold them when they come on. The French, as you know, are holding our right, Namur, and down the Meuse.

See plan A, earlier, to show the situation as it was known at G.H.Q.

The morning wears on. You picture the countryside as not unlike one of our own mining districts, the little villages and low-roofed houses giving that curious smoky, grimy effect of mean suburbs bordering on a large industrial town. Here and there great heaps of slag or disused pits and quarries; gaunt iron stems carrying great wheels and heavy machinery.

The soldiers are billeted all through the houses or make a shake-down in odd barns and yards. Look over the garden gate of one little house and you will see the company cooks of one regiment getting the Sunday dinner ready, peeling the potatoes, swinging the pots on to the camp fires.

From a barn hard by you'll hear the sound of singing. A *padre* has looked in as the rollicking chorus of "Who's your lady friend?" swung out into the roadway, and with gentle interruption has improvised a short service, suggesting "Rock of Ages" as a substitute for the music-hall ditty,

Down the road a couple of sergeants of the West Ridings lean idly over a gate smoking and watching the folk going off to Mass.

---

1. I have simply turned paragraphs of Sir John French's dispatch into imaginary spoken words.

2. A German cavalry division numbered, approximately, 5,200, all ranks, including 2 batteries Horse Artillery and 1 machinegun battery.

Out over the canal line the men are hard at work trench-digging, pausing now and again to look skywards as the drowsy hum of an aeroplane propeller sounds over them. Whether the machine is friend or foe they have no idea.

Three girls saunter down the road, arms round waists, and stop to look with interest and amusement at some of the West Kents washing out their shirts. One of the men is stripped for a wash and Marie exchanges a little repartee with him, to run off laughing as a burly lance-corporal plants a sounding kiss on her cheek, by way of finishing the argument.

So peaceful it all is, with just that undercurrent of excitement which the presence of strange troops would give. Imagine a Lancashire or Yorkshire village on a summer Sunday morning and you have the picture.

It is now eleven o'clock and the people are streaming home from church. The service seems to have been cut rather shorter than usual and there is just a hint of anxiety to be seen on their faces. What was it the *curé* had said, something about keeping quietly in their homes and trusting *le bon Dieu?* But there is no danger, the English are here to protect us. Still, those aeroplanes have an ugly sound, something of *un air menaçant.*

Another aeroplane—and look, it has a great black cross under the wings! *Un Boche?* No, it cannot be. Ah, see, see, a French one, ours! It goes to meet it. *Mon Dieu!* they fight! And dimly from the sunny heaven there falls the crackle of revolvers.

A motor dispatch-rider hurls himself from his machine straight upon the astonished group of West Kents.

"Where's the officer? Get moving; you're wanted up there!" and he jerks a thumb over his shoulder.

The men rush for their kit and rifles. Away to the west there is the crack of an 18-pounder.

Down the street the cyclist pants. A subaltern bursts in on the Sunday dinner of the Bedfords.

"Fall in outside at once!"

Another aeroplane sails over. It hovers for a moment over the Scottish Borderers in their trenches. A trail of black smoke drops down, and instinctively the men cower below the parapet. Slowly it falls. Nothing more. The men raise their heads.

"Eh, man, but a thocht yon werre one o' thae—"

A sudden, odd hum in the air, and then—*crash!*

The Scots corporal slowly and painfully drags himself out from the pile of earth and debris and looks round. There is a curious numb feeling in his right arm. He sits up with a dazed gasp. There is a hand by him on the ground. His? He looks at his arm, and realises. Near by five of his pals are laid out. He seems to have escaped.

"The Lord ha' maircy—but the regiment's fair blooded this day," and he falls back in a faint.

More aeroplanes, more trails of smoke; and, wherever they fall, within twenty odd seconds a German shell bursts fair and true.

All down the line there springs the crack of rifles. Beyond the canal the outposts of the Lincolns, Royal Scots and others are coming in at the double. A curtain of shell-fire is lowered behind them as the British batteries come into action. A curtain of fire rolls down before them as the German guns take the range.

It is now close upon one o'clock, and enemy shells have begun to creep nearer and nearer in from the suburbs upon Mons itself. The good *curé* and his words are forgotten, for what living things can remain? And so there begins that pitiable exodus of old men, women and children which streamed steadily southwards, ever increasing as it crowded through the villages and towns.

But there is no time today to think of them. They must go, or stay and perish—anything so long as they do not interfere with the great game of War.

North of the town, where our lines necessarily bulged out, making a salient, the fighting was becoming desperate. Here three regiments especially (the Middlesex, Royal Irish and Royal Fusiliers) lost very heavily as they sturdily contested every yard of ground. This particular point had, from the first, been recognised as the weakest in the British lines.

Barely an hour since the first shots were fired, and now by one o'clock practically every gun and every rifle of the British Force is blazing away as though the powers of hell were set loose.

As yet it would seem that the ammunition is being merely wasted for the sake of making a noise. There is no enemy in sight save in the air the circling aeroplanes, and away on the flanks dimly-seen clouds of horsemen. A modern battlefield with its curious *emptiness* has so often been described that here one need only record the fact in passing. There is nothing to be seen. The men are firing, in the first flush of excitement, at corners of possible concealment—the line of a hedge, the edge of a wood, the very occasional flash of a field-gun.

On the left, in the Second Corps, the British fire slackens somewhat as the men pull themselves together. No one has the foggiest notion of what is really happening. It is the officers' business of the moment to steady the ranks and keep them under cover.

But away on the right, out by Binche, where the Guards are, the storm has burst in fullest fury. No slackening there. The extreme right was held by battalions of historic regiments, names to conjure with: Munster Fusiliers, Black Watch, Scots and Coldstream Guards. Ah, those Guards! The glorious discipline of them! But how distinguish between any of the regiments that day, and after?

Almost from the first the senior officers began to realise that something was wrong, especially on the right. The divisional commanders and their immediate staffs, to whom the general idea of strengths and dispositions was known, began to wonder whether a big mistake had not been made. "Well, never mind, we're in for it now, we must do the best we can. But, those guns! There certainly should not be so many out there."

And it was positively uncanny how the German guns got their range. That fact struck everybody almost more than anything else. There appeared to be no preliminary ranging, as was always usual, but guns got direct on to the target at once.

It is difficult at times to avoid launching out into details which are of more interest to soldiers than to the general public, but as everything at this time was so new an occasional lapse may perhaps be excused.

Again, one's brain is so confused with such a mass of detail that it becomes most difficult to disentangle impressions and note them down in dispassionate language. If, however, the reader will take the little pen-pictures of incidents which are given and imagine them, not as isolated facts but as being reproduced fifty times all through the fighting lines, he may get a fair idea of the course of events.

★★★★★★

As the day wore on that uncanny effect of the German fire increased. There is no doubt that it was mainly due to the amazingly efficient secret service of the enemy. The H.Q. of a division or a brigade, for instance, does not blatantly advertise its position, and yet time and time again shells were dropped clean on to the particular building where the staff happened to be. And when they got into another building, plump would come more shells.

Looking back it is a little curious to remember that even in that first week a very considerable percentage of our total casualties were caused by high explosive shell, and the shooting of them was astonishingly accurate.

Yes, the German guns did their work well, but they did not fully succeed in their object. Their local successes were great, especially against British guns and batteries.

Here is a British battery which has made two mistakes—it is not sufficiently concealed, the battery commander is perched up on an observation limber, and the guns are not far enough back behind the crest. (The Germans always "search" for some 300 yards behind crests of hills.) The B.C. is quickly spotted by an aeroplane observer and a perfect hell of fire is switched on by the enemy. In a moment telephone wires are cut, communications are broken, and within five minutes the gun detachments are wiped out.

The effect of a shell from the enemy heavier guns is overwhelming. The flank gun of the battery is hit, practically "direct." Some R.A.M.C. men double up a few minutes later to help out the wounded. There is nothing, save a great hole, fragments of twisted steel, and—a few limbs of brave men. Nothing can be done except, later, dig in the sides of the pit to cover the remains.

The rest of the guns remain, but there is no one to work them. The horses, a little way to the rear, have also suffered badly. A subaltern officer staggers painfully through the tornado of fire from one gun to the next, slowly, deliberately putting them out of action, rendering them useless should the enemy come up to capture them.

Early in the afternoon brigade commanders have got orders round to the British lines to hold up the infantry fire as far as possible. It is now all well under control, for everyone realises that the artillery bombardment was a preliminary only, that the real attack is yet to come. The men have had their baptism of fire and magnificently have they stood it. This is discipline, and now they are ready for anything which may come along.

But already the casualties have been very heavy. Early in the day you have seen that company of the West Kents double up to the support of their battalion entrenched about halfway along the Second Corps line. I find a note in my diary: "W. Kents, Middlesex and Northumberlands" (they were all in the Second Corps) "decimated by shell fire." One or two companies of the W. Kents were, I believe, on outpost duty, which would mean that they were literally wiped out.

And, remember, the British trenches were not those of later days

FIELD-MARSHAL VISCOUNT FRENCH.

round Ypres. They had all been hastily dug in extremely hard and difficult ground, so that there were none of the niceties of snug dug-outs and bomb-proof shelters. In many places it was just a matter of scratching up the soil behind a hump of shale and cramming oneself in as far as one could go. To imagine, as one is led to do by some writers, that our men sat snugly in deep trenches through all that shell fire waiting calmly for the infantry attack is to get a hopelessly wrong idea. And if this was so on the first day when the men started in fresh, the conditions during the days which followed may be vaguely guessed.

Think for a moment of the splendid work the R.A.M.C. were doing all this time. I wonder how many V.C.'s were earned by that self-sacrificing corps during the week. It is easy enough to do what people call a gallant deed with arms in your hands when the blood is up, to pick up a live bomb and hurl it away—little trifles of the moment which no one thinks twice about,—but the courage demanded in walking quietly into a hail of lead to bandage and carry out a wounded man, a feat which the R.A.M.C. men in the firing lines do a dozen times a day, *that* is worth talking about.

On our right the fight does not go well for us, and the suspicion that some mistake has been made becomes a certainty. If it is only a matter of two German corps and a cavalry division in front of our position where on earth have all those guns come from?

Still the British guns out towards Binche go pounding gallantly on, hopelessly outmatched though they are. It's pretty shooting, for our 18-prs. can get in six or seven shots a minute more than the German field-guns, but we cannot compete against their heavier metal. And, just as in a naval fight, it is the heavier metal which tells.

The fighting on the right where General Lomax has the 1st Division has not slackened for a moment, but steadily becomes more intense. Now, for the first time, the enemy is really seen. And as his infantry begin an advance the German shell-fire redoubles in intensity. Every house where British can be concealed, every possible observation post, every foot of trench, every hill-crest and 400 yards behind it is swept and devastated by the tornado.

What communication between units is possible in such a storm? Now battalions and batteries find themselves cut off from their neighbours, each fighting and carrying on by itself.

Chetwode's Cavalry Brigade is caught in the thick of it. The Guards are out there and they hold on almost by their teeth. The 1st Irish are in action for the first time since their formation. They'll see the Germans in hell before they're going to quit. The Munsters are in the hottest corner, if indeed you can see any degrees of difference.

The cavalry have to go; and the Munsters and Black Watch lose horribly as they cover the retirement. No finer fighting regiments in the world than these on the right, but nothing human can stay there and live. The little town of Binche is abandoned; the first enemy success that day. The First Corps has had to swing back its outer flank.

But if you think that the Black Watch, or the Guards, or any of them, have been sitting there quietly to be shot at when there's an enemy in sight, you know little of those regiments. And you don't imagine that the Scots Greys, or Lancers, or Hussars, with such a reputation behind them, are going to sneak out of Binche by a back way without first getting a little of their own back.

No, if the Germans have got to have Binche they must bring up a great many more men than that to take it. There has been much talk of a repetition of that famous charge of the Greys, with the Black Watch hanging on to the stirrup-leathers. If indeed it was repeated that August then this must have been the moment. I am sorry to say that I have never been able to obtain any real confirmation of the story, so I shall not set it down.

But it might well have happened, and one likes to think that it did. Anyway, during that hour or so, there was many a gallant, desperate charge in that corner. A charge against overwhelming odds, when the utmost to be expected was the breaking and rout of the first two or three lines of the advance.

It needs no vivid flight of imagination to picture it. On the far outskirts of the town a railway line runs. Under the lee of a sheltering embankment and bridge the officers collect and re-form some of the squadrons, now grown pitiably less in numbers. Words of command are almost inaudible, but the men understand. Hard by, on their left, you have the flanking companies of the line regiments. One or two brief messages pass to and fro between cavalry and infantry.

The Greys and Lancers are going to charge the left of infantry advancing beyond the wood. Give them all the support you can!

The British fire slackens from loophole and broken window. The Scottish regiment and the Coldstream Guards insist on taking a share. They cut out through the leaden hail and make some yards' advance, dropping again under what cover they can.

A last look round, a final pull at girth-straps, and the word is passed. The enemy infantry is 300 yards away.

"*Tr-rot!*" They are clear of the embankment. All well in hand. The enemy guns have not yet got them.

The Scots and Coldstream Guards make another rush and again drop.

"*Can-ter!*" And men and horses settle down into the steady swing. The infantry who have got the orders to support start blazing away again as fast as they can get the magazine clips home.

Now the German gunners see what is happening and one gun after another drops its range and fuse. The German infantry is 250 yards away.

"*Cha-arge!*" No need to sound it. The officers are in front, and where the officers go their men will follow. Anywhere!

The Scots and Coldstreamers are after them as hard as they can leg it.

The enemy on the flank try to swing round to meet the charge, but there is no time. The German guns mercilessly drop the range still more—what matter if they sweep away their own men as well.

One hundred yards! Fifty yards! A long, sickening crash—and the Greys and lancers are in them. Hacking, slashing, hewing! The Scots are hard on their heels just to their left. A mighty heave as the bayonets get home. The first rank is through. There are no more ranks, only a vast confusion.

Five little minutes (it seems an eternity) and the enemy flank is crushed in, smashed to pulp as a block of stone smashes in the head of a man.

"Who goes home?" Who can? Ten men, a dozen, perhaps twenty have struggled through. A few will cover again the ground over which they charged. A few, such a tiny few, will get back under cover again. "The rest is silence."

But they have done it. The enemy have learned what a British charge is like. They know now what bayonet work is, and the lesson sinks deep. They will not face the steel again. Ask the men who fought at the Aisne, at Ypres.

CHAPTER 7

Mons (continued)

But pardon, gentles all,
The flat unraised spirits that have dar'd.
On this unworthy scaffold to bring forth
So great an object: can this cockpit hold
The vasty fields of France?

It may be of interest at this point if the narrative be broken off for a few minutes to give some details of the methods the Germans employ in their infantry attack, especially as they differ so greatly from our own.

The two main features are (*a*) they consider rifle work as of comparatively little value and rely mainly on machine-gun fire, and (*b*) they attack in dense masses, shoulder to shoulder.

British methods are, or were, precisely the opposite. Our men have brought musketry to such perfection that an infantryman will get off in one minute almost double the number of rounds that a German will; and, what is more to the point, they will all hit the mark. Let it be noted that the British Army owes this perfection to the wise foresight of Lord Roberts. (Ah, if only the nation, too, had listened to him!)

British troops, adopting the lessons of the Boer War, attack with an interval between the files, *i.e.* in extended order.

Now at Mons, and after, a German battalion generally attacked in three double ranks. The rear double rank had with it four or six machineguns. They count upon the first three or four ranks stopping the enemy's bullets, but, by the time these are swept away, the last ranks (with the machine-guns) should be sufficiently near to carry the position attacked: say about 300 yards.

This reckless sacrifice of life is typical of the German "machine," as opposed to the British "individual."

As a matter of fact their method never succeeded over open ground before the British fire, for the front ranks were always swept away at the very beginning of the attack, and so they did not get near enough with the rear ranks.

The German officer who gave me these details remarked that the rapidity and accuracy of the British fire were simply incredible, that they never had a chance.

"Our men," he said, "have come to believe that every one of you carries a portable Maxim with him."

★★★★★

It must have been about 2.30 in the afternoon that Binche had to be abandoned. But it was before this that the German infantry attacks began all along the line.

For nearly two hours our men had somehow or other been weathering the storm of shrapnel, and we have seen that they had by now settled down under it. Let us get back to the Second Corps and see what is happening. You have got some idea of the look of the country in front of our positions, all broken up, uneven ground, little woods here and there. Out on the left flank there are county regiments, men of Dorset, Norfolk, Suffolk, Cheshire, Surrey. They know something about "ground" work, and they have learned a deal more with their regiments.

One end of the Yorks L.I. trench ends in a little stone-walled pigsty. At least it was a pigsty about church time that morning, but a German gunner thought it would look better without any roof or walls.

There is still a fragment three feet high on the weather side, and the Yorks C.O. finds it a convenient shelter for the time being. He is not attending church-parade that day, so it doesn't matter about lying full length in the filth on the ground. The last remaining company colour-sergeant is with him—also embedded in the manure. They are both nibbling chocolate. Tobacco would be particularly useful just now, but they have both run out of it.

For some minutes the C.O. has been intently watching through his glasses the corner of a wood about 500 yards in front. He hands the binoculars to the sergeant.

"What do you make of it? That corner over the little shed."

The sergeant has a look. He returns the glasses and slowly nods.

"It might be a brigade, sir, from the number of them."

"Yes," says the C.O., "I thought it was about time. Get word along

71

that there is to be no firing till the order's given."

"Very good, sir!" And the sergeant scrambles to his feet, salutes, ducks hastily as a shell seems to whistle past unnecessarily close, and dives into the rabbit-burrow in which his men are squatting. The C.O. returns to his glasses. The C.O. of a British battery, in position some distance to the rear, has evidently also spotted that particular target, for puffs of bursting shrapnel have begun to appear over the wood and round the edges.

Now there is a distinct movement of troops emerging from behind the wood. It is a movement only which can be seen, for the men themselves can scarcely be distinguished against the grey-green country-side.

At the very same moment it seems as though all the guns in the world have been turned on to those few miles of British front, and to the batteries behind.

The British gunfire wavers for a minute or so; but soon it picks up again though, alas! not so strongly as before.

The Yorks C.O. has lost his enemy infantry for a minute; they are working forward under the edge of a rise in the ground.

Now the front ranks appear, and the C.O. gives a sharp whistle of astonishment. Four hundred yards off, and it looks like a great glacier rolling down a mountain-side.

Nearer still it creeps, and the German guns have raised their range to give their infantry a chance. "Besides, there will probably be nothing but empty trenches to take anyway," they say.

Fifty yards nearer, and the temptation is too great.

"Let it go, Yorkshires!" he yells down the trench. (The command is not in the drill-book, but it serves very well.)

And the Yorkshires "let it go" accordingly.

"Eh, lads," sings out a lad from Halifax, "'tis t' crowd coom oop for t' Coop Day! And t' lads yonder can't shoot for nuts," he blithely adds as myriads of rifle bullets whistle high overhead.

And he and the lads from Trent-side proceed very methodically to give "t' lads" from Spreeside a lesson in how shooting should be done.

Very methodically; but that means something like 16 shots a minute each man, and you may be sure that very, very few bullets go off the target. No one dreams of keeping cover. Indeed, the men prop their rifles on the parapet and pump out lead as hard as their fingers can work bolt and trigger.

Miss? It's impossible to miss. You can't help hitting the side of a house—and that's what the target looks like. It is just slaughter. The oncoming ranks simply melt away.

And now through the unholy din you can hear a cracking noise which is quite distinct in the uproar. Something like the continuous back-fire of a mammoth motor-cycle. Machine-guns.

The Dorsets have got a man who is a past-master in the use of these infernal engines. How he escaped that day no one can tell. But for many an hour he sat at the gun spraying the enemy attack with his steel hose. His "bag" must have run into thousands.

The attack still comes on. Though hundreds, thousands of the grey coats are mown down, as many more crowd forward to refill the ranks.

Nearer still, and with a hoarse yell the Yorkshires, Dorsets, Cornwalls and others are out of the trenches, officers ahead of them, with bayonets fixed and heading straight at the enemy. A murderous Maxim fire meets them but it does not stop them, and in a minute they are thrusting and bashing with rifles, fists, stones, in amongst the enemy ranks.

Again the German gunners drop their range and pour their shells indiscriminately into friend and foe. It is too much for the attacking regiments and they break up hopelessly, turn and begin to struggle back. It is impossible to attempt any rally of our men. They must go on until they are overwhelmed by sheer numbers, or they must straggle to the lines as best they can in knots of twos and threes, or wander aimlessly off to the flanks and get lost.

Such was one single attack. But no sooner was it broken than fresh regiments would march out to begin it all over again. And here is no Pass of Thermopylæ where a handful of men can withstand for indefinite time an army. What can the British hope to do against such overwhelming numbers? The end, you will say, must be annihilation.

The cavalry, the only reserves, are working, surely, as no cavalry has ever worked before. Squadrons are everywhere at once. Wherever a gap is threatened they are there in support. And wherever they go there also go the Horse Gunners working hand and glove with them. Charge and counter-charge upon the flanks of the attacking infantry, dismounting to cover with their fire a British infantry rally, fierce hand-to-hand encounters with enemy squadrons. Wherever they are wanted, each man and horse is doing the work of ten.

But this cannot last for long. Now it is becoming only too evident that far from there being a reasonable superiority against us the British are everywhere along the line hopelessly outnumbered in every arm. And at 5 p.m. there happened one of the most dramatic incidents of the war, that day or afterwards. You will find the bare recital of the event set forth in cold official language in the G.O.C.-in-Chief's dispatch, beginning: "In the meantime, about 5 p.m., I received a most unexpected message from General Joffre."

It will be remembered that from information received from French G.H.Q. the previous night, and from his own reconnaissance reports, the commander-in-chief had concluded that his right flank was reasonably secured by the French armies, that the fortress of Namur was still being held, and that the enemy strength in front of him was about 134,000 men and 490 field-guns, at an outside estimate.

All the afternoon the enemy had been attacking, and the British right had had to give ground before it, with the consequence that Mons itself had to be abandoned.

Now, like a bolt from the blue, came the message from the French. "Unexpected," one would think, is a very mild term:—

> Namur has fallen. The Germans *yesterday* won the passages over the River Sambre between Charleroi and Namur. The French armies are retiring. You have *at least* 187,500 men and 690 guns attacking you in front; another 62,500 men and 230 guns trying to turn your left flank; and probably another 300,000 men" (the victorious army in pursuit of the French) "driving in a wedge on your right.

This is what the message would look like:—

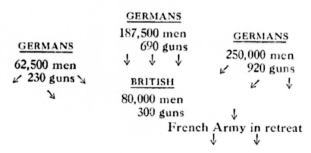

But we have seen that there were really thirteen German corps attacking the positions Tournai—Namur—Dinant.

Thus the *real* figures would probably look like this:—

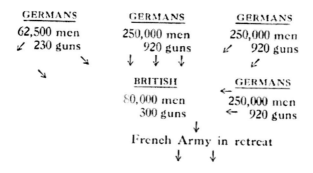

We may, of course, take it that by the end of the day the figures were somewhat reduced all round, British and German; the German losses being "out of all proportion to those which we have suffered." (See plan B earlier).

Such then was the situation at 5.0 p.m. on that eventful Sunday. An average of nearly four times our number of guns against us all along the position. No wonder that senior officers had guessed from the first that "something was wrong."

And G.H.Q.? You imagine, perhaps, that the municipal offices where the General Staff had its abode would now be seething with excitement. You will picture staff officers rushing from room to room; orders and counter-orders being reeled off; the Intelligence and Army Signals Departments looking like Peter Robinson's in sales week; an army of motor-cyclist dispatch riders being hurled from the courtyard towards every point of the compass.

Wrong! G.H.Q. that day, and the next, was less concerned than a little French provincial *mairie* would be on France's national *fête* day. The casual visitor would have seen less bustle of activity than at the Liverpool offices of a shipping firm on mail day.

The Postal Department: "Business as usual." Army Censor: Not much doing. Intelligence: Half a dozen red-tabbed officers looking at big maps with blue and red chalk-marks on them. Director of Ordnance Supplies: "Better see about moving rail-head a few miles farther south." A.G.'s (Adjutant-General) Office: "We shall want orders out about stragglers, what they are to do." And so on, all through the list. If this was an instance of that British phlegm which so amuses the French, then commend me to it! If anybody wanted a tonic against pessimism these days of the Retreat he only had to drop in at G.H.Q. He would certainly come out with the conviction that we should indeed be home by Christmas, with the German Army wiped off the map.

Yes, that week which followed, indeed, welded into one "band of brothers" all the officers and men in the little Force. In those days everybody seemed to know everybody else. Regimental jealousy (if it ever existed) was obliterated completely, and every officer and man, from the General Officers Commanding Corps down to the bus drivers who drove the A.S.C. lorries, worked shoulder to shoulder. And so we pulled through.

★★★★★★

Now there were other units in the Force besides those in the firing-line. There were all those columns which trekked up by road. Normally, most of these should be something like 15 miles to the rear. They know very little of what is going on ahead of them, though the ammunition columns can gauge fairly well by the demands made on them.

So it was that about midnight on that Sunday they began to realise back there that things were moving by a sudden and insistent demand for every scrap of rifle and 18-pr. ammunition they carried.

No sooner was that sent than there came more demands, and there was nothing to send. Wagons and lorries had trundled off at once to rail-head, but it would be hours before they could get back. Thus, on the very first day, the overwhelming nature of the situation pulled at and snapped the slender threads of communication. The threads were soon mended, but, as will be seen later, they never got properly into working order until the Marne.

Nor did those columns altogether escape disaster even at the very outset of the fighting. One, out towards the flank, was attacked and practically destroyed by raiding cavalry, for they do not work with escorts.

In one column, about 10.0 p.m., the alarm was given by an imaginative A.S.C. subaltern. What the men were to fight with is not clear, for only about 25 *per cent*, of the detachment had ever handled a rifle, and no ammunition was issued.

"It's Germans crawling through that field," said the subaltern. "I saw their electric-torch flashes."

The men stood to, peering into the darkness, and feeling certain that their last hour had come.

A farmer came slowly out of the field-gate and begged two of the men to come and help him round up his *cows*.

76

So the detachment turned in again, cursing heartily.

But soon the A.S.C. bus drivers were "doing their bit" under fire as gallantly as everybody else. How and when you shall hear in another chapter.

6.0 p.m.—The enemy have concentrated their fire upon the town of Mons and it has become untenable.

Only six hours, six little hours since the Belgian townsfolk had come peacefully home from Mass to their Sunday *déjeuner*, proud and hopeful in the presence of their British allies. And now their houses, their town, a heap of smoking ruins.

In those short hours how many women have seen their children crushed by falling walls or blown to atoms by bursting shells? How many children are left helpless and alone in the world, with no mother or father to take them by the hand and guide them from the hell of destruction?

Is there no thought for them, you who have been following the fortunes of the day for the British? Many have escaped, with such few household treasures as they can carry in perambulators and little handcarts. They, at least, have some hope of life. These may struggle on for a little while—to faint or die of hunger and exhaustion by the roadside. The strongest may get through.

For the rest, their lives are sacrificed to make a German holiday. They die, but in their death the battalions of these innocents have joined the mighty, mysterious army of souls who shall haunt the German people until Germany ceases to be.

C'est l'armée de ceux qui sont morts
En maudissant les Allemands,
Et dont les invincibles renforts
Vengeront le sang innocents[1]

With such an overwhelming attack working forward in front and on both flanks the only problem left was how to get the British force away with the smallest loss. To remain obviously meant certain annihilation sooner or later. As a matter of course, possible positions in rear had long since been reconnoitred. They were not particularly good ones, but the best that were available.

'Tis the army of those who in dying
Have cursed the German flood—
And whose growing invincible forces

77

Will avenge all innocent blood.—Emile Cammaerts.

From earlier in the afternoon the Sappers had been at work on all the bridges crossing the canal, laying mines ready to blow them up in front of a possible successful enemy advance. By no means a pleasant task this, for the men were working under heavy fire practically all the time. But the Sappers are another of those corps of the Service which are well used to the kicks without the ha'pence, and nothing comes amiss to them. There is no regiment in the army whose work merits recognition more than the R.E.; there is no regiment more surprised and pleased at receiving it.

As the dusk draws on the enemy fire has slackened a little, and the men in their trenches are here and there able to snatch mouthfuls of any food they happen to have handy. Most of them have not tasted anything since early morning, and they have been fighting hard all day. But there is no thought of rest.

The darkening night becomes red day as the glare of burning houses and buildings everywhere mounts to heaven in great shafts of light. It is such a picture as only a Rembrandt could give us on canvas.

The men sit or crouch wearily in their burrows, rifles always ready, heads sunk forward over the butts. Now and again there is a momentary stir as a doctor or stretcher-bearers scramble through the debris to get at the wounded. The fantastic, twisted shapes of the dead are reverently composed and laid down on the ground. The belongings of them are carefully collected, with the little metal identity disc. So far as possible these will reach the wife, mother, or sweetheart at home.

Perhaps those evening hours of the first day's fighting were the most terrible the men were ever to know. The tension had very slightly relaxed, and the brain began once again something of its functions. They began to *feel* things. No one ever gets accustomed to being under the fire of modern warfare, and this was the first day of it. The horror of everything began to crush the senses. Soon physical and mental action became purely mechanical; men ceased to feel, but moved, fired a rifle, fed themselves, with the grotesque jerks of children's toys. But this was not yet. Now they were conscious, if but a little.

One man, a bugler in a county regiment, little more than a child in years, went raving mad as he staggered across a trench and fell, dragging with him a headless Thing which still kept watch with rifle against shoulder. His shrieks, as they pulled the two apart, ring even now in the ears. He died that night, simply from shock after the awful tension of the day.

Consciousness came to the men, yet with it came also amazing cheerfulness even in the midst of the horror. But it was the cheerfulness not of high spirits but of determination, and of pity. They had fought through the day against an enemy which, even to men who did not understand, was in overwhelming strength; and yet they had been able to hold their ground. It was the cheerfulness which, at a word from their officers, would have taken them straight at the enemy's throat.

And pity, if it is to be helpful and sincere, must have behind it a gaiety of heart. No man in the world is more tender to helpless or dumb creatures than the British soldier or sailor; no man more cheerful. And no man in the Force but felt his heart wrung by the infinite pathos of the folk of Mons and round it. History will never record how many soldiers lost their lives that day in succouring the people who had put such trust in their presence.

And how many won such a distinction as no king can bestow— the love and gratitude of little children? One man, at least, I knew (I never learned his name) who, at the tears of two tiny mites, clambered into the ruins of a burning outhouse, then being shelled, to fetch something they wanted, he could not understand what. He found a terror-stricken cat and brought it out safely. No, not pussy, something else as well. Back he went again, and after a little search discovered on the floor in a corner a wicker cage, in it a blackbird. Yes, that was it. And, oh, the joy of the girl mite at finding it still alive!

"Well, you see, sir," he said afterwards, "I've got two kiddies the image of them. And it was no trouble, anyway."

About 2 a.m. (the 24th) orders to begin retiring were issued from G.H.Q. Some four hours before a few of the units—those north of the canal—had begun to fall back; and so the beginning of the move was made. As the last of these crossed the bridges the detonator fuses were fired and the bridges blown up.

For the rest, the men crouched ever in their places, bayonets fixed, rifles always ready—waiting, waiting.

CHAPTER 8

The Retreat Begins

The poor condemned English,
Like sacrifices, by their watchful fires
Sit patiently, and inly ruminate
The morning's danger.

To follow now the fortunes of the British Force you must imagine it, if you will, divided, like Caesar's Gaul, into three parts. There is the First Corps, which still holds its position, save that extreme right by Binche; there is the Second Corps, which has begun at 3 a.m. to retire to a new position; and there is the cavalry, Allenby's Division and the remainder of Chetwode's Brigade, which turns up wherever it is most needed to lend a helping hand.

If you glance through Sir John French's dispatch (at the end of the book) you will see that he had in mind to retire in what is called "echelon" formation. That is, one-half retires and takes up a new position, while the other half stays behind to act as a rear-guard and hold up enemy attacks. Then, in turn, that other half retires behind the first half, and so on.

That was the idea, and on the first day it worked very well. But after that it was found simply impossible to keep to it, partly through the enemy's thunderbolt movements, and partly because our men became more and more exhausted.

Now, it is also a cardinal principle in rearguard fights that you must not only check your enemy, but must also, whenever possible, make a counter-attack. In fact, the counter-attacks are part and parcel of the checking movements. This is where cavalry comes in very useful.

Let us, then, take the three divisions of the Force separately.

Night attacks, especially in the early morning (it sounds rather Irish), are horribly uncomfortable things. The nerves are continuously on edge and you are apt to loose off guns or rifles at the merest suspicion of a movement.

"If ye should see a wee brrown beastie in frront o' ye," a canny Scot sergeant told his men, "ye mauna fire, because likely it'll be a bit rrabbit, and rrabbits are guid for the pot. But if the beastie should walk upon twa legs, then ye may ken it's no a rrabbit, but a Gerrman, an' ye will tak a verry quick but carefu' sicht o' him."

All through that Sunday night the men had snatched odd minutes of sleep just where they had fought through the day. And very little rest did the enemy allow them. For one can well imagine how exasperated by this time the enemy were at being held up by a handful of a "contemptible little army." It was most difficult, too, to get any food up to the lines, for the German guns had "registered" all the approaches and persistently dropped their shells across them.

But the men hung on cheerily enough, and if they couldn't get any sleep they made up their minds that the Germans should not either, especially where they were dug in only a few hundred yards in front.

So the short summer night was passed. And with the first hint of dawn the news ran quickly round that, far from dreaming of retiring, the First Corps was going to attack. The news was as good as a big breakfast. Somehow or other the A.S.C. got up rations to most of the units, and so it was the cheeriest of 2nd Divisions which swung out of their trenches and loop-holed houses and headed for the enemy's left flank in Binche. The 1st Division acted as supports.

In the attack there was something more of a hint of that method and timing which, eight months later, were brought to such perfection in Flanders. The British batteries had by now recovered somewhat from their severe handling during the day, and at the given moment every gun got well to work in support of the infantry, and very fine practice they made.

Of course the attack was really no more than a ruse, daringly conceived and successfully executed. Binche could not have been held even if it had been recaptured. But it is not difficult to imagine the enemy's astonishment at finding an Army Corps, which they had fondly imagined as good as wiped out, coming to life again and actually having the cheek to attack them. Kipling's remark about the Fuzzy-wuzzy who is *generally shamming when 'e's dead*" was an excellent motto for that morning's work.

When the attack was well launched General Lomax began to withdraw very carefully some of his regiments from the supporting 1st Division. The task of the British guns of the two divisions (working together) was to lower such a curtain of fire in front of the 2nd Division as to make it as difficult as possible for the enemy to counter-attack or, indeed, to advance at all. As soon as the 1st Division have retired a little, it will be the turn of the division which has made that excellent sortie.

It is easy enough to say "the guns will check an enemy advance," but think for a moment what that means. There is already a big enemy superiority in guns, and, what is more, these have already got the ranges to a nicety.

Our batteries, or most of them, were in quite good positions, but at this early date we had not yet learned the art of concealing them sufficiently. The enemy aircraft were very active, and against them our own aircraft were hopelessly outnumbered. And so it was not long before our guns were "spotted," with the inevitable result.

Imagine, then, how gloriously those gun detachments must have worked to have accomplished what they did that day, "enabling Sir Douglas Haig, with the First Corps, to reach the new line without much further loss about 7 p.m." For it was undoubtedly the devotion of the guns which made possible this and succeeding retirements. Unless facts like this are realised, the astonishing work of the Force in its retreat can never be appreciated.

THE SECOND CORPS

If that Monday was an anxious day for Sir Douglas Haig, what must it have been for General Smith-Dorrien and his men? One looks hopelessly at the blank writing-pad in despair of giving even the most primitive description of the anxiety, the work, and the accomplishment of it.

Here is a corps which has gone through, for the first time, the awful ordeal of a day's modern shell-fire and massed infantry attack. The men have supped full of horrors, and, at 3 a.m., hungry, weary and with nerves stretched to their utmost tension, they have received orders to move. There is not a regiment which has not lost heavily, especially in officers, and there is not a man but receives the command with his senses tangled in bewilderment.

Now it should be remembered that up to this time all our dispositions had been made for an advance. The impedimenta to the rear of the firing-line were so arranged that they might the more easily follow up a British attack. There was no real thought of retiring. The British were in the place of honour on the left of the line, and intended, with our French comrades, to drive the enemy back again through Belgium. I will not say that all this was a foregone conclusion, but at least it was "confidently anticipated." Remembering this, you will perhaps realise more vividly how staggering were the contents of that telegram from French G.H.Q.

The work, therefore, of clearing the roads of the transport was exceedingly difficult. This devolves upon the Q.M.G.'s department, and General Smith-Dorrien has placed on record the wholly admirable way in which it was accomplished by General Ryecroft and his staff. But proper staff work for all the retiring troops during the hours of darkness was even more complicated.

Thus some few of the companies, with no one to guide them, start off in the wrong direction and march straight into the German lines; they are shot or captured. Others wander off to the east, struggle painfully through the shell-fire on Mons, and drift into their comrade ranks of the First Corps. Others, again, march off to the west, and are hopelessly lost; they are either captured by the flanking German corps or they get through and meet with friendly peasants, to turn up eventually at base ports or other towns.

Night marching across unknown country is not always easy in peace time, with guides at the heads of columns. Now there was the added confusion of the crowds of emigrants, a perfect network of roads to choose from, and, above all, continual alarms of enemy attacks which the British had to turn to meet. The whole of the night and all the Monday was one long period of marching, fighting, marching and fighting.

Early in the morning another infantry brigade, the 19th, arrived by railway, detraining at Valenciennes, and it is no exaggeration to say that the men went straight off the trains into the thick of the fight. It was a very welcome reinforcement of about 4,000 men.

By 8 a.m. the enemy had burst through Mons, across the canal line, and were in hot pursuit in overwhelming numbers. Away on the left flank they had attacked Tournai, which was occupied by French Territorials and also, I believe, by a British battery, though how it got there, or why, I do not know. That bit of fighting was over by midday with the capture of the town and the destruction or capture of its defenders. The Germans were then free to resume their victorious advance.

About the middle of the morning, then, the line of the Second Corps extended from a little Belgian village called Frameries, five miles S.W. of Mons, through the village of Dour. The right flank was the more forward, partly because the regiments there had to encounter the more furious attacks and could not break away.

It was at this point that there was made one more of those splendid but hopeless cavalry charges of which we so often read in military history. It is, curiously enough, almost the only definite incident mentioned by Sir John French in his dispatch. But the incident, or rather the sequel to it, caught the public imagination, mainly because of the fine work of that most gallant gentleman, Francis Grenfell.

Of all the noble, lion-hearted men who have "gone west" in this bloody war, no man more worthily deserves the description applied to the Chevalier Bayard, "*sans peur et sans reproche*," than Francis Grenfell—he and one other whom I shall name hereafter. Gallant soldier, brilliant sportsman, graceful poet, and true lover of Nature, a genuine statesman in his dealings with men, and the most loyal of friends, he died later on the field of honour, and Britain—nay, the world is the poorer for his loss.

The charge was made by the 9th Lancers, which regiment, with others of the 2nd Brigade, had been moved forward to ease the pressure on the right flank.

About 400 yards from the German infantry and guns the lancers galloped full tilt into barbed wire. There was nothing for it but to swerve across the German front. How a single man or horse escaped the hail of shell and bullets which was turned on them one can never understand. But a poor remnant, under Captain Francis Grenfell, did indeed get across, mercilessly pursued by that storm of lead, and eventually found some little shelter under a railway embankment.

An R.F.A. battery was in action here. At least, the guns were still there, but officers and detachments had been gradually wiped out until there were just one officer and two detachments left to work the battery. It was only a matter of minutes before the remainder must be killed and the guns fall into the hands of the enemy, for the German guns had the range and the German infantry were crowding up.

The 9th Lancers and the Gunners are old friends, and the Lancers do not leave old friends (or new ones) to finish a losing fight alone.

"The Germans don't get those guns while any of us are left," said Grenfell. "I'm off to see how we can get them away."

Now Grenfell was already badly wounded, but he stuck on his horse somehow, and *walked* that gallant beast out into the storm to see where he was to run the guns to. (Why does not His Majesty create a decoration for horses? But I'll wager Grenfell hung his V.C. round his charger's neck a month later.)

Well, he walked him out and he walked him back, just to show his men what poor shots the Germans were.

"Now then," said Grenfell, "who's for the guns?"

And, since (as I have said) the lancers always stand by old pals, every man of them was.

They tied their horses up, and lancers and gunners set to work. One by one of those guns they got at the wheels and trails and worked and worked. Down went more gallant lancers and more gallant gunners, but there were still a few left, and, by Heaven, those few stuck to it.

"Come on, lads, just one more!" sang out Grenfell, with his coat off.

And they worked and heaved, and did it. Every one of those guns they saved.

But then, be it repeated, the lancers and gunners always were good pals.

★★★★★★

By midday General Smith-Dorrien's task had become one of the gravest difficulty. And this was but the opening phase of a movement which, I venture to think, will be accounted by the historian as one of the most astonishing pieces of work in military history. I refer not to the Retreat as a whole, but to the work of the Second Corps and its leader from 3 a.m. of the 24th to about midnight of the 26th—27th. An eternity of years was encircled by those few hours.

The difficulties of the movement can probably be appreciated at their full value only by the military student with a vivid imagination, so I will just suggest what had to be done. First of all, General Smith-Dorrien had to get his men away from the Mons line in the early dawn in the face of overwhelming numbers, numbers which he could only guess at, for at any moment a big attack might be made by another army upon his left flank. This was very much complicated by his men having been severely handled all through the Sunday, and getting no food nor rest. In fact, it was the human element which really made all the movement so difficult. The feeling that at any moment the tremendous strain upon the men's endurance would stretch to breaking-point and snap.

Then the G.O.C. had not merely to get his men gradually back, but they had to show a bold front the whole time. It was a matter of fighting backwards without a moment's rest. A couple of regiments, say, with some cavalry, would halt for half an hour on a certain line, and hold up with the heaviest fire they could the attack on their particular section. Then, when the enemy got nearer, up they would jump and go straight at the Germans with the bayonet, the cavalry backing them up all they knew. The same with the guns.

A battery would manoeuvre into a position, come into action, and pound away for a quarter of an hour. Then, at the right moment (and it called for the nicest judgment to select that moment) four guns would be run back, limbered up, and got away, while the remaining couple would continue an intermittent fire to cover the retirement. These in turn would slip away—if they could.

The casualties under conditions like these must, of course, be very heavy indeed. That they were not infinitely heavier was due to the splendid use the men made of the ground, taking cover and so on, and to the noble spirit of self-sacrifice for comrades which animated every unit.

Thirdly, the G.O.C. had to remember that he was not playing a lone hand, but that he had to consider the retirement of the First Corps on his right. He had to play the match for his side. Just at the moment Jessop, in the person of Sir Douglas Haig, was in with him, and Jessop had to hit out against time to make the runs while Leveson-Gower (Smith-Dorrien) kept up his wicket at the other end.

And, fourthly, to carry on the metaphor, when Jessop was forced to "retire hurt" Leveson-Gower had to begin to hit at just that moment when he felt that he had "collared the bowling." In other words, the G.O.C, having held a certain line of defence for a couple of hours or so, had to judge to a nicety the exact moment when he had, for the time, broken the enemy's attack sufficiently to permit of retirement another two miles to the next position.

Those four points, then, constitute in very broad outline the task which General Smith-Dorrien had to perform. Our people have not been slow to recognise how magnificently he and his men accomplished it.

The enemy were now, by accident or design, beginning to drive in a wedge at Frameries between the two corps. Always a serious situation, especially when, as now, units had become very scattered in the gradual retirement. The gap was filled to some extent by the 5th Brigade, which General Smith-Dorrien borrowed from the First Corps.

★★★★★★

Impressions gleaned from the other side are always of interest. Another German officer, whom we got a few days later, gave me his opinion of the British work somewhat like this.

"All our text-books," he said, "about rear-guard actions will have to be rewritten, and you have certainly taught us a lesson. It has been just like advancing into a wall of fog. The fog is elastic enough when one enters it, but soon it clings all round and chokes you. We pushed in all right, but never came out at the other side."

Personally, I felt inclined to apply the metaphor the reverse way, and that is how the men felt it. The dense, overpowering cloud rolling down, the battling against it with impotent anns, and the fog penetrating into every gap in the lines.

The men were dazed, stunned by the continuous onslaughts. There seemed no end to them. As fast as one German company was mown down another would spring up. It was as though their aircraft flew over with watchful eye to sow in every field another bushel of the mythical dragon's teeth. And everywhere more and more German guns would come into action to support their infantry, and everywhere more and more machine-guns would be rushed up by their very mobile transport to rake and enfilade the British companies or gun detachments.

At the time all these things were not realised, for there was no sitting down for five minutes to ruminate. But now, after eighteen months, when one pieces together this fact and that, and learns something of what the actual numbers were, one hesitates to set it down on paper for fear of being flatly disbelieved.

Any record of feelings during those hours is blurred. But there was one thought which, I know, was uppermost in every man's mind: "Where on earth are the French?"

When a thought like that has been born it is easy to guess how it will grow and run through the ranks. If only now and again they had seen a French squadron swoop down upon the enemy's flank in front of them everything would have been well. They would have cheered their French comrades on, and gone in for all they were worth to avenge their death, if called upon. But never a French soldier did one of our lads see.

So far as I know, our Allies have published no official account of their retreat from Namur, although they have very frankly admitted, in an official Government report, the mistakes which were then made and have shown how they were since rectified. It is by no means clear what happened to the 5th French Army on our right after Namur had fallen; we only knew that we never saw them.

But at the time it must be remembered that no one in the British Force, save G.H.Q., knew what was happening even to themselves, so it was hardly likely that they could learn anything definite about the French. So there the subject may rest.

★★★★★★

In the early afternoon General Smith-Dorrien learned that the First Corps had "made good" during the morning, and were fighting their way back with sufficient success to admit of his own retirement when he was able to break away.

Although, perhaps, too little space has been given in this chapter to the work of the First Corps, they had nearly as hard a fight as the rest of the Force. The task before Sir Douglas Haig was probably not quite so delicate as General Smith-Dorrien's, but it was obviously one of as grave a responsibility. However, in the late afternoon he got safely back, as we have seen, to the position determined by the commander-in-chief.

The Second Corps then succeeded in breaking away, and by the evening a new line of the entire Force was formed, reaching from the fortress of Maubeuge on the right to two little villages, Bry and Jenlain, on the left. The 19th Brigade, which had come into the fight in the morning, was posted on and across the extreme left.

It should be noted that, with the fall of Tournai and the destruction of the French troops in that neighbourhood, the whole country on the west was open to the invaders. Their victorious army corps operating there was now able to swing round to attack the British left, and their cavalry was already sweeping in flying squadrons and patrols over the countryside. In fact, the French Channel ports, from Boulogne to Havre, were there for the taking, and the French coast line, for which the enemy fought so valiantly a few months later, would have been theirs without a struggle.

But these facts were only vaguely realised in the Force, and the men, of course, knew nothing of doings save only upon their immediate front. At every moment they fully expected to make a definite stand, with an advance to follow, and thus they remained in good heart, secure in the conviction that though badly mauled they were

not even at the beginning of a defeat. But some of us knew and realised, and it was a hard task to keep the knowledge from the men and
from the friendly country-folk.

Chapter 9

The Second Day

Gloucester, 'tis true that we are in great danger;
The greater, therefore, should our courage be.—
God Almighty! There is some soul of goodness in things evil,
Would men observingly distil it out.
For our bad neighbour makes us early stirrers,
Which is both healthful and good husbandry.

During the night of Monday the whole Force was on or about the line already indicated, with the fortress of Maubeuge on their right flank. But let it not be imagined that the men settled down quietly at 9 p.m. to a cosy supper with a night's sleep to follow. There was no such thing as a halt for any time. Incidentally, most of the horses went through the whole business without being off-saddled once. The first regiments in were the first to move off again. The men just dropped down in the road where they halted and, if lucky, snatched ten minutes' sleep. Many of the men seemed to sleep while they marched; although, as one has often done it on night manoeuvres at home, there was nothing curious about that.

By midnight I do not think that anybody very much cared what happened. There was a certain amount of trench digging going on, and there was, in consequence, some idea that a stand would be made. But the men were really too exhausted to care one way or the other.

It is all very well to remark upon their invariable cheeriness, as most writers seem to delight in doing, but it gives a hopelessly wrong impression of the hardships. A certain form of "cheery spirit" is inseparable from the British soldier when he is up against a tough job, but you can't very well be lively and make funny remarks (as reported in the Press) when you have become an automaton in all your movements.

Had the French held firm, in all probability a stand would have been made on this line. But there is no object in speculating about it now. The view adopted by the commander-in-chief, which determined a further retreat, may best be given in his own words:

> The French were still retiring, and I had no support except such as was afforded by the fortress of Maubeuge; and the determined attempts of the enemy to get round my left flank assured me that it was his intention to hem me against that place and surround me. I felt that not a moment must be lost in retiring to another position.
>
> I hoped, that the enemy's pursuit would not be too vigorous to prevent me effecting my object.

This hope was, fortunately, fulfilled, and the second day's retirement was, on the whole, less eventful. Later I will hazard a suggestion why it was so.

The necessary orders had been given overnight to be clear of the Valenciennes—Bavai—Maubeuge road by 5.30 a.m. The Second Corps got clear by the time specified, but the First Corps could only begin their move at that hour, and so got behind. This fact tended to make inevitable the fight which took place that evening at Landrecies.

It was, as I remember, a baking hot day, with a blazing sun in a cloudless sky. Along English country roads and through our own little dappled-grey villages it would have been trying enough; but French roads, built Roman fashion, do not try to be picturesque and charming, and they certainly have no sense of humour like ours. Thus, the day's march was simply purgatory to a tired force. The fruit trees with their harvest really saved the situation. But, oh, those green apples and pears!

Once again, do not imagine the regiments trekking along straight for their next destination. The day was less eventful only in comparison with Monday and Wednesday. It was a rear-guard action most of the way, and there was quite enough fighting to break the monotony, with some big cavalry actions and the 5th Brigade heavily engaged.

Take, for instance, a field battery in the 2nd Division. The timetable would be something like this: 5.30 a.m., open fire; 6, cease fire and limber up; 6.10, *en route* to new position; 6.30, halt, open fire; 6.40, cease fire, limber up, and start off for new position; 7.15, halt, open fire; and so on all through the day. In fact, that was the ordinary day's programme.

The particular battery I have in mind had a little adventure all to itself on Tuesday. It is of interest as revealing another side of German thoroughness.

The battery was in action, but had temporarily ceased firing, and the detachments were lying by the guns.

A big grey "Sunbeam" drew up on a road to the flank of the battery, and a couple of red-tabbed staff officers jumped out, walked up to the nearest gun, and started to chat with one of the gunners.

After a few remarks about how well the battery had been doing, they asked some questions about casualties, positions of neighbouring batteries, the infantry near them, and the usual facts which the Staff come to inquire about.

The major had been watching from the far flank, and, as the staff officers turned to get into their car, he remarked to the sergeant-major:

" I don't quite like the look of those two officers; there's something wrong about them." And he had a look through his glasses.

Some distance along the road there was marching down a company of R.E.'s.

"Call up those sappers (by flag) and tell them to hold up that car."

The sergeant-major repeated the message to the flag-wagger.

"Stop grey car—suspicious."

The R.E. sergeant ran up to the subaltern in charge:

"Battery signals 'stop grey car.'"

"Well, stop it, then," replied the subaltern irritably.

So the grey car was stopped, very much to the annoyance of two staff officers who were in a great hurry to get back to G.H.Q.

"Very sorry, sir," said the subaltern, "but it's a telegraph message from that battery. The O.C. has probably got something special to send to G.H.Q." And the car was escorted back again.

The O.C. had "something special to send" in the shape of a couple of German officers, very carefully disguised as British. A drumhead court-martial was held at Corps H.Q., and as the Germans in question were hopelessly compromised by the very full notes which they had managed to collect from various units about the Force, the case was clear.

"Guilty. To be shot at dawn."

They were plucky fellows, but—well, a spy is a spy, and that's all about it.

★★★★★★

Less than a week before the country folk had watched with delight and relief the passing of mighty transport columns of British, had welcomed and cheered the men forward, proud and confident in the anticipation of early victory.

Now imagine their feelings, their alarm, at the sight of British regiments, war-worn, weary and battered, trailing back as fast as they could move.

Of what use was it to tell them that this was only a strategical retirement? Panic spreads quickly, and once the hint of calamity is given it is impossible to check the alarm.

But even then it was some little time before the stolid peasants of Northern France could grasp the meaning of what they saw, and I remember well how the inhabitants of a certain little village crowded out to watch the extraordinary (to them) behaviour of a regiment which was in the extreme rear of the retiring First Corps.

The village overlooked a valley, and there was a splendid view of the British lines retiring in open order up the hill towards the little hamlet. They came up panting heavily and, just under the brow of the hill, set to work to dig up some rough shelter. The folk stood watching, laughing and talking, until an exasperated lance-corporal threw his tool in front of an oldish man.

"'Ere, it's about b—— well time *you* did a bit"; and the corporal sat down to wipe off some of the dirt from his face.

In a few minutes all the men and women had started digging as though for buried treasure, and the British sat still for a spell and encouraged them with happy comments.

Very soon down the opposite slope thousands of little grey-blue ants came swiftly, and from the ridge behind them dim flashes shot out.

"Now, then, you'd better 'op it!" said the lance-corporal.

And even then they didn't understand what those ants really were.

"Allmonds!" was the lance-corporal's laconic remark.

The arrival of a shell settled it, and the villagers ran helter-skelter for their houses and little treasures. In a quarter of an hour another pitiable reinforcement had joined the ranks of the refugee army flying southwards, and only the old cure remained, ever true to his charge. They were gallant gentlemen those French cures, and bravely they

93

faced the death which nearly always overtook them at the hands of those murderers.

It was not until the British had turned to advance from the Marne that they began fully to realise the nature of the Germans. As yet they encountered no evidence of the atrocious, bestial work of the enemy. But already rumour was busy, and even on this day I had recorded authentic details that the Germans were placing women and children before their advancing infantry, and that they were stabbing the wounded with the bayonet.

On the Sunday another British Division, the 4th, had arrived at Le Cateau, the little town to which the Force was now moving. This meant a reinforcement of some 14,500 men, together with three field batteries. They were there waiting to come into action on the Wednesday, and in the meantime had begun to entrench.

The general line of retirement on the Tuesday was:

(*a*) First Corps, Bavai—Maubeuge, to Landrecies—Maroilles .
(*b*) Second Corps, Bry—Bavai, to west of Le Cateau.

A glance at the picture-map will show the position of these places. It will be noted that the various divisions kept together pretty well. Also that between Landrecies and Le Cateau there was a gap in the line which the 6th Brigade could not properly fill. The commander-in-chief remarks in his dispatch that the men in the First Corps were too exhausted to march farther so as to cover this gap.

You picture, then, the regiments arriving one by one at the end of that most exhausting day. The men dog-tired, hardly able to drag their feet over the burning ground, no proper meal since a hasty breakfast at dawn, fighting on and off all day, and now simply done to the world.

Now, it is a golden rule in the service that, however tired the men may be, they must set to work at the end of their march to entrench themselves or otherwise prepare against possible attack. I leave it to your imagination to realise the meaning of "discipline" when you learn that the men did entrench themselves that evening. And never was that rule more finely vindicated.

I conceive Marshal von Kluck at German G.H.Q. soliloquising that Tuesday morning something in this wise:

My friends von Buelow and Hansen have between them settled with the French on this side, and *they* won't give any more trouble. Von Buelow and I have pretty well pounded and demoralised the English, and one more effort should finish *them*.

Now, I will just give them enough to keep them busy through today, keep them on the run and exhaust them thoroughly, and then tonight we'll have a really hot attack and crumple up the First Corps. They'll never stand that; and we shall then have the rest of their army surrounded.

And that is the suggestion about the day's work which I venture to make. We have seen how the daylight hours went for the British, and how the Force drifted in to their destinations. Now we will see how von Kluck crumpled up the First Corps with his night attack.

The 1st Division was halted in and about Maroilles, and the 2nd Division at Landrecies. They were therefore on the extreme right of the line, with their flank more or less "in the air," for no French seemed to be near. Landrecies was held by the 4th Brigade, battalions of the Foot Guards, Grenadiers, Coldstreams and Irish, under General Scott-Kerr.

The torrid heat of the day had been the prelude to a cool, rainy evening. Room was found for about two-thirds of the Brigade in the houses and halls of the little town—a typical French country-town, with its straight streets and market-place. The remainder of the men got what little comfort they could on a rainy night outside.

By 9 p.m. they had hardly begun to settle down, after "clearing decks for action"—in case. Outposts had been placed, and the men were congratulating themselves on a comfortable shelter after so many nights of foot slogging. At 9.30 lights were out, and town and country-side were in pitch darkness.

A battalion of the Coldstream Guards had not yet arrived, but was about a quarter of a mile from the town, marching in. The colonel was at the head of the column with the guide. This man persisted in flashing an electric torch to and fro towards the left, and the C.O. peremptorily ordered him to put it out.

The man obeyed for a few yards, and then flashed the light again.

The C.O. at once grasped the situation, drew his revolver, and shot the spy dead.

It was as though that bullet had been fired straight into a mountain of gunpowder.

With a terrific crash German guns opened fire. Simultaneously, on front and flank, rifles and machine-guns blazed out.

A German night attack is no question of feeling a way in open order until the enemy's outposts are driven in; it comes down like a smith's hammer on the anvil.

The Coldstreamers, with miraculous discipline, swung round and got into a kind of line with the outposts already there, then continued retirement to the town at the double.

The outpost line was crushed through almost in a moment like tissue paper, and before anyone could grasp what was happening the Germans were pouring their massed columns into the town.

Thus began perhaps the most critical and certainly the most remarkable fight in which British regiments have ever been engaged.

Tired out, the men tumbled out of the houses; three privates and a corporal here, a dozen men and a sergeant there, a subaltern, a private and a machine-gun at another corner, half a dozen men at two first-floor windows somewhere else. And the only light came from the flash of the rifles.

There was no idea of forming ranks, even had it been possible. Slowly, steadily up the streets the great German mammoth crept, and, like tigers at their prey, the men of the Guards sprang at head and flanks, worrying with grim-set teeth to the heart of the beast.

Now the British machine-guns opened fire straight upon the head of the column, swept it away, swept the succeeding ranks, until the mass was brought to a standstill.

More Guardsmen threw themselves straight at the ranks, firing as they could, crashing in with bayonet and clubbed rifle.

Now the column shivers; but the Germans are brave men. They rally, for their comrades are pouring into the town to help them. Up side streets and lanes, by all the approaches they come, and everywhere the men of the Guards spring at them.

But surely numbers must tell. What can four battered regiments, fighting by handfuls, do in face of such thousands of a fresh army corps!

From Maroilles right down the line the British are fighting for their lives, for von Kluck has staked heavily on this throw, and it would seem that the dice are loaded. He pushes his guns up still closer until some are firing into the town almost at point-blank range. Again, what does it matter if his own men are swept away? There are thousands more to fill their places.

The houses have begun to blaze fiercely in the torrents of rain, and there is plenty of light at last. And now the Guards rally for a supreme effort. The last, the forlorn hope—but it is the Guards, and at least they will go down fighting to the last man.

One mighty heave—in at them—again—they are breaking—heave!

They have done it. Broken them. Driven them out. And behind them the enemy leave close upon 1,000 dead.

Away up by Maroilles Sir Douglas Haig has fought his men like one possessed, and there, too, he has broken the German attack, just as two French Reserve Divisions came up to his aid.

Slowly, sullenly, von Kluck withdraws his legions. Slowly and fitfully the firing dies away, and by 2 a.m. all is still once more.

CHAPTER 10

An Interlude

. . .As many ways meet in one town;
As many fresh streams meet in one salt sea;
As many lines close in the dial's centre;
So may a thousand actions, once afoot.
End in one purpose, and be all well borne
Without defeat.

There is something more than magic in the poetry of Shakespeare's *Henry V.* when it is read to illustrate the stirring events of these opening phases of the War. To set it side by side with the recital of the story is to listen to the voice of a singer supported by the gravely-sounding, deep-toned brass instruments of an orchestra.

There is more than beauty of accompaniment, there is the magic of prophecy. I can hardly find an incident of those August days which was not mirrored three centuries ago in the verse of this play. Thus, I have sought in no other for the musical preludes of my chapters; and I confess often to have rubbed my eyes in astonishment at the aptness of the poetry to the incidents of the moment.

Now those few bars of introduction suggest another *motif;* let me try to expand the theme a little.

In reading the cold, semi-official language which states that the British Force halted at such and such an hour along a line extending from So-and-So to Somewhere, one is apt to gain an impression which is far removed from reality.

You picture, perhaps, the various units retiring along routes carefully assigned by gilded Staff officers, and duly arriving at the scheduled times in various villages and hamlets. That there they are met by courteous billeting parties, who proceed to allot the men to more or less unwilling householders. That at the hour specified in the report you find the Dorsets in one place, the Irish Guards next to them, the batteries with their guns neatly parked, and so on all down the line. The various H.Q.'s of Brigades, Divisions or Corps all in readily accessible spots, and everybody connected up with everybody else by telegraph or telephone, so that any unit can be set in motion at any minute.

That is the ideal. Well, that delightful ideal first assumed definite shape after the Battle of the Marne and not before. Here is a little sketch of a tiny village on the line of retreat on the evening of Tuesday, August 25th:

★★★★★★

M. le maire, old Pierre Godolphin, sat slowly pulling at a new clay pipe as he looked with unseeing eyes up the long dusty road which led out of the village away over the northern uplands. A trimly kept hedge of privet bordered his rose-garden and the road, and his favourite seat was set in a little niche of the greenery whence he could command all that went on in his tiny kingdom and, without moving, could see exactly what *Madame la Femme du Maire* was about in the stone-flagged kitchen.

That afternoon an avalanche of three-ton motor lorries had descended upon the village, weird vehicles which announced in blatant language the superiority over all others of Mayflower's margarine or the outstanding merits of Pulltite's corsets. The men in authority were obviously, from their uniforms, English officers, and not travellers for the firms in question. But, frankly, old Pierre was puzzled. They had come from the south, and why did they not continue their journey? Two of the officers were actually proposing to stay with him, for an indefinite period.

M. le boulanger walked slowly across the road to confer with him about the baking of more bread. "But these English are like a locust swarm, and I have no more flour," he explained.

"A glass of cider for *monsieur*, Henriette."

"I do not understand," Pierre went on, "what it is *ces braves garçons* do here. It is the third week of war, and by now surely *ces bêtes de Boches* should have been driven back into their own pigsties——*Mais, nom de Dieu, qu'est ce que c'est?*"

Down the village street a four-seater car came lurching from side to side like a drunken man. Crash! It has caught a stone post and turned over. In an instant the road is full of people running.

Two men lay dazed as they had been thrown out. Both in the yellow-green uniform of the British, one, certainly, an officer. Willing hands lift them tenderly, and someone dashes a jug of water over their heads. Then one sees what has happened.

Between the shoulders on the officer's tunic there is spreading a great dark stain. Very carefully they take off the coat and shirt and try to stanch the blood. But it is too late; there is a bullet through the lungs, and, with a little gasp, the officer lies still.

In a few minutes the other man recovers sufficiently to tell how they were taking a dispatch through to the rear. The officer was driving the car when they ran straight into a patrol of enemy cavalry. They had got through, but the enemy opened fire, and now his officer lies dead. Things are going badly up there—and the man vaguely indicates the country up north: our men are retiring as hard as they can; whole regiments are getting wiped out; and "Gawd knows where the French are." Can he get a motorbike to take on the message?

An A.S.C. officer runs for his car, the man is put in, and off they start again.

Only the A.S.C. lorry drivers understood the story, but the villagers were quick to realise that something serious was happening. Old Pierre remembered 1870, and he knew what war meant; but to the rest it was a new, hideous thing, dimly realised, but now, at last, with this mute witness before them, very real.

Then things began to happen. No one ever knows how a crowd will spring up in a city street, apparently by magic, and here suddenly the village began to fill with men.

Four soldiers—two Scots, a Dorset and a Bedford man—black with grime, three days' growth of beard, hollow-eyed and limping painfully, appeared in front of Pierre and asked where they were to go. A captain of the Guards, riding a tired farm-horse, with a colonel walking by his side, one hand on the horse's flank, came behind, and, tackling the A.S.C. captain, asked for something to eat.

"We've been on the trudge for twelve hours," said the colonel, "and could get nothing. No one knows where anyone is. The regiment? Badly cut up last night and all scattered, heaven knows where."

"Is the mayor about anywhere?" And a young staff officer, with a French interpreter, pushes his way through the crowd.

"A cavalry brigade ("or what's left of it"—he adds in an undertone) "will be here tonight. What barns and houses have you available? How much hay can you get?"

Old Pierre is beginning to lose his wits in the amazing turn of events.

"If *monsieur* will come into the house I will try to arrange."

The officer follows, with a shrug of the shoulders which might have meant many things.

The long summer's day is closing, but there is no hint of the evening's cool in the heavy air. All over the little village green, where the church tower has thrown a grateful shadow, lie groups of men worn with exhaustion and sleeping with gulping breaths. In one corner Henriette is busy with water and clean linen, bathing and bandaging horrible, staring wounds. And the men lie patiently, with now and then a moan of pain, gazing up at her with the great round eyes of a hurt collie dog.

And now the vanguard of the retiring army begins to stream in and through—all arms, all regiments. Overhead a flight of aeroplanes circle, like homing pigeons, seeking where they may alight. It is incredible that these are the regiments which a little ten days ago swung gaily down the Aldershot roads.

At the head of the column there marches a field battery. Two days ago the major took it into action six guns and wagons strong, with perhaps a couple of hundred men; so proud in his command, his men, his horses.

Now, stand by the path and watch the battery pass! And, as it passes, uncover your head, for it has returned from the very gates of Death.

Two guns—with three horses each to draw them. There are still four drivers left, and there are still half a dozen gunners. On the first limber ride a subaltern and the sergeant-major, and by the gun walk another sergeant and the quartermaster-sergeant. That is the battery.

On the second limber three men sit, swaying dizzily. A captain of a cavalry regiment and two privates of a Scottish regiment.

Here marches a battalion of the Guards. Two days ago it went into action perhaps 1,100 strong. Uncover your head once again as it passes, for these men too have looked Death in the face.

At the head there paces slowly an ammunition-mule. On it, wearing a peasant's slouch hat, with breeches cut off above the knees, and with left arm held close by a rough bandage, there rides the colonel. Count the men as they march past in fours: 80, 120, 160, 180, 220. No, that is the next regiment you are counting in. Just 200! That is the tale of them.

Blackened by dust and powder, bearded, breeches cut short like those of their commanding officer, the few *puttees* that are left to them wrapped round their feet for boots—otherwise bits of sacking or cloth, bloody bandages round heads or arms, some with hats like the colonel's, most with none at all slowly they limp by. And, as they pass, the A.S.C. drivers silently offer such biscuits or bread as they have. God, how they wolf the food!

The colonel turns round on his "charger," and in a hoarse shout:

"Battalion! 'Tention! Pull yourselves together, lads; a French village!"

Ah, the pride of them! The glory of race and blood! This is not the Mons country, with its blood-soaked memories; 'tis the Horse Guards Parade, and we're Trooping the Colour!

The click of rifles coming to the slope runs down the ranks. The fours line by magic as the men straighten themselves; it is a new regiment, marching into action, which the French villagers see pass before them.

"Defeat? Why, this is part of the joke! Just to draw the Germans on into the trap." And at a word they would have turned to charge an army corps.

And so the regiments pass. And as the last of the division goes through, lights twinkle from the tiny windows of the cottages and the great yellow moon climbs slowly over the poplar trees. An A.S.C. sergeant mounts a lorry with a copy of the Paris *Daily Mail* in his hand, and entertains an ever-growing audience with the news that the Russians have invaded Germany and are marching on Berlin.

"It will be all over by Christmas—but I'd 'ave liked just one slap at them Germans, so as I could tell the missis," says a late bus-driver.

But on the outskirts of the crowd the staff officer is talking to the A.S.C. captain:

"I've no orders for you, but you've evidently been forgotten. You ought to have had your park fifteen miles farther south by now. Things are bad, and there will be the hell of a scrap round here tomorrow morning. I should clear out if I were you."

Away up to the north there is a blinding electric glare coming fast down the road. Nearer, and it is the headlight on the first of a long train of R.F.C. light motor-lorries, slipping silently down on rubber tires. The dust rises in clouds above and about them. Halfway through the village a motorcyclist rides, meeting them. The dust takes his shadow, and as he approaches the headlight the silhouette rises higher and higher until it mounts to the sky and disappears. Just as when children play a shadow pantomime and vanish by jumping over the lamp.

The lorries pass, and the dust slowly settles once more. The little lights twinkle clearly again, and the moon now floods the countryside in a sheen of silver.

But the A.S.C. captain talks earnestly with his sergeant-major and *M. le maire.*

"We must move, but how can we possibly carry all those wounded and stragglers?"

M. le maire is of opinion that as *les Boches* are being driven back into Germany, the wounded might well remain until ambulances can be got.

The O.C. looks at his sergeant-major. They have both guessed the meaning of that retirement, and they guess also something that they dare not tell the mayor.

A few minutes suffice to rouse all the men and to get the wounded made as comfortable as possible in the lorries. Lights are switched on the cars, and within half an hour the column is clear of the village on its way south.

An hour later the advance patrols of a German cavalry division ride in from the north; and old Pierre finds that the hay he had collected for *les anglais* does not go very far with his new visitors.

Poor old Pierre, and *Madame* the mayoress, and the pretty little rose-garden!

Such is a little pen-picture, not one whit exaggerated, of an evening of the Retreat. And perhaps those few lines will serve to convey some trifling idea of the wonder of the achievement.

Everywhere regiments and units forgotten, or lost, or acting on their own initiative. And yet, somehow or other, making a composite whole to turn and repel the attacking hordes. Staff work practically ceased to exist, and yet the threads of communication held fast, though only by a little.

Now you have had a glimpse of the men who, the very next day, fought and *won* perhaps the most glorious fight a British Army has ever shared in.

So may a thousand actions, once afoot,
End in one purpose, and be all well borne
Without defeat.

CHAPTER 11

Wednesday, the 26th of August

We few, we happy few, we band of brothers;
For he today that sheds his blood with me
Shall be my brother; be he ne'er so vile,
This day shall gentle his condition.
Westmoreland. *Of fighting men they have full three-score thousand.*
Exeter. *There's five to one; besides, they all are fresh.*
Salisbury. *God's arm strike with us! 'tis a fearful odds.*

The night attack which the First Corps had so magnificently repulsed was but the prelude to the greater attack of August 26th. So imminent did the danger appear to the Commander-in-Chief, so tense was the anxiety, that immediately after the firing had died away at midnight orders were issued to the First Corps to march again at daybreak. I cannot attempt to dwell upon the condition of the men after the battle of Sunday, the fighting and marching of Monday and Tuesday, and, finally, the great fight of Tuesday night. One can but quote the words of Sir John French: "*They were too exhausted to be placed in the fighting line,*" and "*were at the moment incapable of movement,*" and so leave the rest to the imagination.

To that extent, then, had von Kluck succeeded in his scheme. The First Corps were temporarily out of action; the French, as the commander-in-chief remarks, "were unable to afford any support on the most critical day of all "; and to the Second Corps was left the task of withstanding the whole German attack, designed to outflank them on the left and roll them up. And the odds against them were, as at Agincourt, "five to one;" in guns, more than six to one.

Apart from his 3rd and 5th Divisions, General Smith-Dorrien had taken under his command the detached 19th Infantry Brigade (composed of the 2nd Royal Welsh Fusiliers, 1st Scottish Rifles, 1st Middlesex, 2nd Argyll and Sutherland Highlanders), the infantry and some of the R.F.A. of the 4th Division, and two brigades of cavalry, out by Cambrai.

The line of the Second Corps on the Tuesday night extended, roughly, from Le Cateau on the east to a little south of Cambrai on the west, or a front of about fifteen miles. Trenches had been hastily dug since the previous afternoon. East of Le Cateau was a big gap between the two corps. This could not be bridged owing to the exhausted condition of the regiments in the 2nd Division.

Some hours before battle was joined General Smith-Dorrien realised that it was absolutely impossible for him to carry out the commander-in-chief's instructions and continue his retirement in conjunction with the First Corps. A retirement in face of such overwhelming numbers would have meant annihilation. At 2 a.m. he decided to fight, and reported so to his chief. Sir John French replied that the retirement must continue.

My only chance is to do my utmost in weakening the enemy's attack, and then seize such a moment as I can to retire.

General Smith-Dorrien was on the field of action; Sir John French was at G.H.Q., some twenty miles to the south. The man on the spot, realising that the only hope of stopping the enemy lay in a successful action, proceeded with his plans of battle. The fight began at daylight.

About 7 a.m. General Smith-Dorrien informed G.H.Q. by telephone that the battle was in progress, and that he was confident that he could deal the enemy a smashing blow sufficiently heavy to gain time to withdraw his weary troops.

"General," said the senior staff officer over the telephone, "yours is the cheeriest voice I've heard for three days. I'll go and tell the chief."

The commander-in-chief, who did not approve of the decision to fight, in reply instructed him "to use his utmost endeavours to break off the action and retire at the earliest possible moment."

★★★★★★

Le Cateau, after which this battle has come to be named, is a pleasant enough little town set in a country-side not unlike the Sussex uplands between Tonbridge and Hastings—broad, open pasture- and meadow-land, cut by tiny valleys, rolling away south to the dip of St. Quentin. Through the town runs one broad street, and here, in the town hall offices, G.H.Q. had its habitation for a short spell earlier in the week. Opposite there was a little bun-shop and *café* combined, which proudly announced: "English five o'clock tea." The two buxom ladies who dispensed the refreshing beverage must have overheard many a little confidence exchanged between their unsuspecting officer clients, and we heard later that one of the two had been shot as a German spy.

With the earliest dawn the firing began along the front with such a curious spitefulness (if one could so call it) that many of our men afterwards remarked about it. There were evidently to be no half measures about this attack, for the German infantry came on almost with the first rounds from their guns, advancing in their usual masses and making big play with their machine-guns. It was good country for this kind of work, while the cover our men got was generally only such as they could make for themselves by digging.

The morning came on radiantly sunny, with the sky a lovely pale limpid blue, washed clear by the downpour of the previous night.

"An' 'tis a foine morning they'll be having in Lismore for the fair this day," remarked a lad from County Cork; "but I would not be missin' the fair *we'll* be having for all the porter in Daddy Breean's ould tent. Ah, will ye look at that now! Shure, 'tis the bhoys are coming early for the knocks they'll be getting. Will I be seeing how the little gun is shooting this morning, yer honour?"

The platoon commander nodded, for Jerry was a privileged favourite. He was also a remarkably fine shot.

So Jerry nestled his cheek cosily down to his little gun and took a deep breath, while the two or three near him looked on with interest. Jerry lifted his head again, for he was an artist and knew the value of arousing expectation.

"And will it be a golden sovereign if I take the coat-tails of the little ould gentleman with the spy-glasses?" This was Jerry's way of making a bet.

"Yes; I'll bet you a sovereign you won't down that officer on the right, and he looks like the colonel," said the platoon commander. It was a 500 yards' shot, and hazy, too.

Jerry carefully judged the distance by a halfway haystack, adjusted his sight, and settled down once again. "For the ould counthry!" he breathed, and slowly squeezed the trigger.

The "little ould gentleman" was seen to clap his hand smartly to his leg, while two men ran up to him.

"Will ye double the stakes, yer honour, for me to take the three o' them?" said Jerry over his shoulder, clicking his bolt back and forward again.

"A fiver, Jerry, if you do it."

Jerry wedged his rifle between two stones, took a slightly fuller sight, and almost before you could have counted them three shots cracked out.

"Have you that fiver on you, yer honour, or will I be taking an I O U?" And Jerry leaned back with a sigh of satisfaction as a mighty cheer ran down the trench, and the platoon officer shook him hard by the hand. What the enemy thought about it one could only surmise, but a few of the men shook their fists threateningly in the direction of the British lines.

★★★★★★

Now let us follow for a little the fortunes of a brigade in a particularly warm corner of the line close to a small town where a very strong German attack soon developed. The guns of the Brigade opened fire at daybreak. They had managed to dig some serviceable pits, and were as snugly ensconced as time had allowed.

For an hour, perhaps, the German guns pounded steadily away without making very much impression; and our R.F.A. as steadily replied. Many of the outlying farms and houses were badly knocked about and began to burn fiercely. About 7.30 the enemy made a determined attempt to get hold of a flank position for their machine-guns to enfilade our infantry; and it was then that one regiment lost horribly before our cavalry could get round in a counter-attack. So heavy were their casualties that, as a regiment, they were simply out of action, and an urgent message was dispatched to the next Brigade for anything they could possibly send in the way of reinforcements. Badly off though they were, two battalions were promptly transferred. Just one more instance of working shoulder to shoulder.

It was curious how certain regiments suffered very heavily while other units next to them got off comparatively lightly. One R.F.A. brigade, for instance, was right in the thick of the fighting from Mons to the Aisne, and yet had very few losses until the middle of September, while the battery next on their left on this Wednesday suffered very badly. Of two other batteries I came across, one was in action right through to the Aisne, and did not have a single casualty, while a second (most curious of all), in the First Corps, never fired a shot until the big advance of the corps at the Aisne on September 14th.

GENERAL SIR DOUGLAS HAIG

About 9 a.m. things began to look serious. Several enemy infantry attacks had been met by desperate counter-charges; but numbers were bound to tell. A German cavalry regiment had succeeded in working round to the flank, and now they made a gallant effort to capture the British guns. This was, I believe, one of the very few occasions when the enemy cavalry had a real chance of getting any of our batteries by a charge. There was a clear field, and they had got to within 500 yards of the battery, when the guns opened on them. Our men had heard about the fatal charge of the 9th Lancers, and now it was their turn. The battery commander dropped to "fuse to, open sights," and the detachments worked as though the devil were behind them. In the next 250 yards the cavalry lost a good two-thirds of the regiment, and they got no nearer than 200 yards from the guns. A British squadron luckily came out at the moment, and charged clean through the remnant, wheeled, and cut up what still remained. And that was the end of that very game attack.

If only the Germans would always play fair, there would be nothing to grumble about. Their infantry cannot, of course, be compared with the British, and our cavalry have always come out better than theirs in a clean fight; but the Germans have always fought courageously when it was a case of genuine fighting. Indeed, it is a very poor compliment to our men to suggest otherwise.

But the main attack, instead of being checked, seemed to gather strength, until it became manifestly impossible to protect and hold the little town any longer. The infantry accordingly gradually withdrew under cover of the guns, and at last the guns were limbered up and marched back to another position farther south, the Brigade having held the corner for something like four hours.

Most of the townsfolk had begun their flight late on the previous evening, but a good many still remained. Had they only known the fate in store for them, the invaders would have found an empty town.. But, at least in this case, vengeance was swift, as you shall hear.

The brigade, then, took up its new position, and the men were able to make themselves fairly snug before the enemy had finished with the town. Fortunately, too, many of our wounded were got away from the hospital, for the Germans had begun to shell that some time before. But it was a very trying business, as there were not enough ambulances for the very large number of casualties, and many had to be carried on the already overloaded regimental transport.

★★★★★★

Now, it must be remembered that General Smith-Dorrien had absolutely no reserves on which to draw if any part of his line began to bend back. The usual plan is, of course, to keep certain fresh regiments concentrated at given spots to move up in support as and when required. But now, if the Inniskillings were getting badly cut up and a gap was being made, the G.O.C. could only call upon the Cheshires, say, a mile off, who were not being so strongly attacked, to send a company or so to the help of their comrades.

Another thing. I have hinted in a previous chapter that the threads of communication with the ammunition supply were badly stretched to breaking-point, owing to the astonishing speed at which the British had to retire. Normally, the ammunition parks (motor transport) draw the ammunition supplies from railhead, and carry it up to the divisional ammunition columns. These, in turn, distribute to brigade columns, and the actual units draw upon the last named. Thus there are several links between railhead and the firing-line, and the motor-lorries should not come within about eight miles of the line.

But on this Wednesday and the two or three following days all this arrangement literally went to pieces. How could it be otherwise? And that is how the A.S.C. drivers came to do their bit with all the rest. Speed was vital, and the lorries could cover the distance in a third of the time taken by the horse transport. In fact, the horse transport was ignored or forgotten, although there were exceptions. One saw the divisional columns aimlessly trekking about the country, at one moment under orders to go to a certain village, only to find on arrival that the enemy were just a mile off; back they would come again as hard as the tired horses could do it.

Time and again an urgent message would go back from a battery for more 18-pr. or howitzer, and the dispatch-rider would have instructions to get the stuff wherever he could lay hands on it. He generally managed to find a few lorries of a "park," and so off the bus drivers would start with their three-ton vehicles, little dreaming that they were going under fire.

"Gor blimey, sir," said one of them next day to his officer, "I tell yer it wos a fair beano! We'd gone abaht a couple o' miles, when the sergeant wot wos along o' me on the box 'e sez: 'Stevens,' sez 'e, 'can yer knock anything more aht of 'er? 'Cos they're firing acrost the road.' Lor lumme, I nearly put 'er in the ditch at the turn 'e giv me! Yer see, sir, I didn't enlist to get knocked aht by no b—— German. I'm a peaceable man, I am, wot likes my grub and pint o' bitter reg'lar like, and the missus the same. But, as I wos a-sayin', I turned to the sergeant an' I sez: 'Yer don't fink there's no danger, do yer?' An' the sergeant, 'e sez, sarkastic-like: 'Ho no, they're only bustin' the shells on the road, an' we've got a few tons of fireworks be'ind wot's bahnd to bust too if we gits 'it!' S'welp me pink, sir, I turned that cold you could 'ave 'eard my teeth going louder nor the enjin.

"'E 'adn't 'ardly spoke when there was the 'ell of a bang some-wheres just be'ind, and—well, you can bet your life, sir, we did a guy for all we wos worth. Lord, 'ow we 'opped it dahn that road! I tell yer, sir, we knocked forty-five miles an hour aht o' that ole bus, and she come up to it like as we wos knockin' spots orf of a pirit bus dahn Piccadilly.

"The sergeant, 'e jammed 'is 'eel dahn on the accelerator, an' I just 'eld on to the wheel wiv bofe 'ands. It wos a fair old Brock's benifit we wos in. But we got frew orl right, and wen we got to the place where we wos to drop the stuff, there weren't no guns wot wanted it. An', as old G. R. Sims sez, '*hit wos the unkindest cut of orl.*' Well, I wasn't coming back agin frew that pyrriteknikle show not for the ole bus full o' suvrins, an' so we come 'ome rahnd by a place I forgit the name of, and that's 'ow we're late; but it was worf the hextra thirty miles rahnd, an' I 'ope, sir, yer won't mind this time.'"

There was another occasion on this day when three of these lorries went forward under the charge of an officer. He was quite unaware that the village whence the call for howitzer shell had come had been captured by the Germans half an hour after the message had been sent. On the way he picked up another officer who was lost.

Rounding a corner by a wood, about a mile from the village, they came straight upon a small German cavalry outpost. The Germans sprang to their feet at the rumble of the approaching lorries, and a sergeant stood in the road to bar the way.

There was not a moment for thought, and the second officer whipped his pistol out and took a snap shot. Luckily, he killed the sergeant outright. The officer in charge jumped down into the road as the lorry pulled up, with his own revolver in hand, and levelled it at the group by the roadside. One of them got his carbine off from the hip, and the shot just missed the first lorry driver on his seat. The officer promptly sent a bullet through the man's chest. Over his shoulder he shouted to the drivers to reverse the lorries, while he and the other officer held up the Germans.

Now, reversing three big lorries in not too wide a road needs some doing; but they all backed and advanced and sidled and backed until it was done. Then one officer jumped up behind the last one, the second officer followed, and off the lorries went.

There was nothing remarkable about the little experience, and it is only recorded to show the difficulties in ammunition supply at this time and also how the A.S.C. drivers were doing their job.

★★★★★★

You must imagine that while we have been at the rear with the A.S.C, the fighting all along the British line has been growing in intensity. A big flank attack, with the idea of rolling up the whole line like a ball of string, is always a favourite move of the Germans, and this time they were trying to crush the British left.

But although the left was the main objective, the enemy still had a big superiority in numbers for frontal attacks, and these they kept up without ceasing. It was just like the crashing of many mighty hammers from one end to the other.

Following up the policy of making counterattacks whenever possible, a bold offensive was made against the little town from which we had just been driven. The enemy had now been in possession for two or three hours. So word was passed to the batteries, some of the indefatigable cavalry was concentrated, and the infantry, with the two reinforcing battalions, received the cheering news that they were to advance.

How they all went at it! Under the heaviest fire our guns could pour in, the infantry rushed the outlying houses, the main street, and the town itself, the cavalry sweeping up on the flank. The gunners, after raising the range to put a curtain before the infantry, limbered up, and had the satisfaction of marching back through the town which they had just been forced to evacuate.

Then it was that our men first saw a little of the hideous work of the invaders upon the civilian population. And if anything more were needed to brace them up to fight to the last man, they had it in that brief hour in the recaptured town.

The hospital was burning fiercely, just as that at Mons had done. Such a building, with its Red Cross flag, was always a convenient ranging point for the enemy. In it there had been some 400 wounded and other casualties. A large number of these had been got away, but a number had, perforce, to be left. Their end must have been too cruel to dwell upon.

Up the main street everywhere was horrible evidence that *they* had been at work. Mingled with dead or wounded combatants were bodies of women and children, many terribly mutilated, while other women knelt beside them, with stone-set faces or gasping through hysterical weeping. From behind shutters or half-closed doors others looked out, blinded with terror.

But there was one thing which, for the men who saw it, dwarfed all else. Hanging up in the open window of a shop, strung from a hook in the cross-beam, like a joint in a butcher's shop, was the body of a little girl, five years old, perhaps. Its poor little hands had been hacked off, and through the slender body were vicious bayonet stabs.

Yes, close your eyes in horror, but it is right that our people should hear and know these things. There must be no false, vapid sentiment in refusing to think about them. There should not be a home in the British Empire where the facts of German atrocities are not known, and where, in realising them, hearts are not nerved to yield their last drop of blood in stamping out from the world of men the hideous Thing which has done them.

After that the brigade "saw red." There was no more talk of taking prisoners, and if there was another ounce they could put into their work they did it. The sight of those poor distracted women kneeling down in the road before our men, or hanging round their knees praying to be taken away, would have melted the stoniest hearts. The situation was serious enough, for another German attack in force was bound to follow, and the brigade had little hope of getting away safely themselves. But they could not possibly leave the women behind again—nor did they. Somehow or other they escorted, on guns, limbers and vehicles, all they could find safely on to the southward road, sullenly retiring once more before the new counter-attack.

CHAPTER 12

Wednesday, the 26th of August (continued)

A many of our bodies shall, no doubt.
Find native graves; upon the which, I trust,
Shall witness live in brass of this day's work;
And those that leave their valiant bones in France,
Dying like men, . . .
They shall be fam'd.

By midday the tide of battle had begun to roll southwards, though only by a very little. The British lines were forced back, a mile here, half a mile there, but they still held on with superhuman energy and determination. And not only did they hold on, but, wherever there was the least chance, a regiment or cavalry squadron would launch a counter-attack. But it all seemed so hopeless, just as one might throw pebbles into the waves of the sea as they break upon a beach.

Some day it is to be hoped that an adequate record will be published of the remarkable work which the cavalry performed during the Retreat. Sir John French, perhaps because he was himself a cavalry leader, hardly mentions them in his first dispatch. Wherever they were most wanted, there they were in the thick of the fighting. How the horses "carried on" and where and how fresh animals were obtained remains a mystery, in view of the muddle in which everything was.

But where every unit and every man worked as they did, it seems almost invidious to single out for mention any particular regiment or episode. Take a single half-hour of the fighting on the left, and you have an example of what was repeated fifty times that day across the whole British front.

A blue-grey mass of enemy infantry appears advancing with steady, swinging pace. At 500 yards or a trifle more one of our regiments opens rapid fire upon them. You can actually see the lanes in the German ranks ploughed through by the British rifle-fire. Still they advance, for the gaps are filled almost immediately. Nearer and nearer, until that regiment which began the advance has almost ceased to exist. The remnant breaks and scatters in confusion, and as they break away another new regiment is disclosed behind them. Such is the method of the German massed attack, overwhelming by sheer numbers.

But rarely did they get near enough to the British lines for a hand-to-hand fight. Regiment after regiment would be held at bay by the murderous rifle-fire of the little handful of British; regiment after regiment would appear to fill the gap. Now and again the weight of the attack would tell, and the Germans would get close enough for a final rush on the British trench. Then, at the critical moment, a British company, slightly forward on the flank, pours in a withering enfilade fire, and while the German infantry stagger under this unexpected attack the British cavalry charge through our own lines straight on the front and flank of the enemy. There are a few minutes of mad cut and thrust, and the Germans, who always dread the cold steel as a Chinese dreads rain, break and run as though all the fiends of hell were after them.

★★★★★★

Just about this time General Smith-Dorrien and a couple of his staff officers were following the fortunes of the battle from some rising ground not far from the centre of the line. A sudden outburst of heavy and incessant firing was heard from the direction of Cambrai, where, it will be remembered, the enemy were trying to outflank us.

"Good heavens," cried the general, "the Germans have got round our left!" And, jumping on to his horse, he galloped off towards the firing.

To his astonishment and delight he found, as he drew near the flank, that the firing came not from victorious Germans, but from some of our French comrades.

Never was help more opportune; seldom can it have come in more dramatic fashion. By all accounts General Sordêt with his cavalry should have been sitting by the roadside, forty miles away on the British right, tending his worn-out horses. Yet, at the call for help, by sheer grit and determination he and his corps had carried through that long forced march (Heaven knows how the horses did it!), and swept up on our left with his squadrons and horse artillery. Everyone knows what splendid work the French gunners can do, and—well, this was one of their best days.

It was a thrilling episode, and why, in common justice to our gallant Allies, the details have not been published I do not know. You will find General Smith-Dorrien's record and appreciation of the invaluable help thus given by General Sordêt in the second appendix at the end of the book.

While such were the conditions about midday up with the front line, the situation immediately in the rear was fast becoming indescribable in its confusion and complexity. Looking back at it now, after the lapse of so many months, it seemed very much like a theatrical performance where a "front cloth" has been lowered to conceal from the audience a strike of stage hands and the despair of the actors at setting the stage and getting on with the play. Before the front cloth a special "turn "is performing to gain time and appease the growing impatience of the audience.

There was, for instance, a particular centre of cross-roads, nearly a mile beyond where German shells were bursting. It was just outside a large village, and the inhabitants were streaming out with their belongings, yet uncertain whether there was actual danger or no.

At the cross-roads were gradually arriving ammunition columns, remnants of battered regiments, motor-lorries, and odd cavalry patrols; and no one had the vaguest idea as to why they were there nor where they were to go next. A staff officer standing there was as much at sea as the rest. Every moment more and more transport would roll up, and more and more stragglers, while hanging on to the outskirts of the crowd were increasing numbers of frightened women and children. An old cure alone seemed calm and collected. Over another village a little way back down the road the German shells come bursting ever nearer. It must be remembered that even the staff had but a hazy idea of the trend of events, and that outside the Staff not a soul had any notion of what was really happening to the Force. It was just a matter of doing your own special bit.

Right into this confused mass came running some R.A.M.C. orderlies. "The Germans are just behind!" they shouted. There might have been a bad panic with all those civilians about, but there was only rather more confusion. The Staff officer gave a general order to retire on St. Quentin (a large town about seven miles to the south); and then there was one mad rush.

Motor-lorries blocked the whole road, trying to reverse, while wounded and stragglers made a dash for the nearest vehicles. Ammunition columns struck off the road on to the open down-land. The refugees streamed straight across country. Down the road the heavy lorries went pounding, and soon outdistanced everyone else. At one corner there were two R.F.A. drivers in charge of five heavy draught horses. "Germans be'ind us," yelled a lorry driver; "better move!" And they did move. The sight of those old "hairies" clopping down the road at a hand gallop after the disappearing lorries was too ludicrous for words.

★★★★★★

By 3 p.m. the weight of the enemy's attack had begun to tell, and, to quote the commander-in-chief's dispatch:

> It became apparent that, if complete annihilation was to be avoided, a retirement must be attempted; and the order was given to commence it about 3.30 p.m.

Now came the most critical time of all. At the beginning of the day the enemy must have imagined that a retirement would be made at the earliest opportunity. But as the hours passed, and the British line still held, the impression may have spread that they intended to fight the day to a finish where they stood. Certainly it is impossible to think that had they realised a definite retirement to be in progress, they would not have thrown every man they had upon the rear of the corps.

Slowly and cautiously, then, regiment after regiment fell back. I have tried to show in an earlier chapter what that means and how much depends upon the guns at such a juncture.

Again I can only quote the commander-in-chief's words:

> The movement was covered with the most devoted intrepidity and determination by the artillery, which had itself suffered severely.

I will just give one instance of what that devotion meant, a devotion which, as has everywhere been agreed, saved the situation.

Close under a ridge a battery had been in action without a moment's rest for the last six hours. One gun after another had been knocked out, the battery commander and every officer save one killed, all the men of the detachments killed or wounded, until there was left just one gun, one subaltern, and one driver. And still they kept the battery in action; still they loaded and fired, as they had been doing all through that ghastly day.

"Got a drink?" said the subaltern; "a cigarette? Good! Thank God for a white man's cigarette again!" And he went on with his job. That was what "covering the movement" meant.

But the battle had been won. General Smith-Dorrien, his officers and men, had accomplished the almost superhuman task thrust upon them. They had not merely held the German attack through all the long hours of that blazing August day; they had *broken* it. For the remainder of the Retreat it never recovered its sting and energy, and so the Force and Paris were saved.

Events have had time to shape themselves during the months that have lapsed since August, 1914, and it is possible to view them in a certain perspective. It has been urged that we British have exaggerated the importance of the work of the Force in the Retreat; that while we were holding a line of no more than 20 odd miles, the French were extended over a front of 400 miles against an equally strong attack; that, by the prominence given to the work of the Force to the neglect of that of the French, a distorted picture has been given of the operations during August from Alsace to the sea.

To these arguments I would reply that Germany was staking everything upon that rush to Paris. For years past we had known that her intentions were to bring France to her knees within the first month or so, to admit of turning to meet Russia before that country had fully mobilised. And so, with this definite task in view, Germany concentrated her main attack through Belgium and south by Mons. She had not only her greatest strength in the armies of von Kluck and von Buelow, but she included in these masses of troops the flower of the German Army, picked regiments like the Prussian Guard, the "Iron" 3rd Corps of Brandenburg,[1] and others. Add to these facts the sustained violence of the invasion, and the concentrated hate which was levelled against Belgians and British by the invaders when the attack was continually and successfully checked, and I think that there is sufficient evidence to indicate the vital importance of the work of the British Force.

Moreover, the French people themselves had, with fine generosity, recognised that it was the British Force, under God's hand, which had saved Paris: for on Sunday, August 30th, prayers of thanksgiving were offered up in the churches on behalf of our troops.

---

1. This corps is always regarded in Germany as the finest in the German Army.

118

★★★★★★

And now, hopelessly inadequate as this record has so far been, words utterly fail me in attempting to describe the events of the next twelve hours, and how the Retreat was continued. It was one long, ghastly nightmare.

As regiment after regiment received its orders to retire, the survivors staggered to their feet, blinded by the ordeal of the day, and crept back until they reached a point where ranks could be formed. Then they got moving. Their destination no one knew, no one cared. . . . Keep moving! Men licked their blackened lips with parched tongues. "Any chance of a drink?" "Not here; perhaps we shall pass a village." Keep moving! "Got a fag on you?" "Smoked the last this morning; perhaps get some in the village." "Where the b—— 'ell is your village?" "Gawd knows." . . . Keep moving!

Ten minutes later. "Where the 'ell are we going? and why the —— are we retreating? Give 'em socks, didn't we? And where the —— are them Frenchies?" "Oh, shut yer 'ed, carn't yer?" . . . Keep moving!

There was a tiny village called Estrées in a hollow of the downs about three miles out from St. Quentin. Here at 4 p.m. the confusion was indescribable. Lorries, stragglers, refugees, transport columns, guns—all inextricably mixed up. It was, I believe, supposed to be a bivouac point for the night, but no one knew definitely. In any case, they were all tightly wedged in that hollow, and the Germans were but a very few miles behind. Had an enemy battery come within range, as it might well have done, it would have meant certain death for every soul there. Later in the evening news got to G.H.Q. of the position, and rations were sent up to the starving troops, with definite orders about further retirement.

Staff work simply went to pieces. It was not that men lost their heads or anything like that, but the various H.Q.'s found it impossible to keep pace with events. A regiment would be in a certain position, then it would be completely forgotten (or so it seemed), and no orders would arrive to move. Many C.O.'s retired entirely on their own initiative, and so got clear. Others decided to await instructions, and so got wiped out or captured.

As dusk gathered into darkness the confusion grew worse, while discomfort increased (if possible) with the steady downpour of rain which followed. But there was no moment's rest for the exhausted troops, save when a regiment came up against an obstacle across the road—a broken-down motor-van or gun-wagon. Then, if there

119

were any sappers handy, the vehicle would be blown up and the road cleared. . . . Anyhow, keep moving!

And the dreadful agonies of the wounded. At St. Quentin there was a big hospital which had been gradually filling during the past twenty-four hours. Now, on this afternoon, G.H.Q. found it advisable to pack up in a hurry and leave for farther south. And the hospital—would it share the same fate as those of Mons and Le Cateau? Once again the movable cases were hastily got into ambulances and other conveyances, and carried off in the wake of G.H.Q. But for hundreds of men there was no chance of getting even so far as St. Quentin for attention. Through the day the R.A.M.C. had worked as hard as the fighters, but it was very little more than first aid which could be given. No chance for deft operation, anti-tetanus serum or the like.

So, mingled with the retreating army were the ghosts of men swathed in bloody bandages, some clinging to vehicles on which they had found a seat, others marching with vague, uncertain pace by the infantry, others, again, just dropping out, to huddle exhausted by the roadside waiting for dawn and a fate which now had no meaning for them.

Keep moving! . . . Horse after horse in the slowly trekking columns of batteries or supply transport dropped down and fouled the wheels. Unhook or cut the traces; push the poor beast out of the road. An old pal, was he? Aye, he was a fine "wheeler," that dark bay! Remember the first time we bad him in at practice camp? Nothing matters now but keeping on the move. Yes, better shoot him. He deserves a clean end.

★★★★★★

Dozens, perhaps hundreds of men got cut adrift from their regiments that day, adrift and hopelessly lost in a strange country. No house, no village was safe as sanctuary, for the tide of invasion lapped at the threshold and would presently overwhelm it. One trivial incident I heard of seems worthy of record as an instance of "individuality "in the training of the British soldier.

A man—we will call him Headlam—got adrift by himself from the 3rd Division out on the left flank. After many hours' wandering, he came to a little farmhouse on the road. Here the good woman took him in, fed him, and gave him a shakedown. There were also there a couple of French stragglers.

A few hours later the little son of the farm came running in with the news that a patrol of the dreaded Uhlans was coming down the road. That meant murder for everyone. There was no time to hide, and the French were at their wits' end.

Headlam's first thought was for cover. Out in the yard there was a big rain-tub. Calling the two French soldiers to help, they rolled it out longways on into the road, and one of them, with Headlam, got behind with their rifles. The moment the patrol appeared, Headlam gave the Uhlans an excellent example of rapid fire, and three saddles were empty before they realised where the attack came from. Then they charged. French and British, side by side, ground away with their rifles, and when the Uhlans reached the little fortress there were only three left out of the patrol of nine. The second Frenchman, by the side of the road, accounted for another, and, with three to two, the Uhlans surrendered.

So our three musketeers found themselves with five excellent horses and a couple of prisoners; and I leave you to picture the triumphal procession which passed through the villages on the southward journey. The order of march was: Jacques and a led horse, Pierre and a led horse, two disconsolate Uhlans on foot (and hating it), and Headlam (with female escort), as G.O.C., bringing up the rear. . . .

★★★★★★

Keep moving! . . . But oh, the inexpressible weariness of it! No torture is more refined than that of preventing a worn-out human being from sleeping; and here it was experienced to the full. The picture of the Force that night might well have created for Dante the vision of one more circle of Hell.

Hunger was long since forgotten, but a red-hot thirst remained. One could appreciate as never before how Dives thirsted when he asked for Lazarus to touch his lips with a moistened finger. On, ever on, for hour after eternal hour, riding or trudging through the inky darkness, never a halt. . . . Keep moving!

How the troops did it I cannot tell. It was not the triumph of will over the exhausted body, for the sense of volition had fled, and men were mere automata in their movements. The legs jerked forwards as those of a clockwork toy. Had the men halted they could never have got moving again; the clockwork would have run down.

In the saddle it was little better. Every muscle of the body ached with an intolerable dull throbbing; a deadly coma crept through the brain and dragged at the eyelids. Nerveless lingers clutched at the pommel of the saddle, and were pulled away by the drag of the heavy arms.

One knows how a single night of sleeplessness will tell its tale in the face of a man or woman. Here was the fourth night of ceaseless fighting and marching, with only an odd hour of rest now and again.

All through the night and on into the daylight hours sounded the plod-plod of marching men, the grumble—creak—grumble of transport or guns. And in the far rear of the moving columns were more regiments lined out, showing a bold front to the still advancing enemy, ever guarding the backs of their comrades so far as was humanly possible.

★★★★★★

One particularly sad disaster befell a regiment in the course of the retirement; it is remarkable that there were not many others of a like nature. The 1st Gordons lost their way after dark, and began to march in a direction across the front of the German advance. About midnight the regiment found itself moving into masses of troops. The first thought was that they were amongst the French, for it was supposed that they had been marching towards French support.

Suddenly fire was opened upon the regiment from all sides, and though the Gordons put up the gallant fight which they have ever done in a tight corner, the odds were too impossible, and ten minutes saw the end.

I think that disaster affected the Force more than anything else in that opening month. Men spoke of it in hushed tones. A magnificent regiment with glorious traditions, and to be crushed out as they were in those few minutes. And yet not crushed out! Though the older generation of the family may die, there is the younger generation which follows, and their sons after them. And well do I remember that younger generation at the Aisne, when the Regiment rose again reincarnate from the ashes of the dead. I see now the stern-set faces of the officers, proud in their determination to avenge their honour; faces shaded and hallowed by the knowledge of what the Regiment had done and suffered, what it must now do and suffer that their dead may rest in peace. As it was, so shall it be,

Rising, roaring, rushing like the tide,
(Gay goes the Gordon to a fight)
They're up through the fire-zone, not to be denied;
(Bayonets! and charge! by the right!)
Thirty bullets straight where the rest went wide,
And thirty lads are lying on the bare hillside;
But they passed in the hour of the Gordons' pride,
To the skirl of the pipers' playing.

CHAPTER 13

The Retreat Continues

We are but warriors for the working-day;
Our gayness and our gilt are all besmirch'd
With rainy marching in the painful field;
There's not a piece of feather in our host,
And time hath worn us into slovenry;
But, by the mass, our hearts are in the trim.

The following days saw no rest for the exhausted troops, and they were compelled to plod on ever farther and farther south. If the rapidity of the German advance was so astonishing, even more so was the speed at which the British retired before them. For it is a hundred times more easy to do the advancing than the retiring. In the former case there is the confidence of success, with the feeling that at any moment the coveted prize may be snapped up. In the latter there is the inevitable feeling that things are going wrong, that the army is suffering defeat, and the constant dread that the troops may not stand the tremendous strain upon their powers of endurance.

So it was that every encouragement was given to the rumour which ran through the Force that this was but a strategical retirement, part of the plan decided on years before between the French and British Headquarters Staffs. And the idea of the Retreat was that the British were to draw the Germans ever southward, while the Belgian forces were gradually closing in behind the invaders on the west, and the French doing the same on the east. Then at the psychological moment the signal would be flashed round, the British would suddenly turn and present a dead wall, the strings of the net would be pulled tight, and—hey presto! we should all be home by Christmas.

There was only one part of the scheme which everyone regretted, and that was that we should be out of the entry into Berlin. It is all very well to keep up your wicket while the other fellow makes the runs, but then the other fellow gets all the credit. You see, everybody knew for a fact that the Russians were only a couple of days from the German capital, and that heartened the Force almost more than anything else. However, one consoled the men by telling them that regiments were sure to be picked by ballot to represent the British in the march through; and as for the newspaper prizes to the first man or regiment in—well, that regiment would surely be sporting and share the prize.

How many times one must have explained this wonderful piece of strategy to the good French folk I should not like to guess. On passing through a little village, generally at dusk, one of the things one always had to do, after dispelling the fears of the ancient policeman who tried to hold up the battery with an antiquated fowling-piece, was to draw maps on the sanded floor of the *café* for the edification of the local magnates.

"Why do we thus retire, *madame?* But it is so simple. It is a piece of strategy of the most clever. The *Allemands*"—here the audience spit profusely—"come thus, the Belgians are here, etc. etc. At any moment we turn to attack, etc. How many English, *madame?* Ah, *madame*, it is not permitted to tell; but for your ear, *madame* (and I would tell no one else), they say that the second quarter of a million disembarked yesterday."

Perhaps our kindly hosts will by now have forgiven us, but at least much of it we believed ourselves at the time. It all helped to keep the men going and prevent sudden panic with the country folk. It is difficult to say whether we did wrong.

By 8 a.m. on the Thursday the retiring; columns were well on their way beyond St. Quentin. The First Corps, during the eventful Wednesday, had also been steadily retiring, and had had comparatively little fighting to do. The condition of the troops will be remembered.

About half an hour later the rear-guard reached St. Quentin. The batteries marched in, watered their horses in the square, and marched out again immediately, the infantry covering them outside the town.

It was a little curious in St. Quentin—the attitude of the inhabitants. No one seemed to take any interest in the British movements, and certainly no one appeared to bother himself one atom about the German approach, St. Quentin is a big garrison town, with fine open places and streets, excellent shops and stately buildings, and the wealth of the place must be great. Yet there was never a hint of an exodus, and the people accepted the whole situation with astonishing *sang-froid*. I believe that when the Germans did arrive, a little later in the day, they surrounded the town and marched in from all sides at once, to find their triumphant entry opposed by—one British soldier. This man had got lost or left behind in a house, and now turned out with his rifle to defend the town. The German division had to open fire with a machine-gun upon the gallant lad before he fell, face to the enemy, riddled with bullets. The war can have witnessed few more remarkable episodes.

The fact that the R.F.A. with the rearguard were able to continue their retirement throughout the day without having to fire a round will show how well the Second Corps had smashed the German attack.

It should also be recorded that on this Thursday and Friday the Force had further help from the French. General Sordêt's cavalry continued its excellent work in relieving the pressure on the left of the Second Corps.

G.H.Q. had moved from St. Quentin on the Wednesday afternoon, and taken up their abode at Noyon, a cathedral town about 30 miles farther south. Here, again, no one seemed to have the slightest inkling of impending danger, and the business of the town was being carried on as usual. The mayor certainly posted a proclamation imploring the "*citoyens*" to remain calm and to pay no heed to rumours, and the *citoyens* obeyed by wondering why *M. le maire* should have so put himself about as to issue such a notice.

That was on the Thursday. But on the Friday the *citoyens* received something of a shock. A number of British regiments marched through in broad daylight, and it was now plainly to be seen that something very serious was happening. After the first gasp of astonishment and utter incredulity, the people stood by the road in dead silence with tears of pity running down their cheeks. So long as I live I can never forget that scene, the intense drama of it, the tragedy, and the glory of achievement which shone radiantly forth.

The remnants of three gallant regiments we watched go by, and we could look no longer. There is no need to say which they were, for they were but typical of all the other regiments in the Force that day. Again there were but a poor 200 men left of each 1,000. Officers and men alike in their pitiable destitution. Barefooted, or shifts of bandages round their swollen feet; torn breeches, cut short like football

125

knickers. Great bearded men they were, with the grime and dust of five terrible days' incessant fighting and marching upon them; but in their eyes the unquenchable light of their native pluck and steadfastness. There was no trace of defeat there, only the hungry, dazed look of men who long for a little sleep before they turn once more to crash their way into an enemy's ranks.

It is not such things as these that our people at home are told, and so I set them down. Tales of gallant deeds in the fighting-line they have now in plenty, but the great human side of this bloody war is passed over in discreet silence. England knows nothing of the meaning of modern war; she has not suffered invasion, save from the predatory attacks of aircraft. Her sons are fighting for her, and the knowledge thrills our womenfolk; but of the conditions under which they have fought, and of the appalling sufferings of tortured Belgium and France and Poland and Serbia, they are hopelessly ignorant. If but a tenth part were thoroughly realised there would be one mighty irresistible cry from the heart of the civilised world:

Stand at nothing to finish this war at once, and it shall be the last!

There are no such things as *neutral* nations. If a nation refuses to be enrolled for Civilisation, then it is fighting by the side of the obscene Horror which has plunged Europe into this carnival of blood and misery.

On the Friday afternoon some of us learned from a wounded French lancer that the German centre had been badly smashed and was actually retiring from St. Quentin, owing to a French counter-offensive; also some of our cavalry had been doing specially good work south of that town. The 3rd Cavalry Brigade broke and beat back the Prussian Guard and another cavalry regiment, and the 5th Cavalry Brigade had a similar success with other German cavalry.

In the meantime G.H.Q. had removed still farther south to Compiègne, and occupied Napoleon's magnificent palace, or a wing of it.

★★★★★★

It had been intended to give the Force a really good rest when they reached the River Oise on the Friday night. By that time the British line (both Corps) ran along the river from La Fère to Noyon. But it was, after all, little more than five or six hours which could be spared; many of the regiments and batteries did not even get that brief respite. "Keep moving" was still the order of the day.

But for the fortunate it was a glimpse of Paradise. It meant, above all else, a proper all-over wash and a clean shirt, even though you had to wash it yourself. It meant the luxury of a shave, if you could manage to get hold of anything in the shape of a razor. There was a square meal served out, and there were two or three hours of blessed sleep, when you lay with next to nothing on (for your shirt was drying) under a shady tree. It was all little enough, and, truth to tell, most of the men could only turn out of the ranks to fall straight into the sleep of utter exhaustion, a sleep of the clock round had it been allowed.

Tobacco in those days was a luxury, and it was needed most. Now there is a regular weekly ration, and in addition kind friends at home see that the supply of cigarettes does not fail. But in the Retreat the usual substitute was dried tea-leaves rolled in the parchment paper of the emergency ration. Tea-leaves are very nasty to smoke, but I am not sure that they are so nasty as brown paper or the seat of a cane-bottomed chair; and I have tried them all.

The men's equipment, too, was a constant source of trouble. They would throw away their greatcoats and packs, anything to march as lightly as possible. The Germans must have had a fine haul, and there were several occasions when they dressed up their infantry companies in British greatcoats and caps, and got well up to our lines before their identity was discovered.

And that reminds me that in Noyon we caught a German spy wearing no fewer than three different uniforms. First, a French; over it a Belgian; and on top of these a khaki greatcoat with cap. It was a very hot day, and the man's obvious discomfort was the first thing to give him away. It did not take ten minutes to settle that little affair.

By the time the two corps joined up again the refugee problem had become really serious. All the way back the army of unfortunates had been steadily growing larger, and it was but natural that they should hang on to the skirts of the Force for protection. How many of the poor women and little children died of exposure and exhaustion, it is impossible to tell. Our men were themselves badly off for food, but, needless to say, they were always eager to share their emergency rations with those who had nothing at all save what could be garnered in wayside village or cottage.

Rules about commandeering are most rigid; nothing must be taken without payment, or at least a voucher. I remember one C.O. buying a couple of fruit trees for his unit. But it went to the men's hearts to leave behind them tender chickens and toothsome bunnies, even though there was no chance of cooking them, to be snapped up by Germans with no such qualms of conscience.

Yet, to give the Germans credit, they did, in many cases, give written receipts for provisions when it was a question of an odd duck or bale of hay; but when a house was properly ransacked the receipt given more usually bore the signature of that redoubtable warrior, Herr von Koepenick. It was one of the very few occasions when they showed a sense of humour, if one can call it so.

Amongst those fortunate regiments which had been able to snatch the few hours' rest there was a very general, and a very natural, impression that a definite stand was now going to be made. The position was a good one, and it was also confidently expected that more divisions were being hurried out from England as fast as ship and train could bring them.

Perhaps, under other circumstances, the stand might indeed have been made. But what we did not know was that the main French Armies away to the east were being dealt a series of such smashing blows by the Germans that they were retiring almost more quickly than we were.

★★★★★★

Although we are concerned here solely with the fortunes of the British Force, yet it must be remembered that the fighting on the west was only a small part of the general engagement, and that the Force had necessarily to conform with the main strategical idea. The capture of Paris would have been of incalculable moral value to the Germans. They recognised this, and therefore made that special bid for it. But the triumphant entry into Paris would have possessed no real value so long as the French and British Armies were still "in being." Just as, later, the capture of Warsaw was of little *real* value (save as a strategic centre), because the Russian Armies had escaped.

The position, then, on Saturday morning, the 29th, was:

(*a*) The Force was retiring, not too severely pressed by the enemy, but with continuous rear-guard actions.

(*b*) Two new French Armies (the 6th and 7th) were coming into position on our left, by Amiens and Roye.

(*c*) On our immediate right was the 5th French Army, the one which had suffered so badly after the fall of Namur.

(*d*) Generally, the French forces on the east were being steadily pushed back by the very strong enemy advance.

On that morning the commander-in-chief received a visit from General Joffre, and this is what took place. I quote from Sir John French's second dispatch:

> I strongly represented my position to the French commander-in-chief, who was most kind, cordial and sympathetic, as he has always been. He told me that he had directed the 5th French Army on the Oise to move forward and attack the Germans on the Somme with a view to checking pursuit.
>
> I finally arranged with General Joffre to effect a further short retirement towards the line Compiègne—Soissons, promising him, however, to do my utmost to keep always within a day's march of him.

It may be noted here (although, of course, we did not know it till much later) that, owing to the German advance on the west, Le Havre was evacuated as the British base, and the organisation, stores, hospitals and everything, were rushed at half a day's notice right down to St. Nazaire, at the mouth of the River Loire. It was an amusing episode in the war, and quite a happy little yarn it would make; "*but that is another story,*" as Kipling says.

On the Saturday evening the Force was got on the move again, heartened and not a little refreshed. The countryside now was as lovely as any district in France. Gentle, undulating downs, crowned by the beautiful forest of Ligues, and besprinkled with dainty little villages and stately *châteaux*. If these lines should chance to be read by the mayor and mayoress of a certain little village hard by Compiègne, I would beg them to believe that the officer whom they so graciously entertained for those brief hours remembers their kindness with the deepest gratitude, and records the day as one of the most perfect he has ever spent. Officers and men made so many good friends even during those crowded hours of life, only to realise with heartfelt sorrow that perhaps half a day later their kindly hosts must have been engulfed by the tide of invasion.

I vividly recall how curious seemed that order to go on retiring when, from all accounts, the German centre had the previous day been so badly beaten. *Madame's* instincts, when the order came, were only too correct. She guessed the truth; we continued our trek hopelessly blind to the real facts.

CHAPTER 14

Past Compiègne

King Henry. *The sum of all our answer is but this:*
We would not seek a battle, as we are;
Nor, as we are, we say we will not shun it.
We are in God's hand, brother, not in theirs.
March to the bridge; . . .
Beyond the river we'll encamp ourselves.
And on tomorrow bid them march away.

The destruction of a bridge, especially if it spans a river, always seems to me so pathetic. Bridges are such companionable things; they fall so readily into one's mood, and there are, I imagine, few persons who do not possess pleasant memories of one or another. Whether in town or country, there is always fascination in staying one's journey for a few minutes to lean over the parapet and watch the stream—the basking of a trout amongst the pebbles, the sway of the waterweeds, the trailing of heavy barges, or the twinkling shore-lights.

In Compiègne there is a particularly handsome structure which spans the River Oise. The French people love a noble bridge to ferry their broad highways over the rivers, and I cannot help thinking that it was not alone special reliance upon the workmanship of our sappers which induced the French authorities to resign to them the destruction. For, whenever possible, British sappers were called in for the work. They made such a clean job of it, the French would say. No; it was, I feel sure, their affection and pride for beautiful works of art with tender associations that made them reluctant to lay sacrilegious hands upon them.

It must have been on Sunday, the 30th, that the last of the Force marched through or past Compiègne, and the bridge, besides many another, was blown up. The R.F.A. of the rear-guard passed through the town and halted, guns unlimbered, about 500 yards out the other side, ready to open fire, if necessary, for they were being hard pressed. The fuses were laid and lighted literally in face of the advancing enemy, and two R.E. officers who were doing the work were killed by enemy bullets. With a terrific crash the bridge fell, cut in two, and the retirement was continued while the Germans hurled impotent curses and (at that time) ineffectual shells after the column.

The Second Corps had now reached country which was very difficult not only for manoeuvre, but especially so for transport. Immediately after you leave Compiègne its glorious forest is entered, and directly that is passed it is a country of very steep ravines, thickly wooded, with little villages clinging limpet-like to the ridges. The heat of the day, too, was most trying.

The First Corps, which had joined up at Noyon, crossed the Aisne, and continued its retirement *via* Soissons.

The German pursuit, which during the last two or three days had seemed to slacken off, began to get serious again on the afternoon of Monday, the 31st.

About 3 p.m. three field batteries and the Brigade of Guards (First Corps) were out by Villers-Cotterets, and the Germans were pushing on almost as fast as they did during the first days. Their guns came into action at about 1,700 yards, and as our brigade there was far outnumbered, orders were given to go on retiring.

Well, the major of one of the batteries was "fed up" with retiring without getting some of his own back, so he put his telescope (a battery carries a telescope) to his blind eye and said he'd be hanged before he retired (or words to that effect), and "let's give them a dressing down first."

So it was "Halt; action right!" and, after a couple of ranging shots, "Two rounds gunfire!" And that was all that battery got in. The Germans put a couple of guns out of action, and then turned their attention to the wagon line, where they made a considerable mess-up with the teams.

That settled it. "Signal the teams up and let's get out of it!" said the major; and it was so. The quartermaster-sergeant put the fear of God, not the Germans, into the drivers; up came the teams, "rear limber up," and away they went, damaged guns and all. The Guards meanwhile had gone on.

There was nothing particularly heroic about it all, but it was very excusable, and it certainly helped to buck the men up a little.

The Guards, however, gave further excellent evidence of their fighting qualities in a series of stiff hand-to-hand encounters in the forest glades. While they suffered badly, they succeeded again and again in beating back the enemy's attacks, and so further relieving the pressure on the rear.

★★★★★★

Now, despite the continuous fighting and marching, there was no doubt whatever that the men were daily becoming more war-hardened and fit. The worst was over, and with that firm conviction their spirits grew lighter. During the first few days the troops were marching perhaps 25 to 30 miles a day, apart from the fighting. Take, for instance, Wednesday, the 26th. The men had begun that great fight practically tired out. They fought all day, and then at the end of it did a retirement of some 25 miles. Staff officers were simply worn out by the nerve-racking ordeal, and General Smith-Dorrien himself says that he did not average more than two hours' sleep during the first six days.

But the week's campaigning had done more for the troops than ten years' peace work. Their self-reliance, their confidence in and affection for their officers were evidenced in a hundred ways; while officers, for their part, had perfect confidence in their men and knew that, however impossible an order might seem, it would be carried out. The Force was, in short, one big happy family. Everybody seemed to know everybody else, and that meant that everybody helped everybody else. After the Marne it was never quite the same, because the Force began to increase in size. New-comers were immediately recognised, and the old hands could never resist a momentary exhibition of very pardonable pride at having "been out since the beginning."

The heavy losses in officers and N.C.O.'s had an inevitable effect on discipline, though it might well have been worse had not the sense of discipline amongst the rank and file been so strong. It must be remembered that so soon as the vanguard of the retiring Force passed through a village, practically the whole of the inhabitants would pack up such few of their belongings as they could carry on light carts, perambulators and any available vehicle, and then join the ever-growing stream of refugees. So the next units to pass through would find nothing but empty houses, and the temptation to carry away a few "souvenirs" was very hard to check, especially in the case of food.

One man of an infantry regiment "found" a horse wandering loose in a field. He was very tired, so why, thought he, should he not take what the gods sent him? He did, and rode the horse for a couple of days. Knowing nothing about horses, the poor beast got little enough to eat, and the man thought that the heaven-sent gift was becoming a nuisance. So he talked the matter over with a pal, and swopped his charger for—a packet of Woodbines! And I don't think the pal was a canny Scot either.

I remember particularly the date September 1st, and going through the little town of Crépy-en-Valois, because we then realised for the first time that something was wrong about that "strategical retirement" business. Our maps included Belgium and all N.E. France, but Compiègne was the farthest point south; and when we had retired below that town we knew that retreat so far south was not a part of the original scheme.

Then most of us saw some French troops for the first time, and, ominous sign, they were always engaged in barricading and mining the roads, opening the barricades to let us pass through.

But Tuesday, September 1st, must ever be a red-letter day in the annals of the Royal Regiment, on account of the famous fight of L Battery, R.H.A., at Nery, hard by Compiègne. I always regard that episode as one of the most wonderful incidents in this war. Nor do I think so because it was my own regiment, though naturally one can appreciate it the more from being a gunner. The story is, of course, well known, but no repetition can mar the effect, however bald the telling of it may be.

L Battery was working with the 1st Cavalry Brigade, which was made up of the 2nd Dragoons (Queen's Bays), the 11th Hussars, and the 5th Dragoons. For the benefit of the uninitiated it may be explained that a horse artillery battery of six guns forms an integral part of a cavalry brigade; wherever the cavalry go, there can go the "Horse Gunners," for the gun is of lighter calibre than that of the field batteries.

About 2 o'clock in the morning word reached Second Corps H.Q. that a strong force of Germans, 90 guns and cavalry, was moving towards the 1st Cavalry Brigade in bivouac at Nery. The Third Army Corps, which was still included in General Smith-Dorrien's command, was also not far away. Our cavalry were actually bivouacked within about 600 yards of the Germans, and I believe that our outposts were, for some reason or other, not sufficiently advanced.

In an earlier chapter, writing of Captain Francis Grenfell, I have remarked that there was one other to whose life might well be applied the phrase: "*Sans peur et sans reproche.*" That other was Captain K. K. Bradbury, of L Battery. All that I have ventured to say of Grenfell I would say also of Bradbury. I doubt whether there ever lived a gunner officer who was more beloved by his men, or one more worthy to be so beloved. And when that is said, what else remains?

Half-past four in the morning, and the mists have scarcely begun to rise above the beech trees. You picture the guns of L Battery parked in line just on the downward slope of a slight hill and in a little clearing of the woods. The horses of the gun-teams are tethered to the gun and limber-wheels; others are down at a little stream hard by, where some of the men are washing and scrubbing out their shirts. The Queen's Bays are in bivouac in a neighbouring field.

"Some of our scouts out there, aren't they?" remarked a shoeing-smith, pointing to some rising ground about 500 yards to the north; "or is it French cursers?" (*cuirassiers*).

"Looks more like Germans to me," said one of the gunners. "Let's have a squint through the telescope."

"What's up?" said the sergeant-major, passing at the moment.

"Half a mo!" mumbled the gunner, eye glued to the battery telescope. "Yes, it is—Germans—I can see the spiky helmets."

"Rot," returned the sergeant-major; "can't be!"

"Anyway, I'm off to report to the captain," said the gunner.

Bradbury was talking to the horses by one of the guns when a breathless gunner of the battery staff appeared with the telescope.

"Beg pardon, sir, but there are—"

CRASH! A percussion shell burst clean in the middle of the battery, followed the next instant by a couple more. And in the few moments' breathless pause it was realised that practically every horse and every driver was either killed outright or wounded.

"Action rear!" yelled Bradbury, who found himself in command.

Their leader's voice above the unholy din pulled them together, and the gun detachments, such as were left, leaped to the trails to get the limbers clear. But no more than three guns could they get into action.

Now a tornado of shell and machine-gun bullets from close range burst over and through the devoted remnant—Bradbury, three subalterns (Giffard, Campbell and Mundy), the sergeant-major, a sergeant, a couple of gunners, and a driver. And in action against them were ten German field-guns, and two machine-guns enfilading from the wood.

Of their three guns, they had now to abandon two.

"All hands number 2 gun!" called Bradbury, who, with the sergeant, had already opened fire.

The others rushed the few yards to Bradbury's gun; but even in that short space Giffard was hit five times. Bradbury acted as No. 1 (layer), the sergeant No. 2, while Mundy acted as observing officer. One of the gunners and the driver carried across all the ammunition by hand, through the hail of lead, from the firing battery wagons.

The range was, say, 600 yards, but in such a nerve-racking storm it was difficult for the little detachment to work clearly with no one to observe the burst of the shells. There was only a little chance, but Mundy took it, and stepped calmly out from the shelter of the gun-shield to observe.

Then No. 2 gun began its work in earnest.

"Five minutes more left," said Mundy; "add twenty-five."

Crack went the report. "One out!" said Mundy.

"Ten minutes more right; drop twenty-five."

Crack again! "Short," murmured Mundy; then, "add twenty-five."

"Two out!" he counted.

When three German guns had been counted out, Bradbury called over his shoulder to the sergeant-major:

"Take my place; I'll load for a bit."

He had barely changed places when a bursting shell carried away a leg at the thigh. Yet, by some superhuman will-power, he stuck to his post and went on loading.

Now Mundy was mortally wounded. Then Campbell fell. But still the gun was served, laid, and fired. And as surely were the German guns being counted out, one by one.

Then there burst true another shell. The gallant Bradbury received his death-wound, and his other leg was carried away. The rest of the detachment were all wounded. Still that tiny remnant stuck to it through the storm.

Now only are left the sergeant-major. Sergeant Nelson, the gunner, and the driver. Still they work. Still they watch one enemy gun after another ceasing to fire, until all are counted out but one.

All the ammunition is finished. Nothing left now but to crawl back out of that hell. I Battery coming up? Well, they can finish it. Lend us some "wheelers" to get our guns back.

So were the six guns of L Battery brought out of action. Torn and battered, but safe. Glorious relics of perhaps the most wonderful action a battery of the Regiment has ever fought—and won.

I Battery opened on the massed columns of the German cavalry now appearing, and rent mighty lanes through their ranks, turned and scattered them. The Queen's Bays, who had been working as infantry, for their horses stampeded when the firing began, collected up, and with I Battery and the Lincolns went over the hill after the retiring enemy.

There they found the German battery out of action and abandoned.

And Bradbury? His last conscious words were an appeal for morphia and to be carried away as quickly as possible that his men might not witness his agony and be unnerved.

So passed that heroic soul away. A life nobly spent, a death nobly encountered.

Nothing is here for tears,
. , . nothing but well and fair
And what may quiet us in a death so noble.

CHAPTER 15

The Final Stages

French King. *'Tis certain he hath passed the River Somme.*
Constable of France. *And if he be not fought withal, my lord,*
Let us not live in France: let us quit all.
And give our vineyards to a barbarous people.

The fighting in the neighbourhood of Compiègne developed into something of a general action, an action in which the British more than held their own. There was some doubt whether the 4th Division would be able to shake off the heavy attack which was being made upon them, so another brigade was ordered to their help. The retirement was then easily effected.

The 3rd Brigade was a little north of Crépy-en-Valois, and, without waiting for the enemy, themselves made a spirited advance for a short distance, and did excellent work with their R.F.A. against the German infantry.

Soon after midnight on Wednesday, September 2nd, the Force continued its retirement. There may have been some little grumbling, and it became increasingly difficult to keep up the old fiction—now indeed a fact—about a "strategical retirement;" but, somehow or other, a genuine conviction was stealing through the ranks that at any moment the real end would come. If our men were very, very weary, so also were the enemy, and every day brought fresh evidence of the fact.

Then, too, news came to us that the French (the 7th Army) were really tackling von Buelow's armies, and were doing well against them. That had a very inspiriting effect.

Now the Force, or rather our left, was actually in sight of the outlying forts of Paris, about a dozen miles off. Great was the excitement,

137

for, of course, everyone jumped to the conclusion that we were making for the capital. G.H.Q. was at Lagny-sur-Marne, just 15 miles due east of Paris. They actually got as far south as Melun, on the outskirts of the Forest of Fontainebleau, before the tide turned.

If you look at these places on the picture-map you will see that, after Senlis was passed, the Force, instead of retiring straight on towards Paris, as it had been doing, now swung round, with the right flank of the First Corps as pivot, and marched in a south-easterly direction. Possibly the enemy imagined from this that their chance had come, and that they would now be able to slip in between our left and Paris. But the new French army was coming up from behind Paris, upon our left, to fill the gap and cover the approaches to the city.

That swinging round movement to cross the River Marne was rather a risky business, for it meant marching for a certain distance *across* the enemy's front. However, it was successfully accomplished, and by the evening of September 3rd the Force was south of the river. That same afternoon our aircraft reported that the Germans had also swung eastwards, and were now apparently making for the large town of Chateau-Thierry, the point of division between our extreme right and the 5th French Army.

The position in which the Force found themselves that evening was well-nigh hopeless from a defensive point of view. To make matters worse, we were very badly off for entrenching tools, the men having lost the greater part in the hurried retirement after the hard battle of the Wednesday. This question of entrenching tools was further complicated by the removal of our base to St. Nazaire, for that meant a much more serious difficulty in getting up supplies.

I forgot to mention that when orders reached the Second Corps and 4th Division on the Thursday night to keep on the move, instructions were given by G.H.Q. to abandon everything, even the ammunition, which might retard the transport, and so to leave the vehicles free for wounded or the more exhausted of the men. Only one division carried out the order, and that only partially, before the G.O.C. Second Corps on the spot realised it was unnecessary and countermanded it.

★★★★★★

During and after the Battle of Le Cateau, as I have said the fight of the Wednesday has come to be spoken of, a rather curious adventure befell one of the motor transport ammunition parks. About ten of the lorries, under an A.S.C. subaltern, had been doing some detached work away from the main body. These had got out of rather a tight corner, but the rest of the park (some sixty odd lorries) had become involved in that mix-up at Estrées.

About 3 p.m. the A.S.C. captain in charge received an order to go back in the direction of Le Cateau. This was, apparently, straight into the advancing enemy, who were only some three or four miles off. The C.O. obeyed his orders and took his lorries back. From that moment those sixty great lorries vanished into thin air, and not a soul knew what had happened to them. At G.H.Q. the unit was officially reported as "missing," and it so appeared, I believe, in the London Press.

The subaltern invented and spread abroad a delicious yarn. I omit his version of his own adventures, for he got a "mention in dispatches" for it, though this was subsequently quashed.

When the order to go back was received, he said, and annihilation of the park seemed certain, the O.C. called his subalterns together and told them the position. They unanimously decided to obey and charge the advancing enemy with the lorries. The drivers (our old friends the busmen) were instructed to go full speed ahead into the enemy column. But the drivers were not having any. So the officers produced their revolvers and threatened to shoot any man who refused to obey. That decided them. "We will die by German bullets rather than—British." So away they went, the lorries bumping along the road straight into the ranks of the astonished Germans. Nothing could stop them, and the column got through (the narrator forgot to mention where to) with the loss of about half the park.

The subaltern carried his arm in a sling for a fortnight afterwards. A shrapnel splinter, he said, when they were rushing the enemy. It had really been caused by the back-fire of a motorbike. Possibly this is the origin of that glorified picture which appeared in certain of the London illustrated papers.

The park was, however, actually lost for nearly a week. They had vanished as completely as though the earth had opened and swallowed them. They were eventually heard of by the merest accident, when a sergeant came in to one of the towns on the line of retreat to get provisions. But even then they could not be found, for the sergeant had gone again without leaving his address. So for days staff officers scoured the country in swift cars, and thus the park was eventually run to earth. No one was more surprised than the C.O. to hear that he had been lost. They had not seen a single German, and they had had such a jolly time, thank you, seeing the pretty country.

But to tell of half the curious or amusing incidents I should need a volume many times the size of this one. Things happened every day any one of which would provide a newspaper with a column of excellent "copy." At the time one thought little about them, for everybody was too busy looking after his job and himself. There was, for instance, the Adventure of the Flat-Nosed Bullet, the Adventure of the Man with the Crooked Ear, the Adventure of the Field Cashier and the Pay Chest, the Adventure of the Blood-stained Putty Knife, the Adventure of the Perishing Cat, and many another.

The great question on the morning of Friday, September 4th, was: "Are we going right back to the Seine, with our left on Paris?" You picture the Force, tired enough but in most excellent fettle, growing hourly more impatient, longing with all their hearts to turn and have a go at the enemy who had caused them all that trouble and discomfort.

"Give a guess," I asked two of my sergeants that day, "how long we have been out here?"

They thought for a few minutes. "Six weeks," they said; "perhaps seven."

And, you see, it was only a fortnight after all. But they would not believe it until a calendar was produced. Unconsciously everyone reckoned each night as another day, for nights and days were alike so far as work was concerned. I think that remark was more telling than pages of descriptive writing.

The days during those final stages were almost tropical in their heat, which told very severely on men and horses. The nights were chill and wet. So altogether one had one's work cut out in mothering the men. Cases of bowel complaints were very common, and one has to be so careful to prevent serious developments. The lads really need looking after like children, bless them! Aromatic chalk-powder with opium (5-grain tablets) I found an excellent remedy, and cured dozens of cases. So there is a little tip for other officers. Calomel is useful, too, and I saved much agony from bad wounds by doses of opium (1-grain tablets), but this must not be given in cases of stomach wounds—most to be dreaded of any. Aspirin, also, is, of course, invaluable. Certainly no officer should be without a small medicine-case, and it is the one thing they never seem to think of when getting kit together. A trivial lapse, this, into egotism, I am afraid. I hope it will be excused for the sake of the hints offered.

★★★★★★

In the evening of September 4th orders came to continue the retirement still farther. The Second Corps marched through most of the night towards the River Seine, the First Corps conforming to the movement on the east. The 6th French Army was coming up well on our left, and thus the western end of the Franco-British line was gradually swinging round and up between Paris and the right flank of the Germans, who were now definitely moving east-south-east. You must remember, though, that these facts were only apparent at the time to a handful of officers of the Headquarters Staff'; everyone else was still in the dark. But how thrilling those hours must have been to an airman observing from above, and who knew the facts.

On the 5th (Saturday), at noon, one battery found itself halted in a field by the 12-kilometre stone from Paris, and the men were confident that *"la ville lumière"* was their next stop. There was an undercurrent of excitement, for another couple of thousand men had joined up to the corps as reinforcements. It was a definite halt and a rest, the first they had had since Mons, and they were making the most of it.

Just about 6 p.m. the major came into the lines with a paper in his hand. There was something in his walk, something about him— the men jumped up as he approached. "Paris?"—the major shook his head. "Not—not—is it advance, sir?"

The major nodded. "We are going to advance," he said.

Advance!

There was a cheer which must have startled the French Government in Bordeaux, or wherever they had gone to.

The drivers rushed at their horses, the gunners rushed to the limbers to help hook in. "Stand to your horses!" sang out the sergeant-major. Then, in a very few minutes: "Battery all ready, sir!"

The major stood up in his stirrups with a splendid laugh in his eyes.

"Sub-sections right-about-wheel! Walk, march! ' '

Another rousing shout, which soon merged into the cheery strains of "All aboard for Dixie," and the battery began a march, this time in the right direction, which only stopped at 2 a.m. for the sake of the horses. The men were ready to go on for a week.

The great Retreat had ended. The Advance had begun.

How and why the tide turned against the invaders at that, for them, most critical moment we cannot exactly tell. It was, as I see it, a combination of circumstances. There was the imminence of the Russian invasion into Prussia, and it was said that the Germans withdrew two army corps from the Western front to meet it. There was the sudden production by the French commander-in-chief of an entirely new French army from behind Paris to attack the German right.

But one thing, at least, is certain. Von Kluck made, perhaps, the biggest mistake in his life in imagining that "the contemptible little army" which he and his legions had been hunting for a fortnight was now too dispirited and broken for further fighting; and, with that conviction in his mind, he started to do the very thing which the most elementary military textbooks tell you is absolutely wrong. He moved his army across the unbroken front of a hostile force.

General Smith-Dorrien had been compelled to do the same thing with the Second Corps only three days before. But he did it with the full knowledge of the dangers, and he took every possible precaution to obviate them. He succeeded.

Von Kluck, in his delusion, saw no danger. He failed.

Sir John French says;

> I should conceive it to have been about noon on September 6th . . . that the enemy realised the powerful threat that was being made against the flank of his columns moving south-east, and began the great retreat which opened the Battle of the Marne.

★★★★★★

And there I draw the tableau curtains on the first act of the drama.

How inadequately the story has been told, or rather outlined, no one is more conscious than the writer. For every omission the critics may find, I will find two. But if I have so written that the great-hearted public may realise a little more of what the Retreat from Mons meant to the lads of ours who worked and fought so marvellously, to themselves at home, to our brothers and sisters overseas, then indeed I am satisfied.

Of necessity I have had to omit a great deal which may not be told until the war has ended. To an officer on the active list freedom of speech is rightly denied. But some day I shall hope to write in fuller detail and to do more justice to the work of individuals. It is only right that the public should learn the actual facts.

The glory of the achievement lay not merely in the hourly repulse, over a period of fourteen days, of an overwhelming attack, and of a continued retirement, which somehow never broke, before such an inveterate pursuit. But there was also the big question of temperament. The Germans knew exactly what they wanted, and they went straight for it, backed by all the resources of their wonderful organisation working to that particular end for a decade of years or longer. The British, on the other hand, were thrust into the breach literally at the last moment, a week late, and then had to fight for a fortnight in total ignorance of the course of events.

I recall a remark once made by General Joffre:

> The better he understands the importance of the movements of the attack wherein he participates, the braver the French soldier fights, and the more trust he puts in the measures taken by his leaders.

While the converse may not always be true, it will, I think, suggest how very difficult is the execution of a delicate piece of strategy when the officers and men are ignorant of the motives which prompt it.

The Retreat was carried to a successful conclusion because, by the inherent qualities of race, it was a piece of work of a character in which the British Army has always excelled; and also, in face of the terrible engines of modern slaughter, because of the splendid discipline of the men and their training as individual human beings.

Of the invariable cheerfulness of the men I have given several examples; but I would again attempt to correct the popular impression that such cheerfulness is no more than the cracking of jokes on all occasions. No, it is something far deeper and finer than that. The casual observer will watch a party of sappers mending a road, under fire, with loads of flint stones. He will hear them grumbling about the shocking waste of the ratepayers' money, and will then write home a letter for publication narrating the incident as a funny remark under fire. He omits to point out that it is only the cheery spirits of the men (and, of course, discipline, etc.) which make possible the clean finish of the work.

So it was in the Retreat. The men were far too exhausted to crack jokes, but the unconquerable soul of them rose high above every obstacle, and so the work was done.

★★★★★★

Looking back over what I have written, I find that, quite unconsciously, I have said little or nothing of the work of the officers. Yet there is nothing else that I can say. It is not for me to remark upon the work of our leaders and of my brother-officers. I can only repeat the words of the commander-in-chief, and I venture to do so because the general public bothers but little with official dispatches.

Sir John French remarked:

It is impossible for me to speak too highly of the skill evinced by the two General Officers Commanding Army Corps; the self-sacrificing and devoted exertions of their Staffs; the direction of the troops by Divisional, Brigade and Regimental leaders; the command of the smaller units by their officers; and the magnificent fighting spirit displayed by non-commissioned officers and men.

But in the commander-in-chief's dispatches there is one officer whose name shines out like a beacon. You who have followed in spirit the work of the Second Corps on August 26th will have realised the imperishable debt which the nation owes to the general officer commanding that corps. The verdict of posterity will but confirm that of the present generation.

Again I can but quote the commander-in-chief:

I cannot close the brief account of this glorious stand of the British troops without putting on record my deep appreciation of the valuable services rendered by General Sir Horace Smith-Dorrien.

I say without hesitation that the saving of the left wing of the Army under my command on the morning of August 26th could never have been accomplished unless a commander of rare and unusual coolness, intrepidity and determination had been present to personally conduct the operation.

At the head of my sketch of that day's work I have set Shakespeare's immortal lines on St. Crispin's Day. May one who was privileged to serve as a member of that "band of brothers" on that day venture to offer his poor tribute to the leader of that band?

From Mons to the Marne, wherever the fight was hottest, wherever his men were working against heaviest odds, there was the general at hand to help and stiffen them. The outposts before Mons were heavily engaged; the general was up with them, under shell-fire, to see how things were going. Through the days that followed, wherever opportunity served, their commander stepped from his car to say a few words of cheery encouragement to the passing troops. Was there a

144

field hospital, a passing ambulance?—again, those few words of kindly inquiry which made the poor sufferers forget everything save only the desire to be well again to give their chief, and Britain, all that was in them. If the commander-in-chief owed so much to General Smith-Dorrien, I can only say that the Second Corps would have stormed the gates of Hell for their leader, and would have trusted implicitly in him to bring them through.

★★★★★★

I seem to have said practically nothing about the Flying Corps, and very little about the Sappers. I am afraid that I saw very little of our aeroplane work until the Aisne, and so I cannot speak from personal observation. In fact, there are far too many omissions in this brief chronicle.

> *But pardon, gentles all,*
> *Oh, pardon! since a crooked figure may*
> *Attest in little place a million;*
> *And let us, ciphers to this great accompt,*
> *On your imaginary forces work,*
> *Piece out our imperfections with your thoughts.*

Indeed, I find it quite impossible to speak of one branch of the Force more than another. It was just one perfect whole. Thus I have, so far as possible, refrained from designating particular regiments. If I have written of the 9th Lancers or L Battery it is because the gallant work of those units is already a household word throughout the Empire. But, so far as that first fortnight was concerned, there was not a single unit, officer or man, who did not achieve something equally as gallant did the opportunity come his way. Indeed, had it not been so, the Retreat could never have been accomplished as it was. Every man played the game for his side, and, in consequence, that side won.

And if that were so, then there can be no question of "mentions in dispatches," D.S.O.'s and D.C.M.'s. Every regiment in the firing-line should be "mentioned." If, by great good fortune, a regiment achieves some specially noble piece of work which comes to the notice of the authorities, then, say I, let the Colour of that regiment be decorated. To single out individuals, to give a Victoria Cross to the colonel, a D.S.O. to the senior major, a Military Cross to the senior captain, and so on, is to create jealousy, and is, also, unfair to others.

★★★★★★

Humanity, the other noble trait in the character of our men, I have barely mentioned, for it seems quite unnecessary to do so. It is a characteristic of British sailors and soldiers which is always taken for granted. One need only recall some of the many occasions in our naval actions when British sailors have rescued Germans at the peril of their lives, and have been fired at while doing so. And set in contrast the murderous attack by German destroyers upon the crew of a British submarine stranded on the Swedish coast.

And so it has been with our soldiers. Our men invariably enter a fight with the innate feeling that it is a sporting contest, where you shake hands with your adversary before and after the fight. If he knocks out his adversary, then the winner is the man to help him to his feet.

We have seen from the very beginning that "chivalry" and "fair play" are words unknown to the Germans. To them nothing matters but to win, preferably by foul means. So, on the very first day, British soldiers were terribly undeceived. They saw German infantry advancing to the attack behind a screen of Belgian women and children, driven on at the bayonet point. From then onwards we lost hundreds of gallant men simply through their feelings of humanity towards wounded enemies, being shot at by other Germans, or being treacherously shot or stabbed by the very man to whose lips they were holding a flask of water.

And yet, with such examples before them of their comrades' fate, the sense of humanity and chivalry was never dulled. Despite the stringent orders on the subject, the men, even now, hesitate to fire when the enemy raises a white flag, and will always, whenever possible, succour a wounded German lying before the trench. These are the men who have only, as yet, learned of German treachery by hearsay evidence. But there are others. There are companies and battalions who know from ghastly experience. These men adopt other methods.

But nothing I can write will make people at home understand what this war really is. Nothing, short of actual experience, can do that. Stay, perhaps there is one thing: the genius of Louis Raemaekers. He, at least, by his cartoons, is bringing home to millions the hideous meaning of this war. And not only of this war, but of all modern war. I would have a volume of his cartoons distributed *gratis* by the government to every household in the kingdom. I would have half a dozen of the cartoons thrown upon the screen in every cinema-house at every entertainment. The people would shudder with horror, but they would see them and learn what Germany is and what war means.

Apart from this, I hold it to be the sacred duty of every man and woman who can use a pen to advantage, or who can command the attention of an audience, to make known this meaning. To cry from the housetops what is this foul thing which Germany has thrust upon the world, and to show the people why and how civilisation must crush it out for ever.

★★★★★★

There is no greater honour today that a man may wear—alas, there are but few left to wear it!—than the honour of having served his King and Country in France throughout August and September, 1914. Just that. He needs no decoration, no "mention." He served through the "Retreat from Mons." In days to come our children, our children's children, will point with pride to that one little word on the regimental colour, "Mons." For in that single word will be summed up the Liberation of the World. It was the victory of the Marne which won for Civilisation that freedom, but it was, under God's hand, the British Navy, the stand of Belgium, and the "Retreat from Mons" which made that victory possible.

Appendix 1

Military Despatches from the Field-Marshal Commanding-in-Chief, British Forces in the Field, Dated September 7th and 17th

7th September, 1914.

My Lord,

I have the honour to report the proceedings of the Field Force under my command up to the time of rendering this despatch.

1. The transport of the troops from England both by sea and by rail was effected in the best order and without a check. Each unit arrived at its destination in this country well within the scheduled time.

The concentration was practically complete on the evening of Friday, the 21st *ultimo*, and I was able to make dispositions to move the Force during Saturday, the 22nd, to positions I considered most favourable from which to commence operations which the French commander-in-chief, General Joffre, requested me to undertake in pursuance of his plans in prosecution of the campaign.

POSITION AT MONS

The line taken up extended along the line of the canal from Condé on the west, through Mons and Binche on the east. This line was taken up as follows:—

From Condé to Mons inclusive was assigned to the Second Corps, and to the right of the Second Corps from Mons the First Corps was posted. The 5th Cavalry Brigade was placed at Binche.

In the absence of my Third Army Corps I desired to keep the cavalry division as much as possible as a reserve to act on my outer flank, or move in support of any threatened part of the line. The forward reconnaissance was entrusted to Brigadier-General Sir Philip Chetwode with the 5th Cavalry Brigade, but I directed General Allenby to send forward a few squadrons to assist in this work.

During the 22nd and 23rd these advanced squadrons did some excellent work, some of them penetrating as far as Soignies, and several encounters took place in which our troops showed to great advantage.

Sunday, August 23

2. At 6 a.m., on August 23rd, I assembled the commanders of the First and Second Corps and Cavalry Division at a point close to the position, and explained the general situation of the Allies, and what I understood to be General Joffre's plan. I discussed with them at some length the immediate situation in front of us.

From information I received from French Headquarters I understood that little more than one, or at most two, of the enemy's Army Corps, with perhaps one cavalry division, were in front of my position; and I was aware of no attempted outflanking movement by the enemy. I was confirmed in this opinion by the fact that my patrols encountered no undue opposition in their reconnoitring operations. The observation of my aeroplanes seemed also to bear out this estimate.

About 3 p.m. on Sunday, the 23rd, reports began coming in to the effect that the enemy was commencing an attack on the Mons line, apparently in some strength, but that the right of the position from Mons and Bray was being particularly threatened.

The commander of the First Corps had pushed his flank back to some high ground south of Bray, and the 5th Cavalry Brigade evacuated Binche, moving slightly south: the enemy thereupon occupied Binche.

The right of the 3rd Division, under General Hamilton, was at Mons, which formed a somewhat dangerous salient; and I directed the Commander of the Second Corps to be careful not to keep the troops on this salient too long, but, if threatened seriously, to draw back the centre behind Mons. This was done before dark. In the meantime, about 5 p.m., I received a most unexpected message from General Joffre by telegraph, telling me that at least three German Corps, *viz.*, a reserve corps, the 4th Corps and the 9th Corps, were moving on my position in front, and that the Second Corps was engaged in a turning movement from the direction of Tournay. He also informed me that the two reserve French Divisions and the 5th French Army on my right were retiring, the Germans having on the previous day gained possession of the passages of the Sambre between Charleroi and Namur.

Monday, August 24

3. In view of the possibility of my being driven from the Mons position, I had previously ordered a position in rear to be reconnoitred. This position rested on the fortress of Maubeuge on the right and extended west to Jenlain, south-east of Valenciennes, on the left. The position was reported difficult to hold, because standing crops and buildings made the siting of trenches very difficult and limited the field of fire in many important localities. It nevertheless afforded a few good artillery positions.

When the news of the retirement of the French and the heavy German threatening on my front reached me, I endeavoured to confirm it by aeroplane reconnaissance; and as a result of this I determined to effect a retirement to the Maubeuge position at daybreak on the 24th.

A certain amount of fighting continued along the whole line throughout the night, and at daybreak on the 24th the 2nd Division from the neighbourhood of Harmignies made a powerful demonstration as if to retake Binche. This was supported by the artillery of both the 1st and 2nd Divisions, whilst the 1st Division took up a supporting position in the neighbourhood of Peissant. Under cover of this demonstration the Second Corps retired on the line Dour—Quarouble—Frameries. The 3rd Division on the right of the Corps suffered considerable loss in this operation from the enemy, who had retaken Mons. The Second Corps halted on this line, where they partially entrenched themselves, enabling Sir Douglas Haig with the First Corps gradually to withdraw to the new position: and he effected this without much further loss, reaching the line Bavai—Maubeuge about 7 p.m. Towards midday the enemy appeared to be directing his principal effort against our left.

I had previously ordered General Allenby with the cavalry to act vigorously in advance of my left front and endeavour to take the pressure off.

About 7.30 a.m. General Allenby received a message from Sir Charles Fergusson, commanding 5th Division saying that he was very hard pressed and in urgent need of support. On receipt of this message General Allenby drew in the cavalry and endeavoured to bring direct support to the 5th Division.

During the course of this operation General De Lisle, of the 2nd Cavalry Brigade, thought he saw a good opportunity to paralyse the further advance of the enemy's infantry by making a mounted attack on his flank. He formed up and advanced for this purpose, but was held up by wire about 500 yards from his objective, and the 9th Lancers and 18th Hussars suffered severely in the retirement of the Brigade.

The 19th Infantry Brigade, which had been guarding the Line of Communications, was brought up by rail to Valenciennes on the 22nd and 23rd. On the morning of the 24th they were moved out to a position south of Quarouble to support the left flank of the Second Corps.

With the assistance of the cavalry Sir Horace Smith-Dorrien was enabled to effect his retreat to a new position; although, having two corps of the enemy on his front and one threatening his flank, he suffered great losses in doing so.

At nightfall the position was occupied by the Second Corps to the west of Bavai, the First Corps to the right. The right was protected by the Fortress of Maubeuge, the left by the 19th Brigade in position between Jenlain and Bry, and the cavalry on the outer flank.

Tuesday, August 25

4. The French were still retiring, and I had no support except such as was afforded by the Fortress of Maubeuge; and the determined attempts of the enemy to get round my left flank assured me that it was his intention to hem me against that place and surround me. I felt that not a moment must be lost in retiring to another position.

I had every reason to believe that the enemy's forces were somewhat exhausted, and I knew that they had suffered heavy losses.

I hoped, therefore, that his pursuit would not be too vigorous to prevent me effecting my object.

The operation, however, was full of danger and difficulty, not only owing to the very superior force in my front, but also to the exhaustion of the troops.

The retirement was recommenced in the early morning of the 25th to a position in the neighbourhood of Le Cateau, and rearguards were ordered to be clear of the Maubeuge—Bavai—Eth road by 5.30 a.m.

Two cavalry brigades, with the divisional cavalry of the Second Corps, covered the movement of the Second Corps. The remainder of the Cavalry Division with the 19th Brigade, the whole under the command of General Allenby, covered the west flank.

The 4th Division commenced its detrainment at Le Cateau on Sunday, the 23rd, and by the morning of the 25th eleven battalions and a Brigade of Artillery with Divisional Staff were available for service.

I ordered General Snow to move out to take up a position with his right south of Solesmes, his left resting on the Cambrai—Le Cateau road south of La Chaprie. In this position the Division rendered great help to the effective retirement of the Second and First Corps to the new position.

Although the troops had been ordered to occupy the Cambrai—Le Cateau—Landrecies position, and the ground had, during the 25th, been partially prepared and entrenched, I had grave doubts—owing to the information I received as to the accumulating strength of the enemy against me—as to the wisdom of standing there to fight.

Having regard to the continued retirement of the French on my right, my exposed left flank, the tendency of the enemy's western corps (II.) to envelop me, and, more than all, the exhausted condition of the troops, I determined to make a great effort to continue the retreat till I could put some substantial obstacle, such as the Somme or the Oise, between my troops and the enemy, and afford the former some opportunity of rest and reorganisation. Orders were, therefore, sent to the Corps Commanders to continue their retreat as soon as they possibly could towards the general line Vermand—St. Quentin—Ribemont.

The cavalry, under General Allenby, were ordered to cover the retirement.

The Guards at Landrecies

Throughout the 25th and far into the evening, the First Corps continued its march on Landrecies, following the road along the eastern border of the Forêt de Mormal, and arrived at Landrecies about 10 o'clock. I had intended that the Corps should come farther west so as to fill up the gap between Le Cateau and Landrecies, but the men were exhausted and could not get farther in without rest.

The enemy, however, would not allow them this rest, and about 9.30 p.m. a report was received that the 4th Guards Brigade in Landrecies was heavily attacked by troops of the 9th German Army Corps who were coming through the forest on the north of the town. This brigade fought most gallantly and caused the enemy to suffer tremendous loss in issuing from the forest into the narrow street of the town. The loss has been estimated from reliable sources at from 700 to 1,000. At the same time information reached me from Sir Douglas Haig that his 1st Division was also heavily engaged south and east of Maroilles. I sent urgent messages to the commander of the two French Reserve Divisions on my right to come up to the assistance of the First Corps, which they eventually did. Partly owing to this assistance, but mainly to the skilful manner in which Sir Douglas Haig extricated his corps from an exceptionally difficult position in the darkness of the night, they were able at dawn to resume their march south towards Wessigny on Guise.

By about 6 p.m. the Second Corps had got into position with their right on Le Cateau, their left in the neighbourhood of Caudry, and the line of defence was continued thence by the 4th Division towards Seranvillers, the left being thrown back.

During the fighting on the 24th and 25th the Cavalry became a good deal scattered, but by the early morning of the 26th General Allenby had succeeded in concentrating two brigades to the south of Cambrai,

The 4th Division was placed under the orders of the general officer commanding the Second Army Corps.

Wednesday, August 26

On the 24th the French Cavalry Corps, consisting of three divisions, under General Sordêt, had been in billets north of

Avesnes. On my way back from Bavai, which was my "*Poste de Commandement*" during the fighting of the 23rd and 24th, I visited General Sordêt, and earnestly requested his co-operation and support. He promised to obtain sanction from his army commander to act on my left flank, but said that his horses were too tired to move before the next day. Although he rendered me valuable assistance later on in the course of the retirement, he was unable for the reasons given to afford me any support on the most critical day of all, *viz.*, the 26th.

At daybreak it became apparent that the enemy was throwing the bulk of his strength against the left of the position occupied by the Second Corps and the 4th Division.

At this time the guns of four German Army corps were in position against them, and Sir Horace Smith-Dorrien reported to me that he judged it impossible to continue his retirement at daybreak (as ordered) in face of such an attack.

I sent him orders to use his utmost endeavours to break off the action and retire at the earliest possible moment, as it was impossible for me to send him any support, the First Corps being at the moment incapable of movement.

The French cavalry corps, under General Sordêt, was coming up on our left rear early in the morning, and I sent an urgent message to him to do his utmost to come up and support the retirement of my left flank; but owing to the fatigue of his horses he found himself unable to intervene in any way.

There had been no time to entrench the position properly, but the troops showed a magnificent front to the terrible fire which confronted them.

The artillery, although outmatched by at least four to one, made a splendid fight, and inflicted heavy losses on their opponents.

At length it became apparent that, if complete annihilation was to be avoided, a retirement must be attempted; and the order was given to commence it about 3.30 p.m. The movement was covered with the most devoted intrepidity and determination by the artillery, which had itself suffered heavily, and the fine work done by the cavalry in the further retreat from the position assisted materially in the final completion of this most difficult and dangerous operation.

Fortunately the enemy had himself suffered too heavily to engage in an energetic pursuit.

★★★★★★

I cannot close the brief account of this glorious stand of the British troops without putting on record my deep appreciation of the valuable services rendered by General Sir Horace Smith-Dorrien.

I say without hesitation that the saving of the left wing of the army under my command on the morning of the 26th August could never have been accomplished unless a commander of rare and unusual coolness, intrepidity, and determination had been present to personally conduct the operations.

The retreat was continued far into the night of the 26th and through the 27th and 28th, on which date the troops halted on the line Noyon—Chauny—La Fère, having then thrown off the weight of the enemy's pursuit.

On the 27th and 28th I was much indebted to General Sordêt and the French Cavalry Division which he commands for materially assisting my retirement and successfully driving back some of the enemy on Cambrai.

General D'Amade also, with the 61st and 62nd French Reserve Divisions, moved down from the neighbourhood of Arras on the enemy's right flank and took much pressure off the rear of the British Forces.

This closes the period covering the heavy fighting which commenced at Mons on Sunday afternoon, 23rd August, and which really constituted a four days' battle.

At this point, therefore, I propose to close the present despatch,

I deeply deplore the very serious losses which the British Forces have suffered in this great battle; but they were inevitable in view of the fact that the British Army—only two days after a concentration by rail—was called upon to withstand a vigorous attack of five German Army corps.

It is impossible for me to speak too highly of the skill evinced by the two general officers commanding army corps; the self-sacrificing and devoted exertions of their staffs; the direction of the troops by divisional, brigade, and regimental leaders; the command of the smaller units by their officers; and the magnificent fighting spirit displayed by non-commissioned officers and men.

I wish particularly to bring to your Lordship's notice the admirable work done by the Royal Flying Corps under Sir David Henderson. Their skill, energy, and perseverance have been beyond all praise. They have furnished me with the most complete and accurate information which has been of incalculable value in the conduct of the operations. Fired at constantly both by friend and foe, and not hesitating to fly in every kind of weather, they have remained undaunted throughout.

Further, by actually fighting in the air, they have succeeded in destroying five of the enemy's machines,

I wish to acknowledge with deep gratitude the incalculable assistance I received from the general and personal staffs at Headquarters during this trying period.

Lieutenant-General Sir Archibald Murray, Chief of the General Staff; Major-General Wilson, Sub-Chief of the General Staff; and all under them have worked day and night unceasingly with the utmost skill, self-sacrifice, and devotion; and the same acknowledgment is due by me to Brigadier-General Hon. W. Lambton, my Military Secretary, and the Personal Staff,

In such operations as I have described, the work of the Quartermaster-General is of an extremely onerous nature. Major-General Sir William Robertson has met what appeared to be almost insuperable difficulties with his characteristic energy, skill, and determination; and it is largely owing to his exertions that the hardships and sufferings of the troops—inseparable from such operations—were not much greater.

Major-General Sir Nevil Macready, the adjutant-general, has also been confronted with most onerous and difficult tasks in connection with disciplinary arrangements and the preparation of casualty lists. He has been indefatigable in his exertions to meet the difficult situations which arose.

I have not yet been able to complete the list of officers whose names I desire to bring to your Lordship's notice for services rendered during the period under review; and, as I understand it is of importance that this despatch should no longer be delayed, I propose to forward this list, separately, as soon as I can.

    I have the honour to be.

        Your Lordship's most obedient Servant,

            (Signed) J. D. P. French, Field-Marshal, Commander-in-Chief,

    British Forces in the Field.

My Lord,

In continuation of my despatch of September 7th, I have the honour to report the further progress of the operations of the Forces under my command from August 28th.

On that evening the retirement of the Force was followed closely by two of the enemy's cavalry columns, moving south-east from St. Quentin.

Saturday, August 29

The retreat in this part of the field was being covered by the 3rd and 5th Cavalry Brigades. South of the Somme General Gough, with the 3rd Cavalry Brigade, threw back the Uhlans of the Guard with considerable loss.

General Chetwode, with the 5th Cavalry Brigade, encountered the eastern column near Cérizy, moving south. The Brigade attacked and routed the column, the leading German regiment suffering very severe casualties and being almost broken up.

The 7th French Army Corps was now in course of being railed up from the south to the east of Amiens. On the 29th it nearly completed its detrainment, and the French 6th Army got into position on my left, its right resting on Roye.

The 5th French Army was behind the line of the Oise between La Fère and Guise.

The pursuit of the enemy was very vigorous; some five or six German corps were on the Somme facing the 5th Army on the Oise. At least two corps were advancing towards my front, and were crossing the Somme east and west of Ham. Three or four more German corps were opposing the 6th French Army on my left.

This was the situation at 1 o'clock on the 29th, when I received a visit from General Joffre at my headquarters.

I strongly represented my position to the French commander in-chief, who was most kind, cordial, and sympathetic, as he has always been. He told me that he had directed the 5th French Army on the Oise to move forward and attack the Germans on the Somme, with a view to checking pursuit. He also told me of the formation of the Sixth French Army on my left flank, composed of the 7th Army Corps, four Reserve Divisions, and Sordêt's corps of cavalry.

I finally arranged with General Joffre to effect a further short retirement towards the line Compiègne—Soissons, promising him, however, to do my utmost to keep always within a day's march of him.

In pursuance of this arrangement the British Forces retired to a position a few miles north of the line Compiègne—Soissons on the 29th.

CHANGE OF BASE

The right flank of the German Army was now reaching a point which appeared seriously to endanger my line of communications with Havre. I had already evacuated Amiens, into which place a German reserve division was reported to have moved.

Orders were given to change the base to St. Nazaire, and establish an advance base at Le Mans. This operation was well carried out by the Inspector-General of Communications,

In spite of a severe defeat inflicted upon the Guard 10th and Guard Reserve Corps of the German Army by the 1st and 3rd French Corps on the right of the 5th Army, it was not part of General Joffre's plan to pursue this advantage, and a general retirement on to the line of the Marne was ordered, to which the French forces in the more eastern theatre were directed to conform.

A new army (the 9th) had been formed from three corps in the south by General Joffre, and moved into the space between the right of the 5th and left of the 4th Armies.

Whilst closely adhering to his strategic conception to draw the enemy on at all points until a favourable situation was created from which to assume the offensive, General Joffre found it necessary to modify from day to day the methods by which he sought to attain this object, owing to the development of the enemy's plans and changes in the general situation.

In conformity with the movements of the French Forces, my retirement continued practically from day to day. Although we were not severely pressed by the enemy, rearguard actions took place continually.

SOUTH OF COMPIÈGNE

On the 1st September, when retiring from the thickly wooded country to the south of Compiègne, the 1st Cavalry Brigade was overtaken by some German cavalry. They momentarily lost a Horse Artillery battery, and several officers and men were killed and wounded. With the help, however, of some detachments from the 3rd Corps operating on their left, they not only recovered their own guns, but succeeded in capturing twelve of the enemy's.

Similarly, to the eastward, the 1st Corps, retiring south, also got into some very difficult forest country, and a somewhat severe rearguard action ensued at Villers-Cotterets, in which the 4th Guards Brigade suffered considerably.

On September 3rd the British Forces were in position south of the Marne between Lagny and Signy-Signets. Up to this time I had been requested by General Joffre to defend the passages of the river as long as possible, and to blow up the bridges in my front. After I had made the necessary dispositions, and the destruction of the bridges had been effected, I was asked by the French commander-in-chief to continue my retirement to a point some 12 miles in rear of the position I then occupied, with a view to taking up a second position behind the Seine. This retirement was duly carried out. In the meantime the enemy had thrown bridges and crossed the Marne in considerable force, and was threatening the Allies all along the line of the British Forces and the 5th and 9th French Armies. Consequently several small outpost actions took place.

Saturday, September 5

On Saturday, September 5th, I met the French commander-in-chief at his request, and he informed me of his intention to take the offensive forthwith, as he considered conditions were very favourable to success.

General Joffre announced to me his intention of wheeling up the left flank of the 6th Army, pivoting on the Marne and directing it to move on the Ourcq; cross and attack the flank of the 1st German Army, which was then moving in a south-easterly direction east of that river.

THE ADVANCE

He requested me to effect a change of front to my right—my left resting on the Marne, and my right on the 5th Army—to fill the gap between that army and the 6th. I was then to advance against the enemy in my front and join in the general offensive movement.

159

These combined movements practically commenced on Sunday, September 6th, at sunrise; and on that day it may be said that a great battle opened on a front extending from Ermenonville, which was just in front of the left flank of the 6th French Army, through Lizy on the Marne, Mauperthuis, which was about the British centre, Courtecon, which was the left of the 5th French Army, to Esternay and Charleville, the left of the 9th Army under General Foch, and so along the front of the 9th, 4th, and 3rd French Armies to a point north of the fortress of Verdun.

This battle, in so far as the 6th French Army, the British Army, the 5th French Army, and the 9th French Army were concerned, may be said to have concluded on the evening of September 10th, by which time the Germans had been driven back to the line Soissons—Reims, with a loss of thousands of prisoners, many guns, and enormous masses of transport.

About the 3rd September the enemy appears to have changed his plans and to have determined to stop his advance South direct upon Paris; for on the 4th September air reconnaissances showed that his main columns were moving in a south-easterly direction generally east of a line drawn through Nanteuil and Lizy on the Ourcq. On the 5th September several of these columns were observed to have crossed the Marne; whilst German troops, which were observed moving south-east up the left bank of the Ourcq on the 4th, were now reported to be halted and facing that river. Heads of the enemy's columns were seen crossing at Changis, La Ferté, Nogent, Château Thierry, and Mezy.

Considerable German columns of all arms were seen to be converging on Montmirail, whilst before sunset large bivouacs of the enemy were located in the neighbourhood of Coulommiers, south of Rebais, La Ferté-Gaucher, and Dagny.

I should conceive it to have been about noon on the 6th September, after the British Forces had changed their front to the right and occupied the line Jouy-Le Chatel—Faremoutiers—Villeneuve La Comte, and the advance of the 6th French Army north of the Marne towards the Ourcq became apparent, that the enemy realised the powerful threat that was being made against the flank of his columns moving south-east, and began the great retreat which opened the battle above referred to.

Here follows the account of the Battle of the Marne.

Appendix 2

August 29th, 1914.

Issued to the troops under his command by the General
Officer Commanding the Second Corps.

As it is improbable the troops of the 2nd Army Corps understand the operations of the last few days, commencing on the
21st instant with the advance to the line of the Mons Canal and
ending with a retirement to our present position on the River
Oise about Noyon, the commander of the corps desires to let
troops know that the object was to delay the advance of a far
superior force of the enemy to enable our Allies to conduct
operations elsewhere. This object, owing to the skilful handling
of the commanders of units and the magnificent fighting spirit
shown by all ranks against overwhelming odds, and in spite of
very heavy casualties, was achieved, and the French Army is
now reported to be advancing.

That the losses were not greater in the retirement from the
Hancourt—Caudry—Beaumont.—Le Cateau position on
the 26th instant is due largely to the support given by French
troops, chiefly General Sordêt's cavalry corps, operating on the
west flank of the British troops, and we may well be thankful to
our gallant comrades in arms.

General Sir Horace Smith-Dorrien, whilst regretting the terribly heavy casualties and the weary forced marches, in which it
has been impossible to distribute the necessary amount of food,
begs to thank all ranks and to express his admiration of the
grand fighting and determined spirit shown by all ranks, and his
pride in being allowed to command such a splendid force.

He is sure that whenever it is thought necessary to again assume

the offensive the troops will be as pleased as he will himself.
The following messages have been received from the commander-in-chief, Field-Marshal Sir John French, to publish to the troops of the 2nd Army Corps—the first dated 25th August.

(1)

Special Army Order.
I have received the following telegram from the Secretary of State for War:

London, 25-8-14.

Congratulate troops on their splendid work. We are all proud as usual of them.

In making this message known to the troops under my command, I wish to express to them my heartfelt thanks for, and my profound admiration of, their magnificent bearing and conduct during the fighting of the last two days.
The most difficult operation which an army can be called upon to carry out was rendered necessary by the general strategic situation of the allied forces extending over an enormous front.
I can only tell you that it was most brilliantly and successfully performed. This happy result was entirely due to the splendid spirit, efficient training, and magnificent discipline of regimental officers and men, and the fine skill displayed by the higher commanders in the direction of the troops.

(2)

28th August, 1914.

A a 67. Following message from Lord Kitchener to C.-in-C. will be communicated to all troops. Begins:

The First Lord asks me to transmit to you the following message from the Home Fleet:—
The officers and men of the Grand Fleet wish to express to their comrades of the Army admiration of the magnificent stand made against great odds, and wish them the brilliant success which the Fleet feels sure awaits their further efforts.

Ends.

(3)

No. 28 G. Following from Lord Kitchener to C.-in-C. Begins: 'Your F 37. Your troops have done marvellously well under their commanders during severe attacks which they have had to withstand practically alone. Express to them all the thanks of the King and Government.'

Ends.

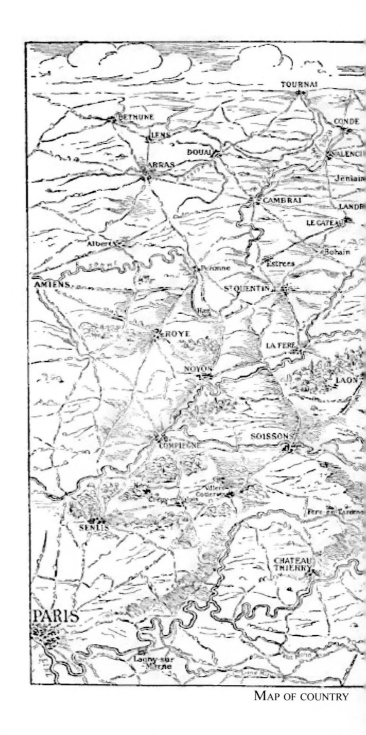

MAP OF COUNTRY

FROM MONS TO PARIS

The Marne—and After

LIEUT.-GENERAL SIR WILLIAM R. ROBERTSON.

Contents

Awake remembrance of these valiant dead.
And with your puissant arm renew their feats
You are their heir.

To
The Immortal Memory
of
The Men of the Old Army
who
Saved England,
August— November, 1914.

Prologue

The Men of Mons
Who shall sing the Song of them,
The wonder and the strength of them,
The gaiety and tenderness
They bore across the sea?
In every heart's the Song of them,
The debt that England owes to them,
The chivalry and fearlessness
That strove—and won Her free.

Merrily aboard at Southampton Quay
(The Horse and the Guns and the Foot together),
Southerly away to the dip of the sea—
(Hey! for a holiday in August weather)
Far to the north the grey ships ride,
But abeam steals a T.B.D. for a guide
'Till they're safely along the French quay-side—
(The Horse and the Guns and the Foot together).

Cheerily ashore by Rouen Quay
(The Horse and the Guns and the Foot together),
As proudly welcoming France flings free
Her gates, aglow in the golden weather.
"God speed!" rings the cry: and with melodies gay
Echoing down the flower-strewn way,
Blithesome as children sped to their play
Go the Horse and the Guns and the Foot together.

On to the drab-grey Belgian land,
With jingle of steel and creak of leather,
Swings into line the jocund band

173

Of Horse and Guns and Foot together.
Away in advance an outpost screen
Of Chetwode's Cavalry intervene;
While flushed with pride, or coldly serene
The marshalling armies press together.

And now while bells yet knoll to prayer,
Or ever the Host is raised on high,
A sterner summons blasts the air
In dread presage that Death is nigh.
Swift overhead in an endless stream
With ghastly wailing the great shells scream,
To plunge the world in a hideous dream
Of murderous carnage and misery.

Hour after hour the raging storm
Crashes o'er Guns and Foot together;
Hour upon hour the ranks re-form—
(Hey I what a game for the holiday weather I)
Out to the flanks the Horse press home
Charge after charge—as the sea-waves comb
And lash the cliffs in eddying foam—
(So work Guns, Foot and Horse together).

Lurid in flame falls the August night
(Shattered the trench and battered the gun),
Yet hurled in vain is the German might,
Scarce a yard of the ground is won.
But harsh is the Fate which aid assigns
To the enemy ranks as his power declines,
And cleaves a road through the stern-held lines
Ere the pale mists rise to the morning sun.

Blinded, bloody, and torn, they reel
(The Horse and the Guns and the Foot together)
Back from the line of glinting steel
They have held through the hours of holiday weather.
Yet hearts beat high, though hands may clench
In the sinister whisper, "Betrayed—by the French?"
As wistful they turn from the derelict trench
The Horse, Foot and Guns have held together.

So it's Southward Ho! for the land of France,
Through the shimmering haze of the August weather;

"And it's we who'll pipe for a merry, mad dance,"
Say the Horse and the Guns and the Foot together.
"With our slim little rifles," the Infantry cry.
"We've shells," call the Gunners, "to darken the sky ";
"While sabre and lance we gaily will ply,"
Sing the Horse as they caper in highest feather.

"They're five to one—but we've piped the tune
Through the blazing hours of the August weather;
It's time to go—maybe none too soon,"
Whisper Horse and Guns and Foot together.
But none would be first to steal away
From the dance they have piped through the summer day;
"'Tis we," cry all, "who've the right to stay"—
All the Horse and the Guns and the Foot together.

Staggering back down the roads they come
(The Horse and the Guns and the Foot together),
And it's hey! for a whistle and a little toy drum
To cheer us along through the August weather!
Thrashed into rags are the uniforms neat;
Blood-soaked puttees to wrap round the feet;
"God! What a game, this merry retreat!"
Cry the Horse and the Guns and the Foot together.

MAP OF COUNTRY

FROM ANTWERP TO THE SEINE

CHAPTER 1

The Turn of the Tide

K. Hen. *We doubt not of a fair and lucky war,*
We doubt not now
But every rub is smoothed on our way.
Then forth, dear countrymen: let us deliver
Our puissance into the hand of God,
Putting it straight in expedition. [1]

"Didn't I tell you we'd be home by Christmas!" and Sergeant Smart threw a leg triumphantly across the pommel of his saddle and came heavily to ground. (It wasn't the proper way to dismount, but Smart evidently meant to emphasise the finality of his remark.)

"Throw them leaders off to the left a bit," he ordered, "and give them Frenchies behind room to pass."

The lead-driver looked over his shoulder and promptly began to pull across to the right. "Left, I said," bawled the sergeant.

The lead-driver evidently didn't hear, for he continued to pull in the wrong direction as a squadron of French cavalry trotted smartly by in half-sections, greeted with a volley of cheers all down the battery.

Sergeant Smart wisely decided to drop the intricate subject of "rule of the road" in outlandish countries like France, and returned to his first argument as two of his pals joined him. The battery was halting for half-an-hour to water the horses after a hard four hours' stretch—in the right direction.

"You mark my words," said Sergeant Smart with an air of absolute conviction, "at the rate we're going we'll have the *Allemons* back over their old Rhine before the month's out. And they won't half be sorry

---

1. The quotation headings throughout the volume are again taken exclusively from Shakespeare's *Henry V.*

they took this job on."

"Bit sanguine, aren't you?" remarked the senior subaltern who was passing and overheard the last words.

"Sanguine, sir? What, after what the general said? Last night's order, sir?"

"No, what was it? I haven't heard," said the senior sub.

"Why, he said—don't remember the exact words—that if all went well he expected to have the German Army scuppered in three days; that it was just up to us to carry out the job." And Sergeant Smart surveyed his audience with a put-that-in-your-pipe-and-smoke-it air that was irresistibly comic.

"Well, you'd better see that you get a new pair of riding pants before you cross the Rhine," said the senior sub. with a smile, "or the German ladies will all be laughing at you." And he went on up the line to report to the major.

"Will have his little joke," said the sergeant, twisting himself round to see the hole through which the breeze was blowing. "And if it comes to that, Mr. Stanion could do with another pair of boots himself."

"It's a treat to see some of those French chaps at last," a corporal remarked. "Can't think what the hell they've been up to all this time."

"Rummy lot, ain't they, them cavalry coves?" the wheel-driver put in. "Wot d'yer think 'o them tin belly-plates o' theirs, Sergeant? Fat lot o' use ahrt 'ere, I don't think."

"All watered. Sergeant Smart?" a voice rang out.

"All watered, sir."

"Bit up, then, and get mounted."

The senior subaltern salutes the C.O. "Battery all watered and ready, sir."

A minute later and they're off once again at a steady trot in the hope of getting in a few rounds at the retreating Huns before nightfall.

★★★★★★

Yes, "by the mass" their "hearts were in the trim." Never did an army, harried and hunted for ten interminable days and nights, battered by incredible weight of shell-fire, marching and fighting, dropping through sheer physical exhaustion, staggering up and on again to face and crush some new attack every hour—never did an army turn at last upon its pursuers with such gaiety of spirits in the unconquerable conviction that the fullness of triumph was theirs for the taking.

Once again it was the ingrained spirit of English race and blood. History is full of instances of it. Never to know when you are beaten. By all the rules of war and human disposition those five infantry divisions,[2] with a cavalry division, had been put out of action more than a week before. So indeed von Kluck believed, or he would not have made the vital mistake he did.[3]

But the gist of the matter was this, and it is difficult to understand when we remember the terrible time through which the Force had passed. The men, or a large proportion of them, had seen how again and again they had beaten down heavy enemy attacks. They knew themselves to be the better men, and it was therefore incomprehensible to them why they were always receiving the order to retire. The prevalent feeling was tersely expressed in the remark I have quoted in the earlier volume. "Where the 'ell are we going? and why the —— are we retreating? Give 'em socks, didn't we?"

In short, the Force had not been fighting as a forlorn hope, with its back to the wall, as it were, but as a victorious army confident in its ability to advance at any moment and fretting at the unreasonable delay in the passing of the word.

Now that the actual facts of the Retreat are known this state of mind seems incredible. When we recall the overwhelming superiority of the enemy in men and material, and the perfect detail of their preparation and organisation, it is indeed a miracle that any part of the British Force escaped to tell the tale. And yet all the time our men thought that they were the victors. I do not attempt to explain it, I can only just state the fact.

There was, too, another factor which seems worthy of mention, for it explains in some degree the difference of outlook between our men and our French Allies in those early days. The French had unforgettable memories of the German invasion of 1870. These, together with subsequent incidents like the Prussian demand, duly enforced, for the dismissal from office of Delcassé the French Foreign Minister, had gradually tended to a belief in the invincibility of Prussian arms. As we remember, this belief was carefully fostered throughout Europe, so that it was not only the French people who were a party to it. And

2. Through the common use of the expression "the First Seven Divisions," the public have come to imagine that these divisions formed the original Expeditionary Force. This misnomer is regrettable. The original Force consisted of one cavalry and four infantry divisions. A fifth division came into line for the Battle of Le Cateau, August 26th, 1914, the sixth at the Aisne, and the seventh in Flanders.
3. *Vide The Retreat from Mons.*

when you are separated from a military menace like that only by the width of a road, and can see for yourselves what it looks like, it is not to be wondered at that the French National Army had a very wholesome dread of its effects.

It was with vastly different feelings that the little professional Army of Britain took the field. For them the might of Germany meant nothing. It was not even a bogey with a turnip head. That it would be a very real and a very stern fight our officers fully realised. But then the professional army, which is always at work somewhere or other on the confines of Empire, is well used to hard knocks. And so they went into this fight, too, simply because it was their job and, so far as this new army was concerned, with the belief that the foeman would probably prove worthy of their steel. That was all. I suppose there was hardly a man in the Force who properly appreciated the reasons for the war. That came later, together with evidence of the hellish methods of the Hun.

So it came about that for one reason and another the British Force had to withstand the main shock of the German invasion. How our two army corps did so, and how, under God's hand, the victory of the Marne was made possible I have already told. The task, a wholly unexpected one, of our army was, for the moment, fulfilled. It became now the turn of our French Allies. And it was our French Allies who won the Battle of the Marne. The British played their part right valiantly, but, from the nature of the contest, it was only a comparatively small part which could be allotted to them. The marvel is that they were in such fine fettle that they could play it at all. And that is where von Kluck miscalculated.

Most people find it extremely difficult to understand just how the tide turned during those critical days. And it is difficult. But as just now we are all soldiers at heart, women as well as men, and as the Marne is one of the decisive battles of the world in which we are all concerned, it is worth giving it a few minutes' study. I will outline the main facts as shortly and concisely as I can.

On the opposite page is a plan to show the Franco–British line on the eve of the advance, and below it is another to indicate roughly how the various Armies were distributed.

6th French Army. Perhaps the first thing you will notice is the appearance of a new French Army on the extreme left, where, up to now, there had only been brigades and occasional troops. This was the 6th French Army. But it was new only in the sense of its appearance in

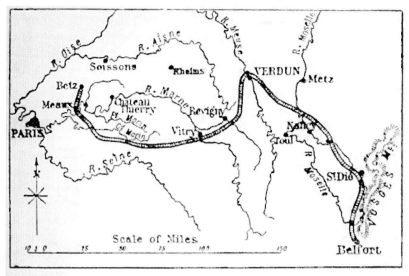

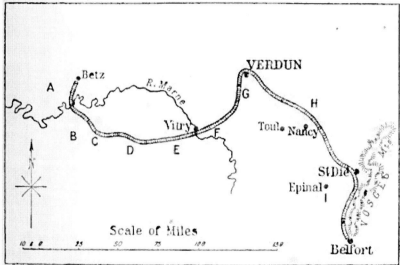

REFERENCE.

N.B.—The letters indicate the approximate centres of the several positions.

A. VIth French Army (General Manoury). B. British Force. C. A Cavalry Corps of Vth French Army (General Conneau). D. Vth French Army (General D'Esperey). E. VIIth (or IXth) French Army (General Foch). F. IVth French Army (General de Cary). G. IIIrd French Army (General Sarrail). H. IInd French Army (General de Castelnau). I. Ist French Army (General Dubail).

that position. As a matter of fact, this force, consisting of rather more than four divisions, had already suffered severely in the previous fighting in the east. We see it in position on the eve of the advance not as a strong fighting force in itself destined to turn the enemy flank, but rather as the nucleus upon which will shortly be concentrated a succession of reinforcements.

Most of these reinforcements were coming from the south of Paris, and history may probably know them as the "taxi-cab army." The story of how motor-buses, taxi-cabs and every possible vehicle were commandeered to rush the troops across Paris to the battle-front is well known. They came into position, division by division, at various times on September 6, 7, and 8. The actual French attack from this quarter on the German right was begun about midday on September 5, 1914, and the main idea was the attempted cutting of von Kluck's line of communications back through Belgium and the outflanking and rolling up of his army on the west, just as he had tried to outflank the British during the Retreat.

British. Still looking at the Plan, and moving from west to east, we next come to our own army. They had crossed the stream of the Grand Morin, a tributary of the Marne, and had halted with the Forest of Crécy between them and the enemy. German cavalry and advance guards were still moving towards them from the north across the Marne.

At this time the British losses had not yet been made good, although a welcome reinforcement of about 2,000 men had just joined the Second Corps. These losses, up to September 7, were put at 589 officers and 18,140 N.C.O.'s and men, or a number not very far below one quarter of the strength of the Force when it came into action only a fortnight before. The Second Corps alone had lost 350 officers and 9,200 men, or more than a quarter of its original strength.

In equipment, entrenching tools and so forth, we were rather badly off. During the Retreat men had discarded pretty well everything they carried except their rifles. Greatcoats and packs were pitched aside during the first couple of days, and what was then left in the way of tools was lost at Le Cateau. The principal base, too, had been moved from Havre to St. Nazaire, and as the line of communication had not yet been properly re-established it was impossible for the moment to get up new supplies.

But the Army Service Corps was putting in some of the finest work that corps has ever done. And only those who saw a little of its organisation from the inside could realise the enormous difficulties which officers and men had then to surmount. Food and ammunition were the only two things to bother about in those early days, and somehow or other the goods were delivered. The man at the head of that department of the army's work, the cool and calculating brain which foresaw every contingency and instantly grasped the best way to meet it, this was Sir William Robertson, Quarter-Master-General. No more need be said. And his right hand man was Colonel C. M. Mathew, an officer who had seen most of the fighting there was to be seen on the confines of the Empire since 1884, and as cheery and lovable a man as any in the Force.

French Armies.—Immediately on the British right, and bridging the gap to the 5th French Army, came a French cavalry corps under General Conneau. Then came the 5th Army, the 7th Army (or 9th), and in succession the 4th, 3rd, 2nd and 1st.

Numbers. As regards the numbers of the opposing forces along that 300-mile battlefront, it is not easy to give even an approximate estimate. We have a fair idea of the strength of the Franco-British line, but we can only guess rather wildly at the numbers of the enemy. No one has made more carefully reasoned calculations of such figures than Mr. Hilaire Belloc, and his estimate is that the Germans numbered at least 75 Divisions, as against 51 or 52 Franco-British (46 French, 6 British). We may place the Franco-British strength at about 700,000 men.[4]

These figures, together with the plan, will, I hope, serve to explain the remark that the British could only play a comparatively small part in the great battle or battles of the Marne. I will now, without discussing strategy or tactics, summarise under three heads how the fighting went:

(1). *East.* An exceedingly heavy German attack was being directed from the north against the line Verdun-Toul-Epinal, and particularly against the centre and the town of Nancy. The importance to the enemy of success at this point may be gauged from the presence there of the German emperor. Here, after delivering the usual address to his troops, he had dressed himself with more than his usual care, and, surrounded by the usual

---

4. For those who may wish to study in fuller detail the numbers and composition of the Armies, reference is suggested to *A General Sketch of the War—Second Phase*, by Hilaire Belloc and Major Whitton's *The Marne Campaign*.

glittering staff, stood waiting to make his triumphal entry into Nancy.

This attack actually began about September 1. It reached its climax just when General Joffre ordered the advance along the Allied line. The French, with far inferior numbers, held and repulsed the attack with a German loss estimated at about 120,000 men—and the German Emperor decided to see for himself how things were going on in East Prussia.

(2). *West.* Von Kluck had swerved S.E. in his advance towards Paris. Apparently he thought that the Allied left (the British and 5th French Army) would crumble before his outflanking attack, and that the 6th Army on his right was not worth bothering about.

As already noted the 6th French Army was being built up to try an outflanking scheme upon the German right. Suddenly, then, appeared to von Kluck this new menace. To meet it he began to withdraw troops from his left (opposing the British). Joffre ordered a general counter-offensive; the 6th Army began their outflanking movement, and the British and 5th Army turned to advance. The weight of this counter-attack induced the Germans to strengthen their right at the expense of their centre, and

(3). *The Centre* was broken into by General Foch and his divisions. A gap was discovered in the German line, the French poured in, and by a brilliant stroke the Battle of the Marne was won. The Germans had to retreat all along the line.[5]

There you have the barest possible outline of this great battle. Nor do I even hint at the sternness of the fighting, how the French were at times driven back, clung limpet-like to new positions, rallied and thrust the invaders back once more. To our Allies it was now or never. The decisive stroke, one of the most brilliant and effective *coups-de-main* in military history, was not actually delivered until the late afternoon of Wednesday, September 9. The story of it, whichever version is correct, is still to be told as it should be. And if Englishmen are not particularly happy in remembering foreign names, let us at least remember and hold in the highest honour the names of Generals Foch and Manoury.

---

5. It is not improbable that official histories may considerably modify this theory. The other theory, ably supported by Major Whitton in his book, is that the leading part in winning the battle was really played by General Manoury and his army on the west. We must wait for the official statement

★★★★★★

It was late in the evening of Saturday, September 5, that the orders got round that at last we were to advance as part of a general offensive. That evening Generals Smith-Dorrien and Haig visited many units of their respective commands, and if there was any shadow of a lingering doubt in the minds of the G.O.C.'s as to the condition and keenness of the men, that visit finally dispelled it. By good fortune, too, the day had been a complete rest for nearly everyone, and that had worked wonders. Thomas Atkins does like to start his job properly washed and shaved. And I well remember a general officer making a sudden appearance amongst a platoon of a certain famous county regiment.

"Tshun," yelled a lance-corporal.

Out came the heads covered with soap-suds before the general had time to stop them.

"Go on, men," said the general, "but you will be glad to hear that we're going to advance tomorrow." And with a salute and a smile he passed on.

There was a moment's pause, and then with a yell up into the air went the buckets of soapy water, deluging everyone near by. The men rushed back to their lines, vigorously rubbing their heads dry, to spread the good news.

That was how the lads felt about it.

Sir John French said in his Order of the Day:

I call upon the British Army in France to show now to the enemy its power, and to push on vigorously to the attack beside the 6th French Army.

Away to the south, through the dim, misty glades of the Forest of Crécy before ever the sun is up, there is a great stirring of marching men. Here and there and on the flanks batteries of field-guns are pushing along hard, for they have some leeway to make up. Close up with the cavalry screens you will find the Horse Gunners. Their moment, too, is at hand. Years ago the German *Kaiser* and his staff recognised them as the finest body of troops in the world; he has seen what they can do in a retirement (L Battery is not forgotten), now he and his merry men shall see what they can do now that the advance is sounded. Yes, it is good to feel that it is the right direction at last.

Back to the riverside town of Melun, where G.H.Q. has its habitation, runs the wireless current of sympathy. Père Joffre has just paid a visit. "*Ça va bien main tenant, n'est ce pas?*" "*Mais oui, ça marche!*" G.H.Q.

has done a deal of packing and unpacking these last days. And they are men of few words those red-tabbed, brass-hatted ones. But this time—*ça marche!* Once again a procession of lordly motor-cars takes the dusty roads and the *mairie* is left empty. The townsfolk are sorry to see them go. *Mais si polis, ces anglais!*

Still farther south and we come to our old friends the motor lorries. Right down to Fontainebleau they have displayed Mr. Johnnie Walker and his eyeglass, Mr. Pulltite and his corsets, Mr. Mayflower and his margarine before an enthusiastic country folk. The colours are not so brilliant as they were a month ago. Some of the pictures, too, are chipped by bullet marks, but Mr. Walker smiles serenely as of old, and brings a feeling of peace to our excitable French friends.

Here, too, the rumour comes that the tide has turned. The lorries fill up to their capacity with shells, a last hurried overhauling of parts, and they, too, are reversed for the north. *Tout ça marche!*

At dawn on Sunday, September 6, the battle opened. The tide had turned.

CHAPTER 2

With the Cavalry

Chor. *Think, when we talk of horses, that you see them*
Printing their proud hoofs i' the receiving earth;
For 'tis your thoughts that now must deck our kings,
Carry them here and there.

Picture to yourselves our own fair county of Kent; enlarge the picture as you would a photograph, and you will see a little of this fragrant countryside of France through which our men are now advancing.

A land rich in orchards, where heavy branches dip down to lazy streams and tell a double harvest of their glowing fruit. A land of yellowing corn, through which, like wind-tracks, run the straight, poplar-lined roads, rising and bending to the gentle hills. A land of tiny towns and sleepy hamlets, of noble chateaux glimmering white against the sky, of tiled cottages and thatched barns dimly seen against the blue dusk of the woodlands.

Into this fair land have the Huns carried their fire and rapine. But thus far and no farther. Along the banks of the little river of the Grand Morin ran the line of their southernmost bivouacs that eve of the Allied advance. And ever in touch with them our own cavalry patrols are now beginning to drive them back. De Lisle is out there with his 9th Lancers, 4th Dragoon Guards and 18th Hussars. Hubert Gough, too, with the 3rd and 5th Cavalry Brigades.

That first day there was comparatively little fighting, at least on any big scale. The French were pushing ahead pretty fast and seemed to be doing most of the work. With us it was more an affair of outposts, in which the cavalry were more particularly engaged. Little disputes over the passage of a stream, the clearing of a cluster of barns, a squadron

189

charge upon a spitting machine-gun, and so on.

Typical of this fighting was a trifling affair near Pezarches. A squadron of Lancers was working in advance of a section of Horse Gunners when their scouts were suddenly fired upon from behind a hedgerow which ran across some farm buildings. Two of ours were hit, one in the arm, one in the leg. The four advance scouts, who were dismounted, at once began to fall back upon the main body, firing as they retired.

In the meantime the C.O. dismounted half his troop and lined a parallel hedge to pour in a hot return fire. The other half-troop worked round under cover of a wood to try to get the enemy on the flank.

The enemy fire seemed to slacken, and some of the Germans were seen making for their horses.

"They're bolting! Come on, boys," and the subaltern was in his saddle and over the low hedge with his men after him in less time than it takes to tell.

But half way across the open a couple of machine-guns opened fire straight in front. The subaltern mixed up a curse with a prayer that the other half-troop would get round in time and held straight ahead.

Over the next hedge and the subaltern launched straight into the middle of a litter of astonished pigs. Down came the horse and two piglets had all the breath knocked out of them. It was rather inglorious, but they certainly saved the officer's life. Before he could get up his half-troop were in amongst the few remaining enemy troopers, while the machine-guns went on spitting death into friend and foe alike.

Now the gunner subaltern had grasped what was happening, and it looked rather serious; nor could he see how he was to lend a hand. Anyway, he decided to trek after the second half -troop. Round the wood the section went at a canter just as the troop was clear and lining up to charge. And then lancers and gunners in those breathless seconds could tell what they were up against.

It was a regular little tactical trick of the Germans. A handful of cavalry would form a screen, and working up behind would come a couple, say, of fast motor lorries, each carrying 40 odd men, *Jaegers* generally, and a couple of machine-guns. The cavalry would hold the line while the infantry deployed, and would then slip away, unmasking the machine-guns. But in this case the enemy evidently had not noticed our flanking movement.

"Mine, I think!" said the gunner subaltern.

You have to make up your mind pretty quickly in a case like that, and the guns swept out into the open without a check of the pace. A sudden wheel. Then, "Halt, action front!" and an admirably placed shell informed the Huns that the game was not to be so one-sided after all. Before six rounds had been fired two of the machine-guns were out of action and the lancers charged, while the gunners turned their attention to the motor lorries. One lorry got away; the other didn't. And a quarter of an hour later one of the first batches of Huns was on its way to comfortable quarters in England.

The whole affair had lasted about a quarter of an hour, and the dear old lady who owned the farm looked on all the while from an upper window, as though it were a stage play arranged for her especial benefit. When it was all over down she came to help with the wounded and dispense drinks.

The subaltern who had jumped on the pigs, and was none the worse for the adventure save for a sprained ankle, tried to explain.

"*Mille pardons, madame,*" said he in his best French, "*très faché j'ai* jumped on *votre petits porcs.*"

That settled it. *Madame* didn't know what he meant, but she recognised "*porcs*" and flew out into the yard.

"Good heavens," exclaimed the gunner subaltern who was helping to carry one of his men into the house, "there's some cursed German after the women." And he drew his revolver and ran, too, as shriek after shriek rent the air.

Round the corner he came full tilt upon half a dozen lancers doubled up with laughter round an old woman who was calling heaven to witness her grievous loss.

"What the—" he began, taking a *trooper* by the scruff of the neck. And then he saw.

Well, quiet was at length restored and Madame eventually pacified by a golden half-sovereign and the first subaltern's cap badge. And that gallant officer is, I am glad to say, still ready and willing to heave you out of the window whenever you may innocently inquire as to the price of pork. But as he is now a major you have to be rather discreet.

★★★★★★

The Germans had certainly brought their machine-gun work to a fine art. In the earlier volume I have described how they used them in infantry attack, and a few more notes at this stage may also prove of interest.

The great importance which the enemy attached to machine-guns is seen from the fact that where the British Army went in for rifle practice and competitions like those at Bisley and elsewhere the Germans held machine-gun competitions. They consider these to be infinitely more valuable. Each infantry regiment carries with it perhaps twelve of these guns, and they are always moved as a part of the regimental transport.

And the ingenuity which has been expended upon this transport is as remarkable as anything in their military organisation. Secrecy seems to be the dominant note. They are carried either on light motor-lorries or two-wheeled carts; sometimes on stretchers with a rug or covering thrown over. And at a short distance away these last look for all the world like a wounded man being carried by a couple of Red Cross orderlies. In fact, on many occasions our men have been completely taken in by the trick and have held their fire.

The carts, too, are generally provided with double bottoms, in which the machine-guns are packed, and perhaps four men ride in the vehicle. The rest of the cart is piled up with odds and ends of various kinds, and no one would guess the real contents. Instances have been recorded at G.H.Q. where some of these carts were captured and the guns never discovered until later someone knocked a bottom through by accident.

Then they have another trick of burying a machine-gun when there is a risk of capture. A wooden cross is put over the "grave," and, of course, no one would dream of disturbing the "body."

But as we have long since come to expect from the Huns, several of the transport tricks are not legitimate. Cases of abuse of the Red Cross were quite common. Knowing the enemy now for what they are it is obvious that they would not miss so excellent an opportunity of getting up close to their opponents by emblazoning their machine-gun lorries with a big red cross.[1] One can recall several instances where our men or French or Belgians have allowed a German Red Cross ambulance to drive close by when, as it passed, the hood (of steel) has been slipped down to disclose a machine-gun which has promptly opened fire.

One particularly flagrant case was recorded a week after the Advance had begun. Here a party of Germans was seen advancing and

---

1. The Germans, with their curious mentality, cannot believe that other nations would not adopt similar tactics in abuse of the Red Cross. Hence their attacks on hospital ships.

waving a Red Cross flag in front of four stretchers carried by orderlies. The British officer ordered the cease fire and the party approached. When they were about 300 yards off a murderous maxim fire was opened. A general mix-up followed, and after our reinforcements had satisfactorily disposed of the would-be murderers the stretchers were found with the machine-guns still strapped on them.

★★★★★★

As our advance pushed on, although it was rather a slow business at the outset, the fighting became more severe. The enemy made the best use of the difficult country, and we were continually checked by their cavalry and machinegun tactics. When it was a question of dealing with their cavalry alone, and our own had half a chance, it was all over in a few minutes. It was the combination which worked the mischief. But even here the balance was not too heavy against us, for our cavalry seemed to be as useful dismounted as they were mounted, while their shooting was well up to the standard of the infantry.

I cannot do better than illustrate these two sides of our cavalry work by two incidents which, oddly enough, happened in the same engagement.

A regiment of German Dragoons had pushed its way south through the little village of Moncel after the retreating British. Now had come the inexplicable order to abandon the pursuit and return the way they had come. It was not in the best of tempers that the dragoons clattered once again down the village street, for the cursed English cavalry had been leading them a rare dance all the afternoon, and the experience had not been a pleasant one.

"Captain Schniff with a squadron will hold the village till further orders," the colonel commanded as he took the remainder of the regiment with him on the northern road.

The captain did not feel too happy about the position, and thought once or twice of telephoning to headquarters for a couple of maxims. However, deciding to make the best of it, he turned his attention to instilling a little wholesome respect for "*kultur*" into the villagers. Unfortunately, his class was likely to be a small one, for everybody had fled with the exception of three old women, two girls, two old men and four or five children.

Nothing daunted, he and his men set to work upon the principles officially laid down by his government,[2] with the gratifying result that

---

2. *The Usages of War on Land*, issued by the General Staff of the German Army. Translated by J. H. Morgan.

193

before nightfall the two old men had both been shot for trying to defend their womenfolk from insult; one girl had been outraged and had escaped somewhere after shooting the man with his own carbine, and the remainder had been reduced to a state of mental and physical paralysis.

Thus the night passed without further incident. But in the early morning the outposts fell back upon the village with the news that British cavalry had been seen in considerable strength moving in their direction. With a hurried order to the senior sergeant Captain Schniff made his way to a small outhouse at the end of the village where the field-telephone line ended, and in a few seconds had informed his brigade H. Q. that he was expecting an attack in force at any minute.

It came before he had removed the receiver-cap from his head.

Three sudden shots and Captain Schniff, running out into the street, found himself in the middle of a whirl of men and horses. Half his squadron had mounted, the rest had just got hold of their horses when the wave of British cavalry swept in from the south. A troop of the 9th Lancers, acting as advance guard, had driven in the outposts, and not knowing, and caring less, what the enemy strength might be, had galloped straight at the village.

A few minutes of mad cut and thrust and the old people were avenged. The lancers cleared the street from end to end almost in a single sweep. By the little outhouse door stood Schniff, pistol in hand. His first shot brought down a trooper with a bullet through his chest. His second tore a cut through a horse's shoulder. Then the wave swept over him. It passed; but the German captain still stood against the lintel, pinned to the wood with a sabre thrust clean through the neck.

Ranks were re-formed, two or three scouts sent forward to the north, and a message was despatched to the main body to report. There with the 9th Lancers were the 18th Hussars, and a brief debate followed as to whether they should push on or hold the village for a spell. The Colonel in command of the lancers knew fairly accurately the enemy strength in cavalry in the immediate neighbourhood, and the odds against the British were rather heavy.

However, the point was soon decided for them. Captain Schniff's telephone message had been promptly acted upon, and some four new German squadrons were already well on the way to support their comrades. Our outposts fell back in their turn with the report that the enemy were approaching fast from two sides.

A squadron of the Hussars was at once sent forward with orders to dismount and get under cover ready to open fire as they saw the best opportunity. The lancers were formed up clear of the village, but still out of sight of the advancing Germans. The joking and laughter have for the moment died away, and every man sits as though carved in stone with that curious, empty feeling inside which will always creep over one when waiting for the moment. Officers nervously fidget at the reins and try to appear unconcerned as they rack their brains for a sentence or two of encouragement or warning for their men. The colonel is well out to the front carefully judging the ground and distance. There is a gentle dip in the ground which his eye at once tells him is the spot where the shock should come. That extra down gradient will be worth to him a score more men.

"We'll get them all right," a subaltern says over his shoulder. "They always pull in a bit when we're on them." He had been through it before with his men, and knew about that odd, sudden shrinking which seems to attack German cavalry at the critical moment. The men knew too, and they instinctively settled to a tighter grip in the saddle, every eye on the man who was to lead them. The eternal seconds passed and the tension grew till it was well-nigh unbearable; just as when a bowstring is slowly drawn back until it seems that the yew will surely snap.

Suddenly the colonel sees that the moment has come. The enemy are riding diagonally across his front, and it may be possible to meet them before they can fully change direction. The signal is given and the lancers have started, so steadily that they might be entering the arena at Olympia for the musical ride.

The pace increases. The colonel has given his men plenty of room, for they'll need every bit of advantage they can get. "Steady, men, steady!" The enemy have begun to wheel—*Now!*

One tremendous bound forward and the gallant horses are stretched out to the uttermost. Down the slope they thunder. Each man tries to pick an opponent, but there is no time. There is one mighty crash all down the line. The lancers have got home. Heave! and they are through. Through, with hardly a check of the pace, and on. The files close in and the men begin to drag at the bit reins. A wheel into section, and so to the village, again.

The Germans, too, have checked and wheeled round, but they are not so steady. Though by far the heavier cavalry they have been badly mauled. It was like the little English ships sailing through and raking the great galleons of the Spanish Armada. Still, they recover and turn to retire the way they had come. Back they trot, re-forming ranks as they go. Now they have reached the northern end of the village. Now three hundred yards past, when there is a sudden burst of rifle fire and a hail of bullets ploughs through the hardly formed ranks.

(You had forgotten all about the Hussars, hadn't you?)

But the Germans know what discipline means, and they are courageous enough too. There is a momentary confusion, but a sudden word of command pulls them together, and about eighty odd men from the inner flank wheel about.

"By Jove!" exclaims the Hussar squadron leader, "they're actually going to charge us." Then, after a moment to make sure, "Cease fire!— we'll wait for 'em," he adds to himself.

The other officers and N.C.O.'s see in a moment what they are to do. It is an old trick, but it calls for nerves of steel to carry it out. The Hussars had been firing "rapid independent" on the retiring Germans, and it is not always easy to get your men quickly in hand again, especially when there is an avalanche of men and horses coming down on top of you. Still, the Germans do not hold a grinding monopoly in discipline, and you might say that a crack British regiment will go one better, for the men are trained and disciplined as human beings, not machines.

"Not a shot till you get the word, and then two good volleys," sings out the O.C. "Aim low."

The German cavalry has covered 150 yards. They are getting alarmingly close, and coming for all they are worth dead straight. Again it is just a matter of seconds, but the O.C. is as cool as though it were practice on the Pirbright ranges.

100 yards! and—"*Fire!*"

Every Hussar had picked his man, and that one volley accounted for practically the entire line of dragoons. They say that only ten got back.

So ended perhaps the most brilliant cavalry engagement of the war up to that date, and, so far as I am aware, up to the time of writing. It illustrates very happily the mounted and dismounted work of our cavalry in those early days. All the world knows how magnificently they fought later in the trenches and not only our own Home cavalry, but those splendid men from India, the Deccan Horse, the Poona Light Horse, and other crack regiments.

The story, too, seems to tell of an adventure in some earlier war. Of a time when the enemy was worth of your steel, and each faced the other for clean give-and-take fighting, with the better man to win. No rancour on either side, but a shake of the hand and a drink shared when it was over. Oh, the pity of it that the Germans cannot always fight so!

CHAPTER 3

Kultur

K. Hen. Now, if these men have defeated the law and outrun native punishment, though they can outstrip men, they have no wings to fly from God.

Never, I suppose, since the dawn of history have a number of men crowded into so small a circle of time so many and such varied experiences as those which fell to the lot of that First Expeditionary Force of ours during the first six weeks of the war. I look back upon those Autumn days of 1914, and they seem no more than "the insubstantial pageant of a dream." A dream from which, on the awakening, a few incidents stand out sharp and clear, but all else is lost save only a sense of atmosphere, of environment.

It was that atmosphere which I sought to recapture for the first part of the narrative. And now, as I embark upon the second part, I find that some subtle change has taken place. "Naturally," you will exclaim, "you have turned from a harassed retreat to a victorious advance. Of course it is different."

No, it is not that; at least, not wholly that. I can see the dividing line between retreat and advance, but it is something bigger, more vague. Somehow the general tone of the campaign is different. The enemy is not the same, the countryside, the inhabitants, all are changed. Before the Advance was four days old there seems to have been, looking back now, some indefinable change even with our own men, some difference in outlook, some subdued note which sounded like a grave counterpoint beneath their natural elation at the turn of affairs. I do not think this lasted, for the inborn gaiety of the British soldier soon reasserted itself. But I seem to have detected it throughout this month of September.

And I am inclined to think that the new mental outlook which did not come upon us until the Advance had well begun was due to this, that we realised for the first time the incredible tragedy of this mighty social cataclysm. Look back for a moment and you may perhaps understand.

Barely a month had passed since that fateful August holiday night. Scarcely had the men realised that the country was at war before they were swept up by a giant hand, thrust into trains and troopships, dropped into a foreign land, hurried through the country and set before this Prussian god of destruction like Hindoo devotees before the car of Juggernaut. Before they could begin to adjust themselves to these astonishing conditions they were swept back again through the mazes of a veritable nightmare. Everything was unreal, phantasmal. Villages, country folk, the pursuing hordes of blue-grey figures, all seemed to dance through the brain like motes in a vampire mist.

Then slowly came the awakening. The dream-cloud lifted and they began to see clearly. Before the Retreat had ended the men were themselves again. They turned to drive their pursuers back; and as they drove them back the British and French *saw*. Now they knew war for what it was; they recognised for what they were the beings who had hurled it upon the world.

So this was modern war; and this was how a great modern and civilised people waged it! "*Kultur* had passed that way!"

★★★★★★

It was along the line of the Grand Morin River, from the town of Coulommiers through Rebais and so beyond La Ferté that our men made their first real acquaintance with German "*Kultur.*" There had been a few isolated instances during the Retreat, symptoms of Hun brutality which had for the moment stricken with horror the unit immediately concerned. But now the troops suddenly crossed the threshold of a new world: a world which revealed as in a blinding lightning-flash not merely the wanton excesses and unbridled licence of an invading army, but the unspeakable depravity of a nation.

Remember that at this time the war was barely a month old. The civilised world had not yet learned of the crimes committed in Belgium; the *Lusitania* had not been sunk, Rheims Cathedral had not been shelled, the ghastly story of Wittenberg camp was yet to come. Even the rumour about Dinant, Termonde and Louvain had barely reached the army in the field, nor indeed was it credited. Personally, the first mail I received after leaving England on August 14, and the first newspaper I saw, was on September 16 at the Aisne. We knew practically nothing of the course of events. I mention these facts to suggest more clearly how unprepared the men must have been for the sights they now witnessed.

The little town of Rebais was the first. There were about two streets of houses still standing, the remainder was merely a ruin. When the first British troops entered after driving out the enemy it was imagined that the town was quite deserted. But after diligent search a few old men and half-crazy women were discovered in cellars and basements. A corporal and a couple of men got into one shop, and in the back room found two young girls. They were trying to climb up the blank wall, legs and arms outstretched, as though they were flies. At the entrance of the men they merely glanced over their shoulders and laughed—a laugh which sent a shudder through the veins. When the corporal touched them they turned round, crouched on the ground and fawned upon him like puppies. In a cot close by lay the broken body of a tiny child. The corporal went out and reported to his officer with the tears rolling down his face.

Rebais, too, was the scene of one of the most extraordinary cases of sexual perversion on the part of some Germans ever recorded. I cannot possibly set down the story here; besides, it has already been published.[1] But it may be remarked in passing that one of the outstanding features of Hun *"Kultur,"* as exhibited in Belgium and Northern France, has been a glut of such obscene and bestial acts as can only be detailed between the covers of a book of medical science as instances of mental and physical depravity.

From this line of country northward to the Aisne the Huns had left behind them one long track of foul deeds, ruin and desolation; a memory which nothing will efface from the heart of the French people till France is no more a nation. Some few places escaped in great measure, but there was not one which did not bear some traces of that trail of slime.

Here is a charming country-house which looks down to Nogent and the smiling valley of the Marne. One wing of the house projects and encloses on three sides a large courtyard. A company of our infantry bivouacked hard by one night, and the officers thought they might find hospitality in the house. Unable to make anyone hear, they went round to the courtyard side. This is what they found. The yard

---

1. *German Atrocities* (T. Fisher Unwin), by J. H. Morgan, late Home Office Commissioner with the B.E.F.

was ankle-deep in feathers—of pigeons and chickens. The gutters ran black-red with the blood of pigs and farm-stock. Hundreds of birds must have been slaughtered—from the number of pigeonries around the owner was evidently a fancier on a large scale.

The officers found a door open and entered the house. Stumbling over some broken woodwork and a big "grandfather" clock which lay across the passage, they came to a room which lay in darkness save for a narrow shaft of light from a chink in the shutters. Through the door there drifted a stench beside which the open sewers of a Chinese city in the height of summer would have smelt like a rose-garden. When at last they had ventured in, candles in hand, it was found that, in addition to the carcass of a pig which had been slaughtered on the carpet, the room had been used, evidently by a number of men, as a latrine. Everything, too, which could be broken lay shattered on the floor, with curtains, blinds, tapestries and chair-coverings smeared with excreta and filth.

To cut the story short, practically every room in the house was in much the same condition. The state of the bedrooms, the linen, ladies' garments and so forth was simply indescribable.

One isolated case? No. Ask the French Government how many of their *châteaux* in those departments of France escaped such a fate.

★★★★★★

In the great majority of cases the destruction or, in its milder forms, the mischief, was purely wanton. Destruction simply for the sake of destruction. Ironmongery shops and houses where there were plenty of bottles and glasses to smash seemed particular favourites. In town after town we came across ironmongers' where thousands of nails and screws were scattered from the drawers and boxes all over the floors; or perfumers' shops where all the bottles of liquids had been broken by pistol bullets or rifle butts.

Cooking utensils would be looted in one town, used and then thrown into the ditch to save the trouble of transport, and the process would be repeated in the next village. At least, this was the only explanation we could imagine for the number of pots and pans found lying about uncleaned.

Systematic looting was quite the least of the crimes committed. And one may give some idea of the extent to which this was carried out by citing the one town of Coulommiers, a place about the size of Tunbridge Wells. Here the Huns, during the two days of their occupation, pillaged the houses and did minor damage to the value of some £16,000. Such was the condition of the town when our troops expelled the Germans from it at the beginning of September.

★★★★★★

Of the outrages and mutilations inflicted upon women and young girls and children I hardly trust myself to write. Their number seemed well-nigh incalculable. Never a town, village, or hamlet, rarely a farmstead did our men pass during those days of victory and horror but poor victims stretched forth imploring arms or lay still with fast-glazing eyes, mute witnesses to the bestial savagery of the invaders, the nation of supermen destined by their "friend" God to inherit the earth. Of a surety will the God Whom they never cease to blaspheme take His count upon them on that Great Day when St. Joseph shall marshal before Him in witness the ranks of those poor tortured souls.

Though vengeance, though repayment are His, yet such is man that he must at times rejoice at the finding of a human instrument. One such case I recall, and I can find no regret in my heart for the fate of one, at least, of these savages.

It was at a farm near Château-Thierry. A patrol of Uhlans rode by. Through the open door they could see the goodwife busy about her duties, crooning the while to her baby as he played by the hearth. Roughly the men demanded food, and, entering, one of the patrol made as if to hurt the child. Food was refused, the woman saying that she had nothing in the house. A search of the house proved fruitless, and they again made their demand. Again she replied that there was none. Thereupon the men seized her, pinned her against the door and crucified her, arms outstretched, with knives through her wrists. The child they seized, broke one of his tiny arms, and threw him down before her. Then they rode away, leaving behind one of their number for some purpose or other.

When the patrol had gone on the man who remained again asked for food and drink. And the woman, in agony, nodded assent. The knives were withdrawn. The man seated himself at the table while the woman staggered out to the back. In a minute or so she returned, holding something under her apron. The Uhlan sat quietly at the table looking through a notebook. The woman came behind him as though to place a dish on the table. A sudden effort and she drew from beneath her apron a heavy chopper. With a single crash she split his skull. Then, seizing her baby, she fled out into the woods.

★★★★★★

There is perhaps no people in the world who have earned a more

202

sinister reputation for ingenuity in torture than the Chinese. Methods employed in our own country during the Middle Ages or by the Spanish Inquisition were bad enough, as we know too well. But Germany, with its *stucco* civilisation, has outdistanced all. The Chinese are adepts in the torture of the body; the Germans torture body and soul. The Chinese may torture the individual; the Germans add the refinement of torturing two or more together. They will outrage a wife in the presence of her husband, a daughter before her mother. They will tie a mother up and mutilate her baby before her eyes. All these things have they done again and again: not in the heat of battle, but under the coolness of rigid discipline; with the connivance and encouragement of their officers. [2]

A company of British infantry was marching through a Marne village. One of the men turned to wave a hand to a little girl whose face appeared at a first-floor window of a cottage.

"Silly owl!" remarked a pal. "Can't you see it's a doll?"

The company marched on. In the evening some men from an Irish regiment joined up, and it chanced that the little incident of the afternoon was mentioned in a joking way.

"It *was* a child," said an Irishman gravely. "Shure, we saw herself. McClusky and me and some of us went in. 'Twas a baby tied across the window, with a cruel bay'net in her. Aye, and an old man, too, and a woman and a boy, all stabbed to the death."[3]

Do you begin dimly to realise what was this new world through which the British Army was advancing? Do you now appreciate a little of the feeling which steeled their hearts?

And since it is of interest to learn how the invaders themselves regarded their own doings, here is the translation of a portion of a letter written by a German soldier, [4] and selected at random from a number of others. The letter is addressed to a German *girl*.

I am sending you a bracelet made out of a shell. It will be a nice souvenir for you of a German warrior who had been through the whole campaign and killed many French. I have also bayoneted several women. During the fight at Batonville (*sic*) I did

---

2. A typical and thoroughly authenticated case, where a German soldier dipped a baby's head into a saucepan of boiling water to make the mother produce some more coffee, is quoted in the Appendix to the Bryce Report.

3. *Cf.* the incident narrated in *The Retreat from Mons*.

4. The name, regiment, brigade and division of the writer are on the original, together with date and town.

for seven women and four young girls in five minutes, etc.

On the other hand, it is pleasant to record that one diary at least has come into the possession of the French authorities in which the author, an officer in a Saxon corps, honestly deplores the vandalism and wanton outrages committed by the soldiery.

"The place," he writes, "is a disgrace to our army." And he adds the significant words:

> The column commanders are responsible for the greater part of the damage, as they could have prevented the looting and destruction.

★★★★★★

With that I close this harrowing chapter. I have tried to set forth those incidents as dispassionately as possible, and have steeled myself to the effort. Of several I write at first-hand. There are others still more horrible of which I know but cannot narrate. To say that the memory of those scenes is seared for ever in the brain is hopelessly inadequate. They have changed the very lives of the men who witnessed them. How could it be otherwise?

And I have made myself write them down partly that this may be a true narrative of those early days of this War of Liberation, but rather that our people may realise—so far as a printed page can compel—the real nature of this enemy of civilisation and humanity.

I have remarked that it is the depravity of a whole nation rather than the individual excesses of an army which is responsible for these things. A national army reflects the spirit of the nation. The German Army was, at the outbreak of war, just such an army as Britain in 1916 had in the field. Representative, I mean, of the nation as a whole. It was not a select body of professional troops such as ours was. And it was that national army—and, through it, the German people—which was guilty of those incredible outrages against all laws human and divine.

For years past, though but a few of us realised it, the criminal statistics of Germany have indicated only too plainly the rapid moral degeneration of the people. It has at length found its expression, so far as the rest of the world is concerned, in the tremendous catalogue of crimes committed by German soldiers and sailors, which, from the number and the ferocity of them, have actually at last dulled the brain of civilisation. We have, for instance, come to accept the murder on the high seas of women and children as a matter of everyday occurrence.

But no national army and navy, recruited as it is from the ranks of the nation itself, could possibly be guilty of such obscenity and criminality were it not that the poison had choked their very blood. It is the German people who are guilty. Have we already forgotten the unholy joy throughout Germany which greeted the sinking of the *Lusitania* and so the deliberate murder of scores of women and children? Or the delight evinced when Zeppelins shed destruction on harmless non-combatants? Or the deliberate torture inflicted by German civilians upon helpless, wounded prisoners of war conveyed through their country? Or, most incredible of all, the calculated and callous cruelty of German Red Cross nurses, the mothers, sisters and wives of Germans?

They say that we fight to crush Prussian militarism; that we will never treat with the Hohenzollerns and ruling caste; that we would *free* the German people from their oppressors. How foolish it sounds! We understand the Germans as little as the Germans understand human beings. What purpose to humanity will be served by a German revolution? The German people remain. Does civilisation hope completely to change the mental and physical outlook of an entire people who, in their nature, have altered not a whit since they emerged from their primeval caves and forests?

These are the things which I would have my fellow-countrymen and women remember when the day of reckoning comes. The men who are now fighting in France and Flanders have not seen things such as I have set down. But there are still amongst them a few—a tiny few—who have seen and who remember. Shall not these be allowed a voice when that reckoning arrives? And France? She will never forget. And it is France and Belgium who will cast the die; for it is they who have suffered. Suffered in such wise as this England of ours has not dreamed of.

Par mes champs dévastis, par mes villes en flammes,
Par mes ôtages fusillés,
Par le cri des enfants massacrés et des femmes,
Par mes fils tombés par milliers—
Je jure de venger le Droit et la Justice.

And if at the last the justice of men cannot reach the criminals, still is there the justice of God, and that shall not fail.

They have no wings to fly from God.

Chapter 4

Days of the Advance

K. Hen. *The game's afoot:*
Follow your spirit, and upon this charge
Cry—"God for Harry, England, and Saint George!"

Half a dozen dumpy, grey motor-buses, newly sped out of Paris, came panting heavily up the hill. They had been converted by French ingenuity into big meat-safes, and as they climbed one caught a glimpse of legs of mutton through the wire gauze which was stretched across the window-frames.

"Benk, 'O'burn, Benk! Penny all the way!" was the greeting all down the ranks of a perspiring battalion incontinently thrust to the side of the road to allow the vehicles to pass.

"We could do with a few o' them, mate," remarked Private Cherry to his next number. "That's wot we want—some of them ole number 'levens orf of the Strand. It's orl right, this foot-sloggin' is, in a manner o' speakin'; but wot I sez is, that yer carn't ginger up the Allemons not 'arf wot yer might. Lumme! They carn't 'arf 'op it! Why, yer —"

"Fall in!"

The men drop back into their fours, and in a few moments are off again after the retreating Germans.

By now that retreat is beginning to look suspiciously like a rout. It was not that, but the men were mightily cheered by the sight of abandoned vehicles and impedimenta of all kinds, and particularly by the steady stream of prisoners being passed through to the rear. You can imagine the curiosity with which Private Thomas A. regarded the first detachments which were escorted by. The general opinion was summed up in the sentence:

"Rummy-lookin' lot of blighters, aren't they?"

And you may take that as an expression of amused affection, criticism, pity, dislike, or sarcasm, as you please. Knowing something of Tommy and his ways, I am inclined to think that there was a generous sprinkling of the first-named quality included. That was at the beginning. After a few days' experience of their behaviour, and until the Aisne was reached, that opinion was somewhat modified.

It ran:

"_____ _____ _____ _____!"

Those Huns became a positive nuisance. You couldn't move without running up against little parties anxious to return to England, and our lads were far too busy ,to bother about providing escorts. Not that escorts were really needed, for Cousin Fritz was remarkably docile. A single uniform of khaki was quite sufficient, even if the wearer carried no more lethal a weapon than a walking-stick.

Long after the wave of pursuit had rolled the Germans back, they still went on surrendering to the bus-drivers and A.S.C. in the rear. One A.S.C. corporal went for a short evening stroll in a little wood hard by. He did not even carry a stick, but he came back decorated with rifles and bayonets and things, and three sheepish Huns in tow.

A special department was needed to cope with prisoners. This was soon improvised, and our men got into the habit of straggling off to round up Huns. It became quite an evening pastime if there was a halt of a few hours for a rest and food. By the way, there is another little habit of Thomas A. You would imagine that he would be only too glad to sit down after a stiff march and a bit of a scrap, have his tea and smoke his "fag" in peace. Not a bit of it. If he cannot find a football to kick about, he'll sit and "buck" on every conceivable subject until he has to fall in again—and then he is so sleepy he can't keep his eyes open.

And the chance of securing a few souvenirs for the "missus" at home was too good to let slip. Some of these little trophies of the chase were quite worth having, although I am not quite sure that Tommy should have taken them. We have a somewhat different standard from the Hun in these matters. Still, as most of the souvenirs were pressed upon the captors out of gratitude, it was probably in order. Of course, a handsome gold watch, or a pair of useful field-glasses, may sometimes have changed hands as an expression of gratitude; but I suspect that cases involving a little gentle persuasion were not quite unknown, for it is difficult to imagine that a Hun would willingly part with such things.

A lad of mine was very proud over one of his captures. I don't know how this particular man was rounded up, but he turned out to be no less a personage than the premier marksman of the German Army. At least, he said he was, and showed the gold Imperial badge on the sleeve of his tunic. The badge now reposes in a little frame on the wall of a best parlour somewhere down the Walworth Road, S.E.

Here is another trifling incident in this wholesale capture of Huns which shall be recorded, not because it was of any particular importance or interest, but because its successful issue was in some measure due (I will be quite frank with you) to one of my own little fads. Most of us have our fads and fancies, and one of mine chances to be insisting on the importance of "observation," keeping your eyes and ears open and making correct deductions from trifles. Incidentally, the men concerned were town lads, who were only beginning such training.

One morning a farmer came along and begged us to settle up with some Huns who were making themselves too much at home in his house. A small patrol of men under a corporal, all being trained in observation work, was selected. They had to try to rush the farm without their approach being seen.

The back of the farm gave on to a copse of trees. "What kind of trees?" asked the corporal. "Beech," was the reply. So the corporal knew at once that as there is little or no undergrowth in a beech copse it would be difficult to get at the house unseen from that side. However, they made a start.

Very quietly they approached the copse. Suddenly a pair of wood-pigeons flew out, disturbed, so they guessed, by someone in the wood. That settled it, for there was no one else about save the Huns. The patrol crept round to the front, got in and surprised four Huns in the back kitchen. A fifth was in the copse collecting wood. Had the corporal not known about beech trees, and had they missed the significance of the pigeons' flight, the little surprise might not have come off so successfully.

★★★★★★

A keen Press correspondent would have given his ears for the chance of being present with the B.E.F. on Tuesday and Wednesday, September 8 and 9, and of standing on the southern ridges above the Marne Valley as the fighting developed. For the moment one seemed to forget the horror of modern warfare in this bird's-eye view of intense movement. Here, at least, was a battle out of the story books, and one may reasonably doubt whether such another will ever be witnessed.

Our front ran along the south bank of the Marne and extended, roughly, from Château-Thierry on the east to La Ferté on the west. Midway between lay the village of Nogent l'Artaud. This was only a small place, but of considerable importance, owing to the main road from the south which passed through and crossed the river by an excellent bridge, a fine specimen of French engineering work. The river at this point is about as broad as the Thames at Windsor. On either bank the ground slopes gradually down, the ridges on the southern banks being rather the higher. The dead level of the valley, with the river flowing through, is perhaps a mile across.

Thus standing on the high ground above Nogent you get a fine panorama of the Marne Valley, and so it is from here that we will watch events for a few minutes. The general position is that you have the German rear-guards crossing the river and following the main bodies which are trekking off to the north as hard as they can move. The British are gradually gaining the southern ridges and then launching down into the valley and up beyond in stern pursuit. But although it is definite, pursuit, the fighting is deadly serious all through, and every point of vantage which can help the enemy is hotly contested by them.

At La Ferté the Third Corps[1] under General Pulteney were having a stiff fight to cross the river, for the Germans had destroyed the bridges. But the good old English county regiments down there were not going to be held up by a trifle like that. They'm coom up from Zommerzet, they be—and Zommerzet breeds good fighting men. And then there are lads from the stiff plough-lands of Essex, as hardy as the soil of that stern county. And there are Hampshire lads, and lads from lovely Warwickshire, and lads fra Lancashire. Wales, too, with her fusiliers, had her share of the fight that day. Add in Highlanders and battalions of three different Irish regiments, and you'll see what a command that little Third Corps was. The G.O.C. should have been a proud man those days.

The bridges are gone and the Germans hold the north bank with a few dozen machine-guns. Behind these up the slopes are batteries of

---

1. This corps (so-called) was then composed only of the Fourth Division and 19th Infantry Brigade. It will be remembered that these commands had been hitherto working under General Smith-Dorrien.

field-guns. No, it does not seem a very easy task.

British batteries, not more than a dozen, have slipped into positions in support of our infantry. To the rear there are a couple of "heavy" batteries. We, too, have a few machine-guns, but very few. It was a weapon which had not been considered by the powers-that-were of particular importance.

All day long British and Germans pounded away at each other with no great effect on either side. Our guns could not always manage to locate and silence the enemy machine-guns, and an attempted crossing of the river by the infantry would thus have been sheer madness, for there was as yet no bridge.

In the afternoon the cheery news came along that both the First and Second Corps had crossed the Marne higher up and were pushing ahead. Third Corps H.Q. was quite seriously annoyed at being left. But their hour had almost struck. It was now up to the Sappers to provide the means.

At two or three favourable points the bridging materials were ready. As the darkness gathered these were rushed down to the bank and the Sappers went at it like demons. The night was pitch dark save for the fitful flashes from the guns and a gleam from burning houses on the north bank; later the rain came down in torrents.

Swiftly but surely the Sappers worked. At one point something like a dummy bridge was made where the burning shone more brightly. This to draw the enemy's fire so far as possible. The ruse succeeded admirably. But a company of the Blankshires, very bored at the long wait, decided to make a little voyage of discovery on some roughly-made rafts. Gaily they slipped from the moorings, and once out in the stream promptly lost all control. A little later some of the "Jocks" who were patiently waiting farther down the river heard a medley of strange oaths, gurgles, and frantic splashings coming from midstream. There was no mistaking a good, honest English "damn," even though uttered in broad dialect, and that probably saved the explorers from a hot rifle fire from the Scots.

"What the de'il are ye doin' oot there this time o' the nicht?" a voice rang out from the bank.

"We're the Blankshires—trying to cross," came the plaintive answer.

"Ye're no the Blankshires"—this very emphatically—"ye're a daft set o' loonies tae gang paddlin' aboot i' the burn this middle o' the nicht. Gin ye maun wash yersels ye dinna need to mak' sic a boast

210

aboot it."

But by the time the little homily was finished the adventurers were nearly out of hearing. Some of them jumped overboard and reached the bank, but for the remainder it was a forlorn little party which drifted into a French outpost in the early morning and was rescued. "Quite mad, all these English," remarked the French captain, and no one bothered any more.

Long before the dawn the Sappers had finished their job and the infantry had slipped across. Once at grips with the enemy there was little further trouble so far as La Ferté was concerned. But the Third Corps, with the Fourth French Corps (8th Division) next on their left, still had a very tough proposition in the shape of a very strong artillery position held by something like ninety German guns. I believe this was eventually solved by the Second Corps driving in a wedge behind the position and forcing a retirement.

The crossing of the Marne by Nogent and Charly was noteworthy because there was no resistance. It was an awkward place to capture, and there was that excellent bridge there which the enemy were certain to destroy. Great were the preparations for the assault, and everyone was on the tiptoe of excitement.

You picture our advance guards spread out down the slope to the village, creeping forward from cover to cover. Nearer still, and not a rifle shot breaks the silence of that early September morning. Not a blue-grey coat to be seen, not a movement in the valley. It was all so uncanny that the men were convinced that they were going straight into some devilish ambush.

At length a couple of scouts went forward. They were watched down to the outlying houses. A woman came out.

"Where's the Allemonds, mother?" asked one of the scouts, keeping his eyes and ears open for any sign of movement.

The good woman replied with a torrent of abuse against the "accursed ones." Then, seeing that the man couldn't understand a word she took him by the arm and drew him towards the house.

"Here, what's the game?" said the man, very naturally holding back.

The woman pushed open the door and pointed in. Then the man saw it all in a flash.

Inside were four Germans lying on the floor amid a heap of empty bottles, dead drunk. And from the gestures of the woman he soon gathered that there were plenty of others about in the same condition. In fact, the village had been the scene of a tremendous drinking bout. The Germans had come across a fine stock of old wine, and the day before a regiment had drunk itself senseless. There were now only about thirty left in the village incapable of moving; the remainder had slipped away on the approach of the British, and were gradually rounded up in batches in the neighbouring woods. And a nice-looking lot of camp-followers they were too!

The bridge had been heavily barricaded, and it took nearly an hour to cut the barbed wire away. They had evidently intended to make a stiff fight for it, but the wine was too good to miss. Incidentally, there were no preparations for blowing up the bridge, and from the fact that several others were left intact General Smith-Dorrien remarked at the time that he suspected they were left so for use on the return journey of the Germans. Well, the bridges are still waiting for them.

★★★★★★

Elsewhere the crossing of the Marne was not so easy. The First Corps, for instance, had some very hard fighting before they gained the northern bank. They had, also, one or two old-fashioned spectacular displays to cheer them on. There was one place where the Germans had run a pontoon bridge across. If you are standing on the crest above Nogent you'll probably be able to pick it out with a pair of good glasses; it is up towards Château-Thierry. One of our airmen reported a mass of enemy troops crossing, streaming down one slope and up the other. A Horse Battery was the first to open fire. I don't remember what the range was, but it was like the dear old pre-war Practice Camp days on Salisbury Plain when a couple of canvas screens representing cavalry used to roll down towards the guns, and you'd plug in shell at about 300 yards' range and go home for lunch.

The Horse Gunners had it all to themselves for nearly a quarter of an hour—the time of their lives. Then a field battery came along, and the major's face, when he saw what they were firing at, would have given Bairnsfather a fine idea for a new sketch. One recalls Jellicoe's too-good-to-be-true message to Beatty and the battle-cruisers at Jutland Bank, "*You can sheer off now; I'll finish the job.*"

Anyway, a compromise was effected; the horse gunners limbered up and clattered off for a still nearer view of the target, while the field gunners set contentedly to work in their stead. I can see that major now, sitting on the No. 1 gun wagon-body with a chunk of hard chocolate in one hand and half a French roll in the other, as he switched the battery from one part of the target to another, as though

212

he were spraying a flower-bed. He did not, however, get so long an innings as the horse gunners, for an enemy battery, with the exact range, began to retaliate, and he had to run his guns back. Still, it was a nice chatty little twenty minutes while it lasted.

Everywhere the roads were littered with equipment, arms and vehicles, and there was no doubt that the retirement was more hurried than the enemy had intended. But, as it turned out, we were only engaged with very strong rear-guards, and critics say that the British should have pushed on a great deal more rapidly than they did. To that I am not competent to reply; I can only remark that the spirit and *élan* of the men could not possibly have been keener, and I do not quite see how they could have speeded up the driving power unless it were with the horses.

For the horses, poor old comrades, were suffering a good deal, especially as the weather had begun to turn wet and cold. Remember what they had gone through in the last three weeks and how nobly they had responded to every call. Remember, too, that in no army in the world is so much care bestowed upon its horses as in ours. To the trooper or driver his horse (or pair) is almost his best pal, and you, an Englishman or woman who reads, will know what that must mean. One of the first things taught to a recruit in a mounted regiment is the idea of making his horse a pet. And, so far as the gunners are concerned, you will find one indirect result of that happy teaching in the reputation which the Regiment has won for being able to drive the guns over the most impossible country and take them any where. What a wonderful combination it would be to have the French ".75's" with English teams and drivers!

But if it was almost impossible to keep the horses in condition the men were in splendid fettle, despite all their hardships. People are rather apt to forget that this was identically the same army which had just won through the Retreat, and that, as yet, there had been no opportunity for any rest and reorganisation. In equipment the officers were as badly off as the men. Most of them had no great-coats, waterproof sheets, nor any change of clothing, for all extra kit had been ruthlessly sacrificed or thrown away. At one point, it will be remembered, orders had been issued to destroy all officers' baggage. [2] In my own unit, for instance, I do not believe there were more than a dozen pairs of serviceable boots left. The men stuck to their work with bare feet coming through what was left of the leather. And this shortage was not made

2. *Vide The Retreat from Mons.*

good for another three weeks.

The base was right away down at the mouth of the Loire, and the farther we advanced the more difficult it became to get up supplies. Also, during the Retreat, a large number of railway bridges had been destroyed behind us, and this meant that in the Advance the trains could not get within some 30 miles of us. The wonder is that the A.S.C. achieved so much in getting up food and ammunition. On the Retreat there was a reasonable chance of getting food and little necessaries in the towns and villages, for the country was then untouched. Now we were moving forward in the track of a plague of locusts, and you could not buy even a box of matches or a stick of chocolate. Perhaps if critics will bear all these little facts in mind they will not be so ready to condemn.

★★★★★★

A typical example of the difficulties of the fighting in the Marne valley was furnished by an episode in which the D.C.L.I.'s [3] played a part. It was a fight for Montreuil aux Lions, a little place strongly held by the enemy and screened by thick woods.

It began with one of those desperate attacks, doomed to failure, by infantry insufficient in numbers across the open upon strong, concealed defensive positions. However, the D.C.L.I.'s were ordered to clear the enemy out, and so they tackled the job straight away.

One company worked round to a flank by a sunken road, deployed into extended order along a hedgerow and waited for the signal. A second company deployed in similar fashion for a frontal attack. With a shrill blast of a whistle they were all on their feet. A twenty yards' rush only brought a few scattered rifle-shots from the wood, and they were on their feet again for a second advance. Then the storm broke. There must have been a dozen maxims protecting that short front of wood, and with a single crash they opened fire on the Cornwalls. Within twenty seconds those two companies lost half their number.

Reserves doubled up to their support, and a second gallant attack was repulsed in the same way, though a couple of our own maxims backed it up so far as they could. Four times at different points did the Cornwalls face the murderous fire. In one corner they got home, and for a few minutes there was fierce work with the bayonet and rifle-butt. Two guns they captured, but the corner was too hot to hold, and they went down fighting to the last man.

---

3. Duke of Cornwall's Light Infantry: serving in 14th Infantry Brigade, Fifth Division.

By now it was the late afternoon, and messages were sent back for reinforcements. With the darkness General Cuthbert had concentrated the greater part of his brigade, and by midnight the men of Kent and Yorkshire had avenged their comrades and swept the woods and village clear of the enemy.

There was much hard fighting of this nature, especially with the First Corps, and in one or two places the Guards suffered badly before they could get to grips with the enemy. But once the machine-guns were beaten down, and our men got to close quarters, the Germans crumpled immediately and put up their hands.

With the Marne safely crossed the going was very much easier, and our men pushed ahead in splendid style. The country was far more open, and there were comparatively few of those awkward woods to be cleared. Thus a few lucky R.F.A. batteries were given a very cheery three or four days' work of a character which will probably never be known again in war. They were sent forward with the pursuing cavalry to manoeuvre as horse batteries, and worry the retiring Boche as much as possible. These were tactics which we had recently experienced at the hands of the enemy during the Retreat, and they had not been pleasant for us. It is rather curious that we should so soon have had the opportunity of retaliating, and with excellent effect, despite the miserable weather and dreadful condition of the roads.

★★★★★★

Looking back over those days of the Advance, and putting this and that together, I cannot help thinking that the Force accomplished very notable work; work such as should not be forgotten. For generations this great turning-point in the world's history will, I suppose, be discussed by critics and historians. We should have done this; the French ought to have done that; the Germans might have done so-and-so. In this volume no attempt is made to contribute to that discussion. But there is one point which I would emphasise; one remark which I would make to the learned sages. Do not ignore the human element! The little flags which you pin into large-scale maps, the little wooden blocks which you manoeuvre as you would chessmen, these are in reality but men like you.

That tiny Force, although it held no more than a tenth part of that long 300-mile front, did the work allotted to it because the spirit of the men soared exultant above all difficulty and hardship. (It is not for me to speak of our French Allies.) You may move your pawns across the board and say, "by such an hour they should have been on such

215

a line," but the pawns which you move are flesh and blood. The men had already achieved the incredible, and, knowing this, you ask why they did not continue to perform miracles.

At this time, with the exception of the 2,000 men already mentioned as reinforcements, the losses of the Force in men and guns had not been made good, despite the statement in the London Press of August 29 that they had. For instance, the Second Corps alone was 42 guns below its strength, or the equivalent of seven entire field batteries.

I cannot resist adding by way of comment the Press Bureau bulletin published in the *Times* of September 7, 1914:

> In all drafts amounting to 19,000 men have reached our army or are approaching them on the Lines of Communication, and advantage is being taken of the five quiet days (*sic*) that have passed since the action of September 1 to fill up the gaps and refit and consolidate the units.

This presumably referred to the Army in India, or to reinforcements being sent to France *via* the Cape of Good Hope. But the "five quiet days!"

If there must be criticism, let it be directed not against the Force, but against the politicians then in power who for seven long years refused to listen to the men who warned them of what would certainly come to pass; who told them the actual month of the year when Germany would make her murderous attack.

The losses had not been made good as they should have been, and the fault did not lie with the military authorities. It was the war-worn veterans of two amazing weeks' campaigning who turned and drove back 60 miles over a 30-mile front an enemy vastly superior in numbers, in guns, in ammunition and in equipment, and it was the unconquerable pride of race which enabled them to do it.

Chapter 5

A Little Music, and a Church Parade

K. Hen. *'Tis good for men to love their present pains*
Upon example; so the spirit is eased:
And when the mind is quicken'd, out of doubt,
The organs, though defunct and dead before,
Break up their drowsy grave and newly move
With casted slough and fresh legerity.

A certain unit was temporarily held up during the Advance at a little village on the Marne. It chanced that they remained there for twenty-four hours. The men bedded-down in a couple of big barns while the C.O. found a room in the adjoining farm. In one of the rooms there was a little piano, and the C.O. hit upon the idea of giving the men a musical entertainment, or rather of helping them to give one.

Now the C.O. was Captain Eldridge (at his request I omit his real name), and Eldridge was a man with no small reputation as a musician, composer and elocutionist. He was, in fact, recognised as one of the finest living reciters of Dickens's *Christmas Carol*, while as a lecturer he had been very popular in many parts of the world for some years past. This by way of introducing him.

The men were delighted with the idea; the piano was soon carried out into the barn, some oil lamps and candles were secured, and Eldridge started in. The proceedings opened with some eight or nine rollicking choruses of popular songs, "Who's your lady friend," "Hold your hand out," "Everybody's doing it," and so on. But artfully sandwiched in were three or four of the old songs, "Heart of Oak," "Loch Lomond," and others.

Then Eldridge gave a little chat about the beauty and value of the old songs, the well-known ditties and the lesser-known folk songs, singing in illustration "Yarmouth is a pretty town," "The Golden Vanity," and others. The men were obviously amazed that such songs could have been created by the country-folk, and before the hour was up they were singing "Golden Vanity" as though they had known it all their lives. And it was a fact, as the lecturer pointed out to them, that the songs which they had sung the best were the old English ones.

This incident seems worth recording for two reasons, apart from its comment on the old tag about "not being a musical nation." One is that the little entertainment was the first given to the men on active service during the war; and that it was from this and subsequent ones, with some stirring lectures on phases of the war, given by Eldridge, that the authorities came to realise the vital importance of this form of recreation for the men. Hence came the organisation of regular concert parties by Miss Lena Ashwell and of frequent tours of the "front" by well-known artists.

The second point of interest is that it shows one side of the work which the "Naval and Military Musical Union" has been doing for several years past in the two services. The value of good music for our fighting men has never been properly and officially recognised. Thus, as usual, it was left for private enterprise to show the way. I believe that General Smith-Dorrien (who, by the way, is President of the Union) begged hard that some of the military bands might be sent to France in the early days. Eventually, after many weary months, some were sent, and immediately they had the fine, tonic effect on the men which he knew would be the case. Who can ever forget the immortal story of Major Tom Bridges collecting the stragglers in St. Quentin and marching them away to the tune of "The British Grenadiers," played on a penny whistle and toy drum?

No, you cannot beat the fine old land- and sea-songs for the men to sing. And once they know them the men are in full agreement. As Eldridge remarked, "I am quite ready to play ragtime by the hour for the boys to sing, but it was 'Heart of Oak' which beat our lads to quarters for the Battle of Trafalgar."

Nor can I resist recording another incident which happened the next day, a Sunday. It looked as though a move would not be made until the afternoon, and as this was the first opportunity since Mons, Eldridge paraded the men and asked if they would like to have a Church Parade service. There was no mistake about the enthusiastic response, and so the Roman Catholics fell out to a flank and were marched off to a tiny church for 10 o'clock Mass, while the Church of England party filed in to the barn where the piano was.

This was the order of Service; and again, unless I am mistaken, it was the first Church Parade service held in the Force since they had landed on French soil:—

General Confession: Lord's Prayer: Preces and Responses: Hymn, "O God, our Help in Ages Past": Lesson from the Old Testament, where Jonathan and his armour-bearer go up against the Philistines: Hymn, "Rock of Ages" (by general request): Prayers, (a) the noble supplication used every morning in the navy, "O Eternal Lord God, Who alone spreadest out the heavens "(but specially adapted that day to the army), (b) two other suitable prayers: Hymn, "Onward, Christian Soldiers": National Anthem.

It may be added that there were only two prayer- and hymn-books available, one of which Eldridge had to use, but never, so he told me, had he heard the hymns and National Anthem sung with deeper feeling or enthusiasm.

The service was repeated, by general request, three Sundays later, when opportunity presented itself, at the Aisne. This time the men, some 300 strong, formed up on open ground in three sides of a square. There was no piano and again only two spare hymn-books. But the congregation made a brave effort over the hymns, and, at least, they knew the National Anthem. And all the while the great guns thundered through the valley. There was no *padre* to take the Service, but I am inclined to think that it owed much of its effect upon the men to the fact that it was their own C.O. who laid with them their offering of prayer and thanksgiving before the Throne of the Almighty.

★★★★★★

I have often been asked about the attitude of the men generally towards religion and spiritual matters, and I have found it very difficult to give an adequate reply. Englishmen have a natural reluctance to speak about such things, and if there is one who does he appears to be regarded with suspicion. After all, it is by noble example rather than by precept that a man wins the confidence and esteem of his fellows in the matter of religion, and active service must inevitably bring out all that is best in the man. If an officer has shown his command that he is a *man* and an English gentleman in the best sense of the word, the rest naturally follows.

There is an old proverb, "*Let him who knows not how to pray go to sea.*" And in this is war like the sea, for both must needs engender prayer

219

in a man. I do not believe that any man can be an atheist in the daily presence of death. The faith in a Supreme Being, the trust in the efficacy of prayer, may not be apparent to his comrades, but it is there, none the less, hidden deep in the heart of a man.

During the opening month there was practically no opportunity for officers and men to partake of the "most comfortable Sacrament" of the Holy Communion, but so soon as it was possible to hold the service in various commands the response to the summons was almost overwhelming. And the same conditions were always to be seen at the Base on the eve of a draft's departure for the "front."

But if the ghostly comfort of the Church Service and the ministrations of a priest were denied them, when through the welter of battle there was no time for thought or prayer, may we not say with perfect sincerity that the men made of their great work a prayer? Who is it will deny that the self-sacrificing devotion of men for their comrades, the succour of wounded under fire, the pity and help extended to the country-folk, even the rescue of dumb animals—who will deny that prayers such as those were not more acceptable to God than the "words of their mouths and the meditations of their hearts"?

And there was another aspect. I can best indicate it by an example. One night I had to look after a man who was badly hit and suffering agony. There was no doctor available, and in the meantime I dosed him with opium to relieve the pain. After a little while he tried to get at his pocket. Helping him, I found a letter and placed it in his hand.

"It's all right, sir," he replied, "number's not up yet—" Then in a minute or so, "Mother—says—she's praying for me—read letter."

I read the letter as he asked, but the words are too sacred to set down. The man pulled through safely, partly, perhaps, owing to a splendid constitution, but mainly, I think, because he willed to live, supremely confident that the old mother's prayer must be granted.

This incident must have been just one of hundreds like it. The men did not talk of such things save, perhaps, in an extreme case like that one. But when they did it was always with a perfect simplicity which carried immediate conviction. People at home, bishops and clergymen, used to assert with professional pride that there was a great spiritual revival with the Army in the field. They suggested that the teachings of the Church were responsible for the awakening. The *padres* working with the troops knew better. Just as the war has altered our outlook on the material life, so has it extended and transformed our *vista* of the spiritual. And one thing, at least, is certain, the time has come when our dignitaries of the Church must needs set their house in order, for "our sons have shown us God."

I think there can have been few men in the Force who did not realise, even if it were but dimly, that the prayers of their loved ones and of the people at home followed them. Nor were those prayers without avail. In all the works of R. L. Stevenson there is no passage of finer truth and comfort than the one in which he asserts that a generous prayer is never presented in vain.

The petition may be refused, but the petitioner is always, I believe, rewarded by some gracious visitation.

It is those at home who have the harder part, for the mental torture and suspense is infinitely greater than mere physical discomfort, greater even than wounds and disablement. Perhaps in the confidence that their prayers are not in vain there may be for those loved ones something of comfort, something of that "gracious visitation."

CHAPTER 6

With the Flying Corps

K. Hen. Therefore let our proportions for these wars
Be soon collected, and all things thought upon
That may with reasonable swiftness add
More feathers to our wings.

In all the departments of our fighting services, hardly one of which has not been completely revolutionised since the outbreak of the war, no developments are more astonishing than those which have taken place in the Air Services. It seems only yesterday that Bleriot made the first cross-Channel flight and so brought great headlines into the daily papers, "England no more an Island"; "Threat to our Island Supremacy," and such-like nonsense. Today our men fly backwards and forwards over the Dover Straits as regularly as an infantry battalion goes on a route march. In the first year of the war there was accomplished in invention and flight more than could have been dreamed of in ten years of peace.

It is well that we should occasionally remind ourselves, and our Allies and neighbours, of facts like these. We are far too modest over our nation's achievements, and since we so constantly belittle and criticise ourselves we can hardly be surprised that our friends and enemies should take us at our own valuation.

At Mons and during the Retreat, as far as the Aisne, in fact, the R.F.C. was represented by four little aeroplane squadrons, Nos. 2, 3, 4 and 5. This meant about 60 machines, and the number averaged about the same until well into 1915. This was due to the fact that we lost so many machines in the earlier months, and the authorities were hard put to it merely to replace them without building additions. But it was not the number of aeroplanes which counted, it was the skill of the

222

pilots and observers. And in this the R.F.C. has been second to none.

In those early days of which I write aeroplane work was in its infancy; no one seemed to realise its actual value, and certainly hardly a man can have foreseen those wonderful developments in the new arm which were so speedily to be in force. One looks back at the old days of peace manoeuvres, trekking about on Salisbury Plain or through the Essex flats, and remembers how suspiciously one regarded aircraft. Co-operation between aircraft and guns, now of the first importance, was then hardly more than hinted at, and signalling was of the most cumbersome description, sheets or large flags spread out on the ground, and so forth.

Now it was as though a veil had suddenly been torn aside from the future. The swift and accurate information of the enemy movements which the R.F.C. sent in left general officers gaping with astonishment. When you are accustomed to rely upon laborious written dispatches brought in by cavalry patrol, dated perhaps an hour and a half before you receive them, it certainly is a little disconcerting to get a message literally from the sky to the effect that an enemy battery is *at that moment* unlimbering to come into action 4½ miles E.N.E. of where you are sitting. I remember how pleased General Smith-Dorrien was when an aeroplane squadron was definitely allotted to him at the opening of the Advance, and how amazed he was at the accurate information wirelessed or signalled down.

It may be noted here that although the R.F.C. had started poor in equipment, yet so rapidly did they make up leeway that we were actually the first of the armies in the field to make practical use of wireless and of photography. Wireless signalling from aircraft was used first, I believe, at the Aisne. The arming of aircraft came later, and it was after the Force had got round to Flanders that the first Lewis gun was mounted. Until then it was a rifle or revolver, and not always these.

But to return for a moment to the Retreat. Like every other arm of the service, the R.F.C. was working under new and untried conditions of warfare. No one could guess just what the German Flying Corps would be like:—how fast were their machines; how were they armed; would their men fight, and so on. Thus on the very first day our airmen went out, and, as General Henderson remarked, no one at H.Q. could tell whether any of them would be seen again. However, to the general's relief, all returned safely.

One fact was very soon established, the German was not out to fight. With the enemy, as with us, observation was the main thing.

BRIGADIER-GENERAL SIR DAVID HENDERSON

And as soon as our men got their air-legs (if there is such a term) the reports they brought back were invaluable. Within two or three days they had begun to mark down the character and direction of every single enemy column.

It was entirely due to our R.F.C, and the fact must never be forgotten, that von Kluck's big turning movement to the south-east from just before Paris was discovered in good time. The news was at once sent on to General Joffre, and the Allied attack at the Marne was the result. A momentous and historical piece of observation work and a big feather in the cap for the corps. It adds another to the list of instances where the fate of an army, sometimes the issue of a campaign, has been decided by a single scout keeping his eyes open and making a correct deduction from what he has seen. [1]

There are so many stories of plucky observation work and hairbreadth escapes one might tell. We lost many machines, but somehow or other the pilot would generally turn up in a day or two in our lines after an adventurous journey from behind the enemy's.

A machine would come down crippled. Word was got back to the R.F.C. H.Q., and a fast motorcar with a couple of mechanics was sent up to the scene of the accident. Here the men would work for all they were worth until an advance patrol of enemy cavalry hove in sight. If they could get the "old 'bus "going in time—all right. If they couldn't the engine would be picked up and carried off in the car from under the very noses of the disappointed Germans.

The aeropark (may I coin the word?) and Corps H.Q. had many a lively moment during the Retreat. When units were continually being left to shift for themselves and escape as best they could, H.Q., awaiting the return of overdue machines, would often find themselves in a very unhealthy situation. Like the old A.S.C. 'bus drivers (you will remember them in the earlier volume), they were not armed and prepared for defence. So on several occasions the R.F.C. lorries were converted into a kind of Boer laager, while the remaining officers and men would stand to with any weapon that came handy. There was rarely, if ever, a protecting force to help them, but they always got away somehow, slipped through the ranks of the retirement, and started in again somewhere ahead.

Here is a striking little piece of observation work which illustrates

---

1. The Battle of Sadowa, for instance, where a single German scout discovered the Austrian Army in an unexpected position, with the result that the German line of attack was immediately altered and with complete success.

admirably the skill and courage of the R.F.C. There was a certain flight commander (now, I believe, a distinguished General officer) who went up one day on an observing "stunt." He brought back a piece of valuable information which no one would believe.

"Righto," said he, "I'll go and have another look."

In due time he returned, made an excellent landing, and stepped out of his machine. It was seen that she was simply riddled with bullet holes.

"Yes, it's all right," he reported, "it was the Nth Regiment."

"Good lord, man, what the devil have you been up to?" they asked him.

"Well," said he, lighting a cigarette, "you're such a lot of unbelieving beggars that I had to make sure. I just landed in the same field and had a look at the number on their tunics. Had rather a job starting again, but they're rotten shots."

By such deeds of cool-headed daring is the tradition of a Service created. We speak with pride of the glorious tradition of the navy, of the gallant deeds and noble chivalry of our seamen; achievements and aspirations which through the centuries have welded into a perfect whole that Spirit of the Navy which lives with us today. But the Air Service, born but yesterday, seems already to have grown old in wisdom and achievement. Yet we can see the record and tradition of it being created day by day before our eyes. The first amazing adventure in the new element is within the memory of each one of us.

So swiftly do the events of this war crowd upon us that we are apt to forget the great debt which we owe to those gallant gentlemen, adventurers all, who created the Flying Corps—men who, like Frobisher and Drake, Raleigh and Hawkins, went a-voyaging in their frail cockleshells through unknown, uncharted seas to dare everything for England's sake. If it is those young lads of ours fresh from school who are so worthily maintaining for us this new-born tradition, remember that it was the pioneers, the old officers who created it and made the Flying Corps. Amongst these Sir David Henderson must ever take pride of place. The first colonel-commandant of the corps, he learned to fly during spare time snatched from his onerous duties as Director of Military Training, and so, with the outbreak of war, he had the proud privilege of commanding the first four little squadrons to go on active service. Nor must the name of Godfrey Paine, Commodore, R.N., be forgotten. As commandant of the Central Flying School during the critical years of the birth of the corps it will be guessed how grave a responsibility was his in the training of the personnel.

★★★★★★

It was many months before our lads (on the ground) learned to distinguish between the markings on the various machines; to decide which aeroplanes were ours, French, or German. The consequence was that whenever an aeroplane sailed over, everyone would start firing away at her as hard as he could and with any weapon that came handy. Of course, no one had the least idea how to shoot at such a target, save perhaps officers who knew something about rocketing pheasants coming over tree-tops in a high wind. But that didn't matter. Orders from G.H.Q. had stated quite plainly that all enemy aeroplanes were to be fired at. And as you couldn't tell which were enemy aeroplanes you decided that it was better not to run any risk in missing a possibility. So you fired, and somewhere in the direction of the machine. I have even seen an old woman in the street throwing stones.

But they were fine sportsmen those flying men of ours. It certainly is annoying when you are just dipping down for a good landing in your own lines to be greeted with volleys of rifle fire from your own friends. Yet apart from a little grousing if the petrol tank had been shot through, or some other like mishap had been caused, they took it all in excellent heart.

Orders were not to fight if you had any special job on hand. If you had to fight, then do it behind the enemy lines. But sometimes the temptation was too great to resist. One particularly thrilling encounter I remember at the Aisne, an encounter which should rank as historic, for it definitely established once and for all the superiority of our flying men over those of the enemy.

One of our men, I believe it was Lieutenant (later Flight Commander) N. C. Spratt, R.F.C., was returning from over the enemy's lines. It was a warm, sunny day, with barely a cloud in the sky. When well within our lines another aeroplane was seen following the first: whether it was friend or foe no one could tell. The second machine was perhaps a mile behind the first when Spratt realised that he was being chased.

With a sharp pull on the "joy stick" Spratt began to climb. Then a steep "bank" over, and in a few seconds, it seemed, Spratt had turned to meet the pursuer. It was an enemy after all.

The firing at the aeroplanes ceased as if by some magic command. No sound now save the whir of the propellers humming like a gigantic sewing machine. From above it must have been a curious sight, those hundreds of white, upturned faces as the great audience gazed spellbound at the combatants.

Spratt went straight for his man like a hawk at a fieldfare. Men held their breath for the crash which seemed inevitable. But, almost on his quarry, Spratt suddenly dived beneath, swung upwards in a climb, and was over the enemy. Faintly was heard the crack of a revolver.

Then followed such an exhibition of flying, of this new mastery of the air, as made each man grip his fellow by the arm and catch his breath at the sheer wonder of it. Over and under, loops and banks, Spratt manoeuvred his machine. Now she hung poised, almost motionless—so one fancied—then she seemed to hold the air, tail on, beating with swift wings. With a sudden dive she would dart away to return and harass her enemy once again with her incredible evolutions.

The end came suddenly. The German had had enough. Turning, he fled in fear from this superhuman enemy. Spratt, with yells of laughter, followed. On, on into the vague distance the two tiny specks vanished from sight. And the hundreds below who had watched spellbound threw their caps into the air and yelled themselves hoarse.

Half an hour afterwards, as dusk was falling, an aeroplane winged her way back to the aeropark. Softly she nosed to the ground, taxied her distance and stopped. A few mechanics ran up to attend to her wants. Spratt hoisted himself out, to lean against the machine shaking with laughter. A brother officer came swiftly across to him.

"So it was you, was it, you old beggar!" he exclaimed. "Did you finish him?"

Spratt shook his head, still laughing.

"Good lord, why not?"

"Hadn't got a gun," said Spratt.

★★★★★★

It was, however, the moral effect which counted on this occasion, and that had been great. Our man had put the fear of God into the Boche, and from that day onwards we knew that our flying men were the masters. The Boche wouldn't fight. That superiority they have never lost, despite the pessimistic head-waggings of croakers at home. The Germans from time to time may produce a better engine, and so for a spell we may have to compete on somewhat unequal terms so far as equipment goes.

But it is not the engine or the machine or the gun which counts in the long run, it is the man in control. Again and again during this war has that fact been established, especially with the Fleet. The spirit and breed of race have ever risen triumphant over incredible disadvantages. That this should be so on the seas we naturally expect, for we are an island people and the tang of the salt is in the blood of us; the centuries-old tradition of sea heritage runs in the veins. It is a sea tradition with which no twenty-years-old navy of landsmen can hope to compete.

But in the new element of the air we started on equal terms. If anything the Germans were ahead of us, and certainly in equipment. For some years they had been experimenting with all types of machines, both heavier and lighter than air. Yet, once again, they have failed. Once again they pinned their faith to the machine and neglected the human element. Germany has failed because Germany does not breed the men.

The gallant deed of Lieutenant Warneford, V.C., when—

In one brief crowded hour
He drew the world's wide wonder and her dower
Of breathless admiration,

—was but typical of the deeds accomplished by our flying men every day that passes. They are made possible because untiring experiments and improvements are giving us the right engines and the best machines. But what avails the finest engineering skill if the right men are not at hand to pilot?

And so at the call of this new mistress England has once again shown to the world the blood that is in her. "Now these her princes are come home again," and with never a thought save that England calls has the budding flower of her manhood leaped to fight for her this new, strange warfare. Pricked by the sharp spur of adventure, as their fathers were before them,

Almost they brush the splendour of the stars,
And sway the low red lantern of the moon
With wind-beats of swift wings.

Thus if it was the old officers who made the Flying Corps it is to the cool brains and gallant hearts of these boys of 18 or 19 years that the future destiny of the Air Service is entrusted. And the old officers will tell you with pride how apt their pupils are, how quickly they learn, and of the glory of their achievement. The destiny of the service is in safe hands. As with Captain Ball, Lieutenant Warneford, and many another, so

> *While such deeds move*
> *An empire, while eyes glow, and wonder starts*
> *And old-time courage kindles in young hearts,*
> *Men will be found to die his lonely death.*

Ladies and Gentlemen, the toast is:

The Royal Air Services of His Majesty's Navy and Army.

Pray charge your glasses, and to the brim!

CHAPTER 7

Between Whiles

Fluellen. I beseech you now, will you voutsafe me look you, a few disputations with you, as partly touching or concerning the disciplines of the war, in the way of argument, look you, and friendly communication.

"Between whiles" is not perhaps a very happy title, for nothing took place during the Marne-Aisne days which was not essentially a part of this horrible business of war. Still there were, shall we say, lighter moments away from the sterner realities, and it was some of these which really suggested the heading.

Then, as now (three years later) the great topic of conversation was the eternal one of the primitive animal—Food. No sooner was one meal finished than you began wondering about the next and what you were going to get. You knew perfectly well, for it was always Bentos bully-beef or Maconochie's Mixture, but it was not unpleasant to pretend about it and order something really scrumptious. I remember Sir Ernest Shackleton once telling me that the same delightful game was a great help to him and his men in the Antarctic. The ideal dinner menu they used to plan ran something like this:—item, a cup of nice hot oily fat; item, a boiled leg of pork with plenty of fat, pease pudding, etc.; item, a boiled treacle pudding; and a cup of strong cocoa to finish with.

The men seldom mapped out meals like that; their desires seemed to run in the direction of special dishes, "something a bit tasty like." The homely kipper, perhaps; a stuffed sheep's heart; a plate of whelks; fried fish and chips. And, oh, the fun there was in trying to make the motherly *patronnes* of *cafés* and *estaminets* understand about fish and chips.

"*Bon soyer*, mother," a hungry Tommy from London's wild-East remarked affably leaning over the counter, "pennorth o' fish and chips, please."

"*Mais oui, monsieur, tout-de-suite*," the good lady replied, not understanding a word.

"Wot did she say, chum?" said Tommy, turning to a pal.

"Dunno! Thought she said 'Moossoo was too sweet.'"

"Too sweet!" this in great astonishment. "Too sweet! Me? Wot, on 'er? My eye, chum, time we 'opped orf ahrt o' this. T'ain't arf a lively spot. My missus allus did tork a lot abaht them French 'ussies—torked frew the back of her neck, I fought she did. But turning on a bloke like this all of a suddin like—I'd never a fort it of 'em. Wot abahrt them fish an' chips? Ain't we goin' to get none?"

"Better make yerself a bit pally like fust," advised his chum.

"O orlright, hif it's the custom o' the country, I'm on." And Private Thomas A., with some dim idea of acting up to Kitchener's famous parting words on the subject, promptly heaved himself on to the counter, reached over, placed an arm around the astonished *patronne*, and gallantly saluted the good dame upon the cheek.

"*Veeve longtong cordiarl!*" sang out Thomas A. No. 2, a cry which was re-echoed by a number of French *poilus* who had been amused spectators.

Madame was far too good-tempered to feel any particular resentment. If anything she was shyly pleased at the little act of gallantry. Unluckily, though, it did not have the effect of producing the fish and chips, and our friends had to be content with a glass of weak beer each. And French beer is not popular in the British Army.

By the way, so great was the demand for fish and chips that later, in Flanders, shops were actually opened in little towns and villages to the rear of the lines for the sale of that succulent if greasy combination—to Tommy's great content.

For a short spell something went wrong with the meat supply, and the edict went forth that every man was to be allowed two *francs* per day in lieu. The men were not to receive the actual cash, but purchase of rations to that amount was to be effected locally. In other words, we were to live on the country till supplies got into working order again.

The C.O. of one unit, who was rather a good caterer when put to it (no, fair reader, you need not smile; your charming sex has not a monopoly in these weighty matters), went one fine morning into a neighbouring town to purchase sheep. He was directed to a butcher's on the market square.

"*Bonjour, monsieur!* How much are your sheep per kilo, if I buy wholesale?"

"For you, *monsieur*, for *ces braves garçons d'Anglais* I will charge but three *francs* per kilo."

"Three *francs!* But that is outrageous, *monsieur.*"

M. le boucher shrugged his shoulders. "*Mais non, monsieur*, it is a fair price. It is the price which has been fixed for the commune, and we cannot sell for less."

"But whoever heard of such a price? And who could have fixed it at that?"

"*Pardon, monsieur*, but it has been fixed by *M. le maire* himself."

"Oh, but I am sure *M. le maire* would not fix so high a price; it is unheard of." The C.O. waxed impatient.

"But yes, *monsieur*, it is certain. *M. le maire* is a worthy man who knows the value of these things."

"Oh, well," said the C.O. with resignation, "if it is so, I must go and see the mayor and talk to him myself. Will you have the kindness to direct me to his house?"

M. le boucher drew himself up with an air of splendid dignity, and, laying his hand upon his breast,

"I, *monsieur*, I am *M. le maire*," he said.

★★★★★★

I do not suppose that our men thought their rations very remarkable, but to our French comrades the commissariat was a never-ending source of astonishment. It is a well-worn platitude by now to remark that never has an army in the field been fed so luxuriously as ours, and that from the very first. The food was there if only the A.S.C could get it up to the men. And to do the A.S.C. justice, they never failed save only when it was a sheer impossibility; and they did not often fail even then. It is true that the variety was not very large. We did get rather a surfeit of plum and apple jam, and fresh vegetables would have been most welcome (ye gods! fancy an army on active service grumbling because fresh vegetables were not issued), but taking it all round we had every reason to be most grateful to the powers that were for their admirable foresight and arrangements.

It may seem a curious confession to make, but it was not until we got to the Aisne, when we were able to shake down a little, that I discovered that a beneficent government supplied free rations to the officers as well as to the men. One was so accustomed to the paying of mess bills for food that it did not occur to me to regard conditions of active service as any different. It was sufficiently bewildering to be in receipt of a daily field allowance over and above the usual rate of pay, so that one quite cheerfully paid for such food as was obtainable. When, a few months later, the daily rate of officers' pay was raised all round I began seriously to study the lists of "best investments." It was very pleasant to find that you could now count upon a comfortable living wage in the army.

The pay which the men received was another fact which used to astonish the French. To the *poilu* with his two *sous* a day (or is it one *sou?*), these men in khaki must have seemed like an army of million-aires. Among the thrifty French the reckless extravagance of the Eng-lishman with his money when holiday-making on the Continent had long been a proverb. It seemed that our lads were now determined to live up to the English reputation. And since they began with the firm conviction that a *franc* was of the same value as a shilling, that a five-*franc* note was the same as a five-shilling piece instead of being only a trifle over four shillings, it is easy to imagine the results.

It is easy, too, to see their unconscious point of view. A summer holiday on "the Continong," with the old tradition of the English milord in their blood. (Remember the thousands of pounds squan-dered in a week's holiday at Blackpool by Lancashire workers.) A shil-ling or half a crown would be thrown on the counter with an air of magnificence for a roll or a couple of eggs. The *patronne* was probably as ignorant of the value of the silver piece as the man himself, and whatever change was forthcoming the man would pocket without a thought. The temptation was too great, and within a week of the land-ing in France the thrifty shopkeepers were coining money wherever our men passed.

Pay for the men would be obtained from any field cashier whom one could discover, and we used to give them five *francs* each about every ten days. The N.C.O.'s would, of course, receive more according to rank. An officer could obtain five pounds at a time from the same source. It must have been a very ungrateful and responsible job that of a field cashier, especially in the early days when they were on the move all the time. One incident well illustrates it.

The scene is a small A.S.C. officers' mess in a farmhouse near the Aisne. The C.O. and three other officers are having dinner. The door is suddenly thrown open and another officer appears.

"At last!" he exclaims breathlessly. "At last I've found you. Thank the Lord! *Where's my box?*" And he pants heavily into a chair.

The diners look at each other in astonishment.

"What on earth are you talking about?" says the C.O. "Have a drink?"

"My box. The one I gave you to look after."

"Box?" says the C.O.; "you didn't give me any box." The other officers shake their heads. "When was it, and what sort of box?"

The newcomer sat up in alarm. "On the Tuesday night at that little village after Mons. Don't you remember I asked one of your lot to take care of it for a few hours? When I came back you'd gone, and I've been trying to find out ever since what unit it was. For God's sake, don't say you haven't got it."

The C.O. shook his head and thought for a minute. Then, "Yes, I do seem to remember a sergeant bringing me a box. Said an officer had asked him to look after it. I took it on my car for about a week, but I haven't seen it for some time. Hope it wasn't anything important."

"Important!"—the field cashier (for such he was) passed his hand over his forehead—"important! Oh, no, thanks; there was only about five thousand pounds in cash in it."

The C.O. whistled. "I say, I'm awfully sorry. I'll have a search made. It may have been put on one of the lorries."

A search was made, and an officer was sent back in a car through the villages, but nothing more was ever heard of box or money. A Court of Inquiry was duly held, with what result I do not know. But this was just one of a hundred similar incidents of which there was no time to take stock during those days of stress. The officer in question had found a Divisional Headquarters, and handed his box to the senior N.C.O. on duty for a couple of hours. He never dreamed (nor did anyone else) that the division, and the army, were then in imminent danger of being wiped out at any moment. And that was the little adventure of the field cashier and the pay chest.

It was extraordinary how little count one took of incidents like that. One of my own men, for instance, on the very first Sunday shot a comrade through the head with a revolver and killed him. A pure accident; he "didn't know it was loaded." We kept the man under arrest for a week, but it was merely a farce under such conditions of hurried retreat. I recall the pathos of the incident because the victim of this misadventure had only half an hour before finished writing cheery letters to his wife and mother.

★★★★★★

Between whiles we had an occasional court-martial or two. Not the interminable, red-tape variety of court-martial they have at home, but a shortened form properly adapted for active service; the Field General C.M. Again, until the Aisne was reached these were very few in number, for there was no chance of holding them when on the move. We shot a goodly number of spies, and there were a few cases where summary treatment had to be meted out to our own men. Every army has its black sheep, and it is absurd to pretend that ours was different from others in the field.

At the same time, one is happy to record that cases of the more serious crimes of active service were very rare indeed; some few were inevitable. For instance, during the first four months I heard of only three cases of looting. The culprits were very promptly dealt with. There were a very few cases of disobeying orders, and again, of course, an immediate example had to be made for the sake of discipline. Even cases of drunkenness were few and far between, and that was rather astonishing in view of the weird drinks the men imbibed in the cafes in place of good, honest beer.

Courts-martial on active service are all very much alike; there is a minimum of writing, and cases are very quickly disposed of, if the president knows his business. One case, I remember, came to a very abrupt end—through enemy intervention.

The court (of three officers) had assembled in a small house a mile or so behind the front lines. A desultory gun-fire by the enemy had been going on since daybreak, but only a stray shell or two had fallen anywhere near the house.

The court was formally opened, and the three witnesses for the prosecution in the second case had ensconced themselves beside a neighbouring hedge to await their turn for giving evidence.

The first case was nearly at an end when a shell sailed over the house and burst about fifty yards beyond. A second burst some seventy yards short. The president quietly finished the case, and, opening the second, sent an orderly for the prisoner and the first witness for the prosecution. The prisoner was marched in and the court waited. A minute later the orderly returned. With face deathly white he saluted.

"Shell, sir! All the witnesses killed," he reported.

CHAPTER 8

The Crossing of the Aisne

K. Hen. *Now set the teeth, and stretch the nostril wide;*
Hold hard the breath, and bend up every spirit
To his full height!—On, on, you noblest English,
Whose blood is fet from fathers of war-proof!

It was on Saturday, September 12, that the Force reached the River Aisne, and never, never will anyone who was there forget the misery of that day. People at home reading despatches from the front may be told in half a dozen words that "the weather delayed further progress," or that "snow rendered operations difficult," and they murmur "Pity they're having such bad weather out there," and think little more about it. But to the men "out there" it means just everything.

You must picture, if you will, the various units, horse, guns and foot, as they came up that day to the south bank of the river; for it is only when you can see them in the mind's eye that you will begin to appreciate the sheer wonder of their continued achievement.

Remember that this was still the remnant of the Force which had fought through from Mons and, without a break, had turned and fought back again. Two hundred odd miles of ceaseless fighting and marching, and through torrid heat alternating with drenching rain. Casualties not yet made good; lost or worn-out kit not yet fully replaced. The men, or a great number of them, were in rags, and that is just the truth of it.

During the few previous days the weather had been getting worse and worse. The climax came that Saturday in a steady downpour of heavy rain which did not stop for an hour. It seemed as though all the rain in the world had been concentrated in that valley. The roads became quagmires for all wheeled traffic, and transport and guns were everywhere held up.

The men left their bivouacs wet through; before half an hour had passed they had all got to that stage when nothing mattered. The orders were to make good the crossing of the river and hold the northern slopes. On that day no one, at G.H.Q. or in the Force, could have guessed what was before them, that it was the end of the Advance and the beginning of many weary months of hammering at a wall.

With the earliest misty dawn everyone was on the move, squelch, squelch through the mud. Teams strained at the guns, dragging them through the liquid glue away over fields of heavy soil wherein carriages sank well-nigh axle deep. Motor-cars with a ceaseless yonking of strident horns thrust infantry aside. And the rain came down in torrents.

One battalion found a few dozen oat sacks in a granary. Wrapped round the shoulders they were at least a reasonable substitute for greatcoats, and there was a mad rush for them. Another company appeared looking like a gang of Chinese *coolies* with bundles of straw tied together and hung over the shoulders by way of capes. Disconsolate-looking cavalry horses, heads and tails tucked down, plodded heavily past, carrying riders who sat grimly in pools of water. Squelch, squelch, and down came the rain. Oh for a glass of hot rum and water, and a pipe of tobacco! Never mind; stick it, lads! The Sixth Division have landed; they are on their way up.

It was on this very day that we got the rumour about those Russians landing in the north of Scotland and being rushed down through England to take the Germans in the rear. The fact seemed so unlikely and improbable that it was quite generally believed, and the rumour had a very heartening effect. We didn't hear till later of the extraordinary sensation it caused at home amongst all classes, even down to the old lady whose son, a railway porter, had actually swept the snow out of the railway carriages.

About 7 a.m. General Allenby with his cavalry had worked up to Braisne, a village some five miles south of the river. Quickly they drove out a small enemy force, but were unable to hold the village without support. This was forthcoming from some of the infantry of the 3rd Division. General Gough, too, with his brigade (the regiments of a previous chapter) had another smart little affair with enemy infantry some three miles nearer to the river.

One may be excused from referring so frequently to those three gallant regiments under General Gough, but they did put the fear of

God into the Germans. When there was a little job like that on hand it was not a case of sending for those lads to do it; they were generally on the spot and half-way through it by the time the need was realised.

Well, this time they just counted out some seventy Germans, captured 150 more, and then went on with their trek to the river. But the bridge at Vailly, with a strong battery of machine-guns to hold it, was too tough a nut to crack just then, so they exchanged a few shots and drew off out of range to await supports and guns.

Elsewhere, all along their sixteen-mile front, the Force pressed steadily forward. On the extreme right the lads of Sussex, Northampton and Lancashire; on the extreme left that splendid little Third Corps which we watched crossing the Marne at La Ferté. Squelch they went through the mud and rain, but it was the right direction, and—we're all going to be home by Christmas. Cheero!

But apart from the distressing condition of the troops, the bad weather was a severe handicap to the Flying Corps. Our flying men were away and aloft as usual, but observation was simply impossible. Thus the several H.Q.'s had to send their troops blindly forward, and trust more or less to luck, and no one knew what we were up against. I wonder what the Force would have done that day and the next had they known. Gone ahead just the same, I suppose. But we didn't know, and this is what it was.

The Aisne about there was sixty or seventy yards broad, in flood and very deep. There was just one possible bridge for the whole front; all the remainder had been destroyed. About a mile north from the river the ground began to climb to a high plateau which the Germans had prepared as a strong defensive position. It was a natural line of defence; they had reconnoitred every yard of it years before, had prepared in secret their big gun positions all along the height, and so soon as they had swept over the country in their advance they had set to work upon it against such a contingency as the present.

Few facts of the war can have revealed in stronger light than this the military organisation and forethought of the Prussian General Staff. I should imagine that there was not an officer on that staff, from William Hohenzollern downwards, who doubted for a moment that their war plans against France would have been precisely fulfilled within their scheduled time—that Paris would have fallen, the French Armies been destroyed, and terms of peace dictated in time to turn upon Russia in the same way before the Holy Empire had had time fully to mobilise. And yet, despite that conviction, the Prussian Staff had worked out the defensive strategy of the Aisne—in case.

Our flying men could not yet tell us all this, and even when the crossing of the river and the subsequent attacks were in progress it was with the greatest difficulty that they were able to discover the German gun positions. The general impression was that the enemy were going on with their retirement, and it was with this idea in mind that the G.O.C.'s pushed ahead.

It was not until the afternoon of the 12th that the several commands realised that it was going to be a difficult task. Our advance patrols arrived at the river at various points, and were promptly held up everywhere. Reports were sent back, and the S.O.S. call went out for the Royal Engineers. And it was then that this splendid corps started upon and accomplished one of the finest pieces of work in its history.

Lieutenant J. A. C. Pennycuick (later Captain and D.S.O.) began it by floating out on some kind of raft (no one quite knows how it was done), and drifting down stream to within 100 yards of the bridge at Missy in order to reconnoitre. He could not well escape being seen, and the Germans as soon as they had recovered from their astonishment blazed away at him as hard as they could. But, to quote Admiral Beatty's delicious remark upon a similar adventure,[1] "this in no way interfered with the clarity of his report." Pennycuick got back safely to tell how the bridge was just a wreck, while the remnant of it was strongly held with the inevitable battery of machine-guns.

Similar reconnaissance was successfully carried out within the next couple of hours at all the points of possible crossing. The Sappers saw what they had to do, and promptly tackled the job with that thoroughness and gay insouciance which have ever marked their work.

The enemy had all the ranges registered for their overwhelming mass of guns, and they were fully prepared to hold up by every means the crossing of the British. But that fact didn't bother the Sappers. It was up to them to provide the means of crossing, and they intended to do it. Within forty-eight hours they had finished the task.

Within forty-eight hours, working under the direct fire of the enemy's massed artillery and machine-guns, the Sappers had constructed or sufficiently repaired no fewer than fourteen bridges along a fifteen-mile front and across a seventy-yards broad river in flood.

Upon such a feat as this any comment is impossible. One can only

1. Reconnaissance by a sea-plane flying at 900 ft. under heavy fire from four enemy cruisers. *Battle of Jutland Bank official despatches.*

record it in the simplest words, and leave the details to the imagination.

The misery and depression of that pouring wet day hung over the troops like a leaden pall all through the night. Towards evening a gale sprang up to add to the discomfort (if it were possible). All the day the men had been halted under arms awaiting the orders to go forward. They had started off gaily enough, but the check had soon come, and that meant moral depression as well as physical discomfort. With nightfall an attempt was made to secure some shelter in the neighbouring villages and barns, but there was little enough available. And the rain poured down unceasingly. Food supplies temporarily broke down, for the roads by this time were impassable for transport. It was a dreadful night, and how the men saw it through, coming as the climax of all their privations, remains a mystery. The wonder is that most of the Force were not on the sick list with dysentery and similar complaints.

And yet before the following night had passed the whole of the British Force, with the exception of half a dozen brigades, had crossed the Aisne. They had "made good" once more. Ah! the wonder of the "contemptible little Army." Never has the world seen such troops. Will it ever again?

To some of the men in the 11th Brigade (Third Corps again) fell the honour of being the first across. Do you remember their nocturnal expedition on the river at La Ferté when they were chaffed by the Jocks? The memory of it had cut deep, and this time they were determined to make a clean job of it. They succeeded admirably, and by 3 o'clock on the Sunday morning they had pushed across on some rafts from near Venizel, and were snugly settled on the other side. A little later the remainder of the 11th Brigade, as well as the 12th, were over hard upon their heels and pushing ahead up the hill.

Thus had the first troops won the northern bank. Their task had been comparatively easy. Not so with the remainder. But I can find no words in which to tell of the achievement of these and the following days. The genius of some great painter displayed upon a mighty canvas might perhaps *suggest* the scene; no author's pen can do so. So would one cry:

O for a Muse of fire, that would ascend
The brightest heaven of invention!

The dawn of that Sunday, the 13th, broke dull and misty after the rain-sodden night, and the first gleam of daylight came as a welcome relief to the men after the depressing hours of darkness. All down the valley the fog-wreaths tumbled and danced before the dull booming of the guns on the northern heights, and shells tore their way through the heavy air to burst with deadly monotony along and over the southern bank.

The cavalry and horse gunners, with an occasional battery of field-guns, are up in the front on the very fringe of the shell storm. Pass down the horse-lines, and you will see the men already hard at work wisping and hand-rubbing, striving to work up the circulation and get some warmth into their dumb comrades before the business of the day begins. They know well enough that it is the first hour or so that will tell.

A little apart from the horses of one squadron are picketed three or four officers' chargers. "Well looked after," you will exclaim; "they've actually got horse-rugs." Look a little closer, and you will notice that the "horse-rugs" are of rather superior quality. They are the officers' greatcoats.

Most of the gunners and drivers have found their night's shelter under their guns and wagons. Rather risky, this, for the horses, tethered to the wheels, will probably kick you during the night. At least one driver fell in that morning with two black eyes and a bleeding mouth.

"If you want to fight," said the No. 1, "why can't you wait for them Germans?"

"Carn't 'elp it, Sergeant," protested the driver; "it was that there 'Ermione. She went and trod on my face in the dark—the old blighter!" he added affectionately, as he slipped in the bit.

And "'Ermione," nuzzling into his hand, was rewarded with a piece of cold bacon which she didn't like and promptly dropped in the mud.

All the C.O.'s have got their orders. The various H.Q. Staffs have spent a very busy night working out the arrangements for the advance. You can see them, some in leaky barns, others in tapestried drawing-rooms of lordly chateaux, one and all poring over large-scale maps, fitting in this and that report, checking dispositions of troops. Right back to G.H.Q. at Fère-en-Tardenois, fifteen miles to the rear, run the threads of communication.

"On that morning," says Sir John French, "I ordered the British Forces to advance and make good the Aisne."

Little enough it seems when resolved into that single paragraph. But it indicates as nothing else can the supreme confidence which the commander-in-chief had in his troops.

The British guns all along the lines have begun their response to the enemy's heavier metal. Effective firing was very difficult, for in many cases battery commanders had but a vague idea what their targets were. The German gun positions on the heights were most cleverly concealed, and until fire was concentrated just over the river crossings a great deal of ammunition was wasted.

On the extreme right the First Corps had to make a double crossing; first a canal which runs parallel to the Aisne, and then the river itself. Just by the village of Bourg another canal runs down from the north, crosses the Aisne by an aqueduct, and enters the first canal at a "hair-pin" angle. This was the spot assigned to the First Division, and they had a pontoon bridge, just constructed, and the aqueduct by which to cross.

A small advance patrol has felt its way forward to the crossing. Good! The enemy have rather neglected that aqueduct, and they have left but a weak post to hold it. Word goes back to the batteries, and nearly all the available guns there are switched on. But the enemy, too, know what is going to happen, and a deluge of shrapnel and high explosive is poured down over the river and banks.

The first to the pontoons was a company of one of the County regiments. Officers ahead, over they went. It was fairly easy going, but the shrapnel took its toll, and perhaps a quarter of the little advance force went down. The bank was quickly won, and our guns by this time had settled accounts with the trifling enemy rearguard on the aqueduct hard by. The cavalry followed close upon the advance company, the boats of the bridge swaying and dipping as they crossed. But the horses are long since accustomed to such a roadway, even though under fire, and the men get them safely over. Once on the bank the squadrons form up as though on the drill-ground, and it is only a few minutes before they are off and away to round up or drive ahead scattered parties of the enemy. By the evening they had occupied three or four of the villages five miles north of the river.

For the remainder of the division the crossing was fairly easy. The aqueduct was, if I remember, intact save for a few broken girders and supports, and the Sappers worked unceasingly to strengthen it and the pontoons. Thus this division got rather ahead of the rest of the Force, and the effect of this was seen during the following days.

A little farther to the west the Second Division had a stiff tussle before they could make good. I wish I could give you a picture of the shattered bridge that Sunday morning as General Haking's Brigade swarmed across. They were the Worcesters, the Highland Light Infantry, the Connaught Rangers, and the Oxford and Bucks Light Infantry.

There was just a single girder and a tangle of wreckage for them to clamber over. On the far side lay the Germans with maxims, while up on the heights the enemy gunners worked hard to finish their task of destruction. For once their gunnery failed them, but it was a near thing. Just as the first of our men set foot on the girder a well-placed high explosive shell burst close under the far end, and twisted up still more the slender support; and that was the last which seemed to do any real damage.

The big difficulty about that crossing was that you could not rush it. Under fire, when the blood is up and a position has to be won, there is no thought of holding back if it can be done at the double. But to clamber in single file across a steel plank, over a swollen river with shrapnel and H.E. hissing and plumping all round—that calls for steady nerves.

There was one big man, in the Worcesters, I think, whose great strength served him and a comrade well that morning. The man immediately in front got badly hit, staggered for an instant, and was on the point of falling over into the river when—

"Hold up, chum!" called the big man, grabbing him by the belt. With a heave he got him round the waist, and tucked him up under his arm. How he got across the remaining fifty yards of that narrow slippery path burdened with his kit, his rifle and a full-grown man with all *his* kit remains a mystery. But he did it somehow by sheer grit; needless to add he was promptly dubbed "Blondin" by his pals.

The next crossing farther west was at Chavonne. This fell to the brigade of Guards under General Scott-Kerr, and was probably the hardest of any; this, and the crossing at Condé. At both these points the northern heights fall sharply down to the river bank; thus the character of the ground helped the enemy very materially in their defence. At Bourg and Pont-Arcy the northern side was comparatively level for some few miles.

If you were to ask any half-dozen officers in the Force to tell you which they considered the best all-round regiment out there, I would venture a wager that you would receive, as I did, the same reply from

244

each. And that answer would be "the Guards." Just that. Not the Irish Guards or Grenadiers, but "the Guards." And in the original Force, where there seemed nothing to choose between the various arms and regiments, that is surely a very remarkable tribute.

"For the press of knights," says Emerson, "not every brow can receive the laurel." And I have often tried to analyse that indefinable quality about the brigade of Guards which has given them a place apart, even in that so great a "press of knights." I think that if I had to define it in a single word, I should say it was "finish." You will find that quality preeminent in everything about them. Their uniform and kit are always a trifle more neat and smart than their neighbours'; their bivouac or camp lines a trifle more straight and well ordered; their movements on parade carry a trifle more spring; and so all through the list.

To the lay mind these factors are of trivial account. But to the sailor or the soldier they spell the word "discipline." And discipline, with all that it involves, is perhaps the greatest asset in modern warfare.

That crossing of the Aisne at Chavonne was the hardest, and, by mere chance, it was allotted to the Brigade of Guards. How they carried it after nearly twelve hours of hard fighting, eventually crossing in boats, and then stormed a strong position the other side, is a story which will rank as one of the proudest in all their magnificent record. By sunset they, too, had "made good the Aisne."

To tell of the work of the remaining Brigades on this day is only to repeat incidents already set down, for these are but typical of the whole. It was work in which all arms nobly played a part: the individual and collective gallantry and skill of the Sappers; the unceasing vigilance and support of the Gunners which made the crossing possible; the superb tenacity and gay courage of the Infantry which carried them over and through every obstacle.

By nightfall the Men of Mons had "made good the Aisne "according to orders.

The Roll of the Sixth Infantry Division

General Officer Commanding—Major-General J. L. Keir.

16TH INFANTRY BRIGADE

Brigade Commander—Brig.-General C. Ingouville-Williams.

1st Batt. East Kent Regt.   1st Batt. Shropshire L.I.

1st Batt. Leicestershire Regt.   2nd Batt. York and Lancaster Regt.

17TH INFANTRY BRIGADE

Brigade Commander—Brigadier-General W. R. B. Doran.

1st Batt. Royal Fusiliers   2nd Batt. Leinster Regt.

1st Batt. North Staffordshire   3rd Batt. The Rifle Brigade
Regt.

18TH INFANTRY BRIGADE

Brigade Commander—Brig.-General W. N. Congreve, V.C.

1st Batt. West Yorks   2nd Batt. Notts and Derby Regt.

1st Batt. East Yorks   2nd Batt. Durham L.I.

Cavalry (attached)

19th Hussars (one squadron)

Royal Artillery

R.F.A. Batteries—21, 42, 53 (IInd Bgde.); 110, 111, 112 (XX-IVth Bgde.); 24, 34, 72 (XXXVIIIth Bgde.).

Howitzer—43, 86, 87 (XIIth Bgde.)

Heavy Battery R.G.A.—24.

Royal Engineers

12th and 38th Field Companies. 6th Signal Company.

CHAPTER 9

At the Aisne

Bard. On, on, on, on, on! to the breach, to the breach!
Nym. Pray thee, corporal, stay: the knocks are too hot; and, for mine
own part, I have not a case of lives: the humour of it is too hot, that is
the very plain-song of it.

With the passage of the Aisne there began the last great fight of the
Men of Mons, the original "contemptible" Army. For four days and
nights it lasted with never a break, and all that mortal men could do
the officers and men accomplished. Yard by yard they won their way
up the plateau, and when they could do no more there they held their
ground. Their attack passed into a defence. Then, with the imperishable tradition of the British infantry, was formed once again "the thin
red line."

Hour after hour, day after day, the waves of German infantry rolled
down upon them. Hour after hour the British stood to meet them,
broke them and hurled them back in disorder. Pounded night and
day by the German guns, to which our own could barely reply, they
clung to their positions. Was a point momentarily lost, a counter-
attack would instantly be launched and the position won again.

There they fought while their ranks grew ever thinner, and still the
remnant struggled on. That little line, with the cavalry all in, held and
fought the enemy to a standstill. For with the fifth day of the battle the
German attacks had grown weaker and weaker and the dreary dawn
of trench warfare had come.

It was the last day's fighting for the original Expeditionary Force,
composed as it had been from the early stages of the Retreat. The
Sixth Division was on its way up from the coast, and on September 16
it had come into line. Of course, this is no more than a trivial point

of sentimental record. But you who read will perhaps appreciate the feeling of pride which was in the hearts of the "old stagers" at having seen the thing through from the beginning.

And the difference, in appearance, manner and so forth, between the new-comers and the old stagers was almost laughable. Can you not imagine the contrast? There was no possibility of mistaking one for the other, although the lads of the Sixth did their best in the way of "make-up."

With the exception of one Irish battalion they were all English county regiments; Kent, Leicester, Durham, Shropshire, Yorkshire and others. And how fresh and young-looking they seemed beside the war-stained veterans of a month! Such nice clean faces and such nice clean uniforms. And overcoats! real overcoats they had.

"Hullo, mate!" (can you not hear the old stager?) "Come up to join the picnic, have you? Proper picnic this, I give you my word. Why, *we* ought to be paying the blooming government for giving us such a jolly old picnic. An' they're paying *us*—five *francs* a fortnight. Robbery, that's what it is, downright robbery to take the money—that's what I sez. You'll see, my lad, after you've been out 'ere a bit. You won't like to take it."

The new-comer murmured something which might have been an expression of somewhat doubtful gratitude.

"Why, mate," the veteran continued, starting backwards in astonishment, "whatever are them things you've got on your feet? *Boots?* 'Ere, let's have a look at 'em. My Gawd! and laces, too, in 'em! Real laces! Leather, ain't they? Gawd!" and he lapsed into incoherence.

"'Ere," he said, "I'll tell you what I'll do for you, chum. Them things ain't no good to you. Wot you want is a nice shiny German 'elmet. Or one of them long stickers wot them cavalry o' theirs uses. That's wot you want. A soovenir like, wot you can send 'ome to yer best gal. Boots! wot's the good of boots? She don't want boots, she wants one o' them 'elmets so's she can do a bit o' swank to her pals on a Sunday night."

The new hand was obviously becoming impressed. In fact, he had been touched upon a very tender spot.

"That's all right then, mate," decided the veteran. "I've got the very thing for 'er. Got a proper dab o' blood on it too, it 'as, an' a regular cut in it where I got the blighter clean through the napper. Dirt cheap it is for them boots, but I'll let you 'ave it cos you're a new chum—see? Come along o' me and we'll 'and over."

Meekly the new chum followed, and the bargain was sealed with a *"petit caporal"* apiece (Woodbines were no more then). But the new chum was not so happy over his bargain the next morning when charged before his C.O. with "losing by neglect his personal equipment," and that shiny German helmet cost him dear by the time he had finished with all the necessary formalities.

However, it was not very long before the new chums had become broken in to the manners and customs of active service, but it took longer for them to get the hang of the fighting. A brand-new company going into the firing-line for the first time is apt to be pretty nervous, especially when it is trench work. A year later on the Flanders side, when things had settled down into a regular routine, a new battalion would go through endless rehearsals of every phase of trench work before it went up into the front line. The only new thing they then had to face was the target hitting them back.

But at the Aisne there was no opportunity for rehearsals. Every man was wanted, and badly too. So after a very few days in reserve new battalions were sent up to replace some which had suffered the most severely.

There was one new half-battalion which took over a certain very warm corner of hastily dug trenches. They didn't like it, and it is no use pretending they did. Who shall blame them? It was a wet, misty dawn when they first found themselves peering anxiously along their rifles at the enemy lines only some 150 yards away. They were cold, they were rather hungry, and the last few hours, when they had been relieving their comrades, had been trying ones for the nerves. So that there were a good handful of them to echo the remark in *Henry V.*, *"Would I were in an alehouse in London! I would give all my fame for a pot of ale and safety."*

And the enemy, with that uncanny secret service of theirs, knew perfectly well that new, untried companies had taken the place of the old guard. "We'll just give them an hour to settle down," said the Germans, "and then at the early dawn we'll have them out of it."

And that is exactly what happened. The officers were probably as nervous as the men, but they kept a tight grip on themselves not to show it. A few minutes' heavy gunfire came almost as a relief, for they knew it was but the prelude for what was coming.

"Stick it, lads; here they come." And with the words down rolled the wave upon them. The front ranks melted away before the heavy rifle fire, but there wasn't quite the same quality about it as usual. You cannot get that nice accuracy and tremendous speed with your rifle when you are feeling cold and wet and rather nervous and everything is new.

So the wave swept on down the slope, over the parapet, and into the trenches. The new chums now were fighting for their lives. One vast confusion of mad stabbing, bashing with rifle-butts, fists, revolvers, anything. Still the wave poured into the trench, flooded it, swallowed up the defenders, stayed there. The trench was won.

The crash of the attack had come to the brigade commander a few hundred yards away. He had expected it, had hoped that all would be well—but he was prepared. Curtly he raps out an order—"The Hampshires will retake Trench W"—the order is scribbled down, signed, and a Staff officer is on his way with it before a couple of minutes have passed.

The Hampshires, in support, are finishing a somewhat sketchy breakfast and feeling in their pockets for any stray fag that might have worked into the lining. Sergeant Stephens is sitting on a little mound gloomily listening to the noise of the attack. Suddenly he jumps to his feet.

"Fall in, B Company," he calls. "We'll be wanted up there in a minute," he adds for the benefit of one of his corporals.

B Company snatches up its rifles, looks to it that bayonets are fixed and all magazines charged. Within a few minutes the Company commander appears, running.

"We're to counter-attack Trench W," he remarks cheerily. "Any pistol ammunition yet?"

"No, sir," says Sergeant Stephens. "Had orders to throw the last lot into the river. You remember, sir."

His captain does remember, and curses again. There had been something wrong with the ammunition originally issued, and orders had been sent round to throw any remaining into the nearest river. For a week or more officers had been without any.

"What's that lot up there in W?" asks a private.

"Don't know. Think it's the Blankshires. Just come up," replies the next number.

"Well, why the hell can't they do the job 'stead of rounding us up?"

"Stop that talking," cuts in a corporal sharply.

The captain casts a quick glance over his company and hurries back to report "ready." A few more minutes and they are off with two other companies, cutting out into extended order as they advance.

The German guns from the very beginning have been plastering with shrapnel and H.E. all the ground just to the south of the won trenches in anticipation of counter-attacks. The gunners and officers cannot see for the mist, but the ranges are registered and so they carry on.

The Hampshires have been through this sort of thing before, and while one never gets really used to it they are not inclined to worry overmuch. The ground is against them, and it is very heavy moving up over that wet, chalky soil.

Just as the mighty breakers crash high upon the beach and roll back in wavelets over the pebbles and sand, so does the counter-attack develop. The enemy have attacked in heavy masses, overwhelming almost by sheer weight. The British counter-attack in thin, extended lines, skirmishing forward. Here and there with a smothered moan men drop and lie still, but the rest do not falter. Now the captain is down, two bullets through the thigh. A subaltern leaps to his place to lead on the company.

Nearer now—50 yards, is it?—and the Hampshires tighten up for the spring. Have you seen an Irish hunter tuck his legs beneath him for a stiff hedge with a broad, peaty stream beyond? So the Hampshires.

Two or three little seconds and they have struck home. Still the shells burst beyond the trench, but within it there is hardly a shot. It is the steel now. The second line is up and in with their comrades. Again the vast confusion, but the end comes more quickly. The Germans do not enjoy the steel.

A few minutes and a hoarse cheer tells the Brigadier what he has been waiting for. The counter-attack has succeeded. The Hampshires have made good. Half an hour later another little party of German prisoners is on its way down to the river and G.H.Q.

★★★★★★

Just one incident out of fifty like it. The whole affair had begun and ended within half an hour. I make no attempt to trace the course of this Battle of the Aisne, I can only suggest by an illustration or two the general character of it. Perhaps you will then turn to Sir John French's despatch or to one or other of the published histories and read between the lines. For instance, in the official despatch the course of the fighting of these four days is very clearly outlined, and with the exercise of a little imagination it is easy to follow.

It will be remembered that the 1st Division was able to cross the Aisne very rapidly, and so to push forward in advance of the remainder of the Force. This is what Sir John French says about the value of it:

> The action of the First Corps on this day (Monday the 14th), under the direction and command of Sir Douglas Haig, was of so skilful, bold and decisive a character that he gained positions which alone have enabled me to maintain my position for more than three weeks of very severe fighting on the north bank of the river.

And again:

> Throughout the Battle of the Aisne this advanced and commanding position was maintained, and I cannot speak too highly of the valuable services rendered by Sir Douglas Haig and the army corps under his command. Day after day and night after night the enemy's infantry has been hurled against him in violent counter-attack which has never on any one occasion succeeded, whilst the trenches all over his position have been under continuous heavy artillery fire.

I have reproduced those two passages because they seem to me to sum up in the most fitting language the general situation of those days. Above everything the Battle of the Aisne, both the first four days and the trench warfare which followed, was fought through, and the enemy held by the regimental officers and their men. Strategy and tactics went by the board, for there was no opportunity to use them. It was a soldiers' battle pure and simple, and never in the history of the British Army have officers and men fought with more splendid grit and determination.

★★★★★★

As I write Sir Douglas Haig's great offensive of Easter, 1917, is in progress, and I am continually reading in the Press that "*now*" or "*at last*" our infantry are beating, or "have got the measure of" the German infantry.

I wonder if editors can realise how foolish such statements really are. Not only are they foolish, but they are actually a libel on the men who were bearing the burden and heat of the day at a time when the men of the New Armies were sitting at office desks, or otherwise carrying on their peace-time vocations.

Our infantry have "had the measure of" the German infantry from the very first day at Mons. There they proved themselves undoubtedly the better in face of overwhelming strength both in men and artillery, and through the months that followed they never lost that superiority. Nor was it affected by such incidents as that just related. Is the work of the immortal Seventh Division at Ypres already forgotten?

Only yesterday I came across this sentence in the *Memories* of Admiral Lord Beresford, writing of the fight at Abu Klea in the Sudan War of 1884.

Once more the British soldier proved that no troops in the world can face his musketry.

It was the same at Crécy and Agincourt with our bowmen, and so it has been from the wars of Marlborough and Wellington down to the present.

And our cheerful newspaper editors express surprise! Well, I, for one, have no patience with the man who finds every country better than his own and is for ever making unenviable comparisons. There is far too much of it with our publicists, and it is not to be wondered at that Germans and others constantly denounce us on the score of hypocrisy.

★★★★★★

Needless to add, the incidents of individual heroism in this soldiers' battle were almost endless. As always, dozens will never be recorded. But some we have which can never be forgotten so long as the recital of great deeds can thrill a people.

There was Captain W. H. Johnston, R.E., who, single-handed, kept a couple of rafts crossing and recrossing the river under heavy fire. On the forward journey he carried ammunition, on the return he brought back wounded.

There was a private of the Highland Light Infantry, G. Wilson, who, again single-handed, attacked and captured a German machine-gun, actually shooting or stabbing seven of the enemy to take it.

But one of the most heroic exploits of all has, so far as I know, not been recorded, and I have never been able to discover the name of the man, another Scotsman, nor the regiment.

An advance guard of Scots with a maxim was on outpost duty on a bridge over one of the waterways just north of the Aisne. The post was rather an isolated one, but supports were coming up.

The advanced sentry suddenly doubled back to the post and reported a body of German infantry coming down the road. The maxim was manned, and with the appearance of the leading enemy files fire was opened.

For a second or two the enemy halted. Then they charged, with another rank firing over their heads from higher ground.

The gun detachment ground away for some fifteen seconds, when both men were killed instantaneously. Another rushed forward. He was dropped almost at once. One by one the men on that little post went down rifle to shoulder, working trigger and bolt till the end came.

Two now are left, one badly hit. "We'll gang oot decently," cried the other and leaped to the maxim, picked it up and ran across the bridge towards the enemy. *Zip-zip* went the bullets all round him; then a couple in the arm and one through the leg.

Staggering forward against the parapet he brought the gun into action once again. Bullets splashed against the gun, against the stones, but he worked steadily on.

"Hold them, Jamie," came the hoarse cry from his comrade behind.

Could he hold them? Hit again and again, the blood streaming across his eyes, one arm powerless, he worked on by some incredible will power, and never could the enemy reach the gun.

Then a shout from behind. Supports at last! A last effort—just one more—one little one—supports, Jamie—hold them!

The gun lever moves again—so feebly. There is a sound in his ears of great waters rushing, and with it the faint echo of the Scottish cry. With a little moan he drops forward over the breech as his comrades sweep across the bridge in irresistible charge.

They found him then, hand still gripped upon the lever, and in his body were thirty bullet wounds. But Jamie had "held them."

★★★★★★

Such were the men who fought at the Aisne.

CHAPTER 10

On Big Guns, Spies and Other Matters

Chorus . . . *The nimble gunner*
With linstock now the devilish cannon touches,
And down goes all before them. Still be kind,
And eke out our performance with your mind.

It was on Wednesday, the 10th, that the first shell from the new "devilish cannon" of the Germans sailed over and made a very horrid mess in the village of Missy, which it nearly destroyed. And an awe-inspiring monster it was; 262 pounds of it. Our heaviest gun in those days threw only a 60 lb. shell, our field-gun 18 lbs. So you will see at once what an enormous difference there was. Incidentally the estimated range of that new gun was well over 5 miles. Of course, that doesn't sound very far when you have just been talking about H.M.S. *Queen Elizabeth* smashing up a fort 20 miles away, but then you must remember that on land transport and platforms for big guns form a serious problem.

Yes, that first shell had a most bewildering effect. It landed well within the village, and the near-by houses collapsed as though an earthquake had passed, while hardly a window in the place remained unbroken. After the first gasp of amazement the villagers fled panic-stricken. The few of our men who were there seemed too dazed to do anything. At first nobody had any idea what had happened, for the explosion was unlike anything they had yet experienced. Until they knew that it was a shell the general opinion was that a great pile of ammunition had been hit and exploded.

Unfortunately from then onwards the men were to endure the

continuous nerve-racking ordeal of these monsters, and although they soon came to laugh at them, as they always do at danger or discomfort, nobody can say that they were popular. If the German gunner scored a direct hit—well, there was nothing left of the target. Otherwise the shell did curiously little damage save when it burst within a "dugout" or on the top of a trench. In that case every soul inside would be buried alive—surely the most horrible of deaths.

I remember being deeply impressed one afternoon by some German gunnery near Bourg. There were a couple of small iron bridges over the canal about 60 yards or so apart. Suddenly, without any ranging shot, one of those great shells plumped right on the bridge and smashed it through.

"Hullo," I could hear that German gunner remarking, "there's a bridge. Better have it down." *Plump!* The bridge was down.

"Hullo," said the German again, "why, there's another bridge! Better have that down too." A second shell. *Plump!* The second bridge was knocked through. No more. Just those two shells to do the job. It was quite uncanny.

★★★★★★

But the successes of the German gunnery, and the accurate finding of targets were in the main due to their extraordinary Secret Intelligence Service. It will be remembered that we had instances of this the very first day at Mons. Now, when a German battery began scoring hits you didn't waste time exclaiming what remarkably fine shots the Germans were—you began to hunt for the spy.

There was one typical instance (of many) in Rheims. General D'Esperey, the G.O.C.in-Chief the 5th French Army, took over a school-house for his Headquarters. Early the next morning something like 50 enemy guns were switched directly on to the house, and the general barely escaped with his life. Several of his Staff officers were killed.

At the Aisne German spies were a regular plague. On one single day sixteen were captured and shot. Of these one was taken with 50,000 *francs* on him, presumably blood money, for he was discovered in the very act of telephoning military information to the enemy.

Even with the little that is actually known of the working of this phase of German activity one is amazed at the ingenuity and money expended—for the comparatively trifling results obtained. Some of the tricks and disguises of these agents read like pages from an Oppenheim romance.

One of our Corps H.Q. took up its abode in a certain village one afternoon. A staff officer chanced to glance up at the hands of the church clock to learn the time. To his astonishment the hands of the clock began to run round and back again, jerking from one figure to another.

Guessing what was wrong he entered the church and climbed the belfry steps. In the tower he discovered the sexton engaged in the gentle art of semaphore signalling to an invisible enemy. Probably in a quarter of an hour Corps H.Q. would have found their house being made into a target for German guns.

A French battery was immediately shelled by the enemy whenever and wherever it came into position. For some days the affair remained a mystery until it was noticed that a shepherd with a flock of sheep invariably followed the battery when on the march. An enemy airman, taking the position of the battery from the flock of sheep, could then signal back accurate information.

One of the cleverest cases of disguise I came across was in a little town where the mayor had just held up a fast motor-car containing two bedraggled and handcuffed refugees on the back seat crushed between a couple of *gendarmes* armed with rifles. The chauffeur was another *gendarme*.

"Ah, *monsieur*," said I, "I see you've got a couple of spies."

"A couple!" said he. "Take another look, *monsieur*. They are *all* spies."

And so they were, both refugees and *gendarmes*. Though how the mayor had spotted them I could not imagine. Naturally, any sentries would let such a car-load pass almost without question. But perhaps they tried it once too often.

It is sad to think that quite a number of the spies captured were French suborned by German money, but I am sure that the number of these was exaggerated. Men are apt to forget the peaceful penetration of the Germans and how they settle in the country for years, assimilating the language and manners, and so are easily mistaken for French.

Cases like that of a leading merchant of a certain town near-by were very common. For some fifteen years this merchant had had in his service a confidential clerk who seemed invaluable to him and to the business, and who came to be treated almost as a son. A week before war broke out the clerk disappeared.

When a German division entered the town the confidential clerk came back, but now as the officer in command of a company. He found his old quarters very comfortable, for he knew where everything was, and with a cellar of good wine he was able to entertain his friends quite pleasantly. The entertainment was made still more attractive by the enforced presence of the two daughters of the house. You will know what that means where the Huns are concerned.

Further, the erstwhile clerk, having had access to all the books of the firm, had acquired a great deal of information about the firm's customers, and that meant most of the principal people in the district. The information proved very useful in the robbery and extortion which followed.

These were some of the ways in which this typical example of German manhood was able to recompense his late employer and the family for fifteen years of trust and affection.

It is very irritating that the majority of our people at home should still refuse to credit the widespread activity of the German agent in foreign countries. When one takes the case of Italy, for instance, where the Germans had succeeded in acquiring the control of the majority of the great banking-houses and had direct interest in many of the important commercial firms; of Russia, where nearly every war and political department was undermined by German interest; of Holland, with its German-owned banks and newspapers; of France, with its elaborate secret service—when all this is recalled how can our people continue fondly to delude themselves that England is free from the German blight? Great Britain, the arch-enemy! We talk glibly of what we shall do in case of invasion, of the defence by the Navy, of the immediate extermination of the raiding force. But with invasion the danger is from within our shores, not from without. And so it will be when we come to set our house in order after the war.

Spies appear to be a necessary evil in war. They have always existed and probably always will. Old Sun Tzu, the Chinese general, stoutly defends them in his famous treatise on the Art of War. And that was written 2,500 years ago.

But the enemy did not owe all their knowledge of our movements to spies. Many a German officer and man, in uniform, were discovered concealed in the middle of our lines at the end of a telephone wire which once or twice was found to be connected up with our own H.Q. lines. One officer was discovered cramped up in a largish pigeon-cote, another in the middle of a haystack, and so on. That was real pluck on their part, for they must have believed that they would certainly be shot if captured. Needless to add, they were treated decently and merely sent back as prisoners. One does not care to imagine the fate of any of our own men taken in similar circumstances.

★★★★★★

For many a weary month to come our men were compelled to face the terrible weight of enemy guns without the glint of satisfaction that it was being replied to. How the infantry faced the shelling was suggested to me by a German officer. "We pound your men all day and even then cannot get ours to attempt a charge on the bayonets."

I cannot remember when the new heavy guns of ours arrived from home, but I have a note under September 19 that they were expected at any moment. But even when they did arrive they were able to make very little difference except in the moral effect upon our own troops, for the Germans fired nearly twenty-five shells for each one that we could send back. On the same date I have noted that there had at last arrived the new 18-pr. Field-guns which were sent to replace those lost in the Retreat. With them came a number of machine-guns.

One is anxious to record facts like these not only for present reading, but rather for the historian of the future. I have already emphasised the fact, and I would do so again and again, that no history of these early days can be a true one which does not take the fullest account of the conditions under which our men worked: of the human element, in short.

You will doubtless have read in histories already published that the infantry were now digging trenches and making "dugouts." Quite true! But imagine how it was being done. The greater proportion of the spades and picks had been lost, as I have said, in the Retreat, and although new ones were being supplied as quickly as possible the work was just now only possible through purchasing tools in the neighbouring towns and villages. And towns do not keep much of a supply of such articles in stock.

Then there was the difficulty of the roads. The bad weather and the ceaseless heavy transport had reduced them to a shocking condition even in a single week. There were not very many French civilians available, but such as there were at once found employment in road-repairing. And a very slow job they made of it.

The one thing which never seemed to fail was the rations; and just about now the first issue of rum was made. I wonder how many hundreds of lives, thousands possibly, that evening tot of rum saved during the winter. Good hefty stuff it was, too; the real Navy brand. At first it came up in great casks, and there was a lot of waste in dealing it out, while some of the men secured much more than was good for them. But proper arrangements were soon made and all went well.

Extra clothing, waterproof sheets, etc., were now being sent up as fast as they could be procured, and these things made life just about bearable. But no necessaries like these (we had not yet arrived at the luxury stage) could relieve the supreme discomfort of this curious cave-dwelling, chalk-quarry life with its incessant wet, exposure and consequent dysentery, and the never-ending stream of shells and bullets. Worst of all was the knowledge which was now spreading that we could advance no farther and could not adequately reply to the enemy guns. The move to Flanders, when it came, was hailed with delight by everyone. But after a few weeks' experience of winter in Flanders the Force looked back with longing to those days at the Aisne.

But about the supplies, the marvel is that the Force was so wonderfully well served as it was. I do not think I ever once heard a man grumble except in the usual, general sort of way. And even then it was not really grumbling, but rather his way of expressing a wistful longing to have the war over and be at home again. How the demands for the Force were being met at home one cannot tell; there was probably much confusion before the machinery of supply was got into working order. But in France only those actually concerned with the quartermaster-general's department could speak justly of the magnificent effort which met and overcame endless difficulties.

As the crow flies the Force was well over 300 miles away from its main base. All supplies had to come up over the network of French railways, a feat which, even in peace time, would have involved no mean effort of organisation. But in war, over a strange railway system, with the greater part of the rolling-stock needed by our Allies, and what was left being manned by a much depleted staff—that indeed was an achievement in organisation to be proud of. If the country only realised half the debt which is owed to General Sir William Robertson for his magnificent work during the first months of the war they would honour him even more than they do today.

And the railway difficulties suggest but one phase of the organisation. There was, for instance, the motor-transport problem. Motor-lorries built to carry Mayflower's Margarine, Pulltite's Corsets and other delightful products over honest English roads in the piping times of peace could hardly be expected to stand for long the strain of war over French pavé roads. And when there are a dozen different types of vehicles for which to provide spare parts, etc., and when spare parts are not to be obtained because they come from Belgium or America or elsewhere, then there are more difficulties. And these, too, are somehow surmounted.

Then I think that we hardly appreciate as we should the exquisite tact and comradeship of our French Allies in those days in this matter of railways and supplies. Tact is not a quality in which, as a rule, an Englishman shines, especially out of his own country, so there were naturally endless possibilities of friction. But the French were always so anxious to meet us in every possible way that they refused to take offence, even when they must have thought English manners and speech very brusque and curt. And as *it takes two to make a quarrel*—

And this reminds me of a very interesting and significant change which we noticed about this time in the bearing of the French towards the British. A single illustration will suggest its character.

One day just after the first bombardment of Rheims an officer had to go into that city on duty. The chauffeur was the only other occupant of the car. About a mile or so outside the city they found encamped in the fields the outposts of the population, mostly women and children, who had fled from the German shells. From there right into the town the road was lined on both sides with people standing or sitting two and three deep all dressed in deep mourning. The sight, he said, reminded him of the London crowd at Queen Victoria's funeral.

But on the approach of the car they all started to their feet, and instead of waving and cheering, as the French had always greeted English troops, they all clapped with their hands, as though applauding a favourite actor. For a few moments the officer was too bewildered to respond to the ovation. Then he began to salute in return, but the farther he went the louder became the clapping. So in desperation he felt compelled to keep on raising his cap. And, as he said afterwards, he realised for the first time what an ordeal it must be for the king to drive through London, and how it was His Majesty wore out so many hats.

★★★★★★

Wednesday, the 16th, was a red letter day for my own unit, for it was then that we received our first mail since leaving home, just a month before. A month! It seemed like six months. With the mail were newspapers up to August 30, a week before, and we were able to get a glimpse of the great happenings outside our own little corner.

We were tremendously excited to hear all about the Retreat and what we had done and why; and oh! so disappointed to find that the Russians had not yet got to Berlin. Nor was there any news about a big fight in the North Sea, and that we couldn't understand. We learned that recruiting was going ahead at a tremendous pace mainly because of the great disaster (how we rubbed our eyes in astonishment!) of the Mons affair: also that there was much distress in Hamburg and other German cities through shortage of food. Oh yes, we should certainly be home for Christmas.

For one or two there were parcels of "woollies." But how clever and thoughtful of the folk at home to think of such things! Socks and lovely soft scarves—however did they guess? One man actually received some bootlaces, to his vast delight and the envy of his fellows.

But the climax came two days or so later. The quartermaster-sergeant appeared in the lines and announced that some tobacco and cigarettes had arrived for us, a present from the *Daily Sketch*—I think that was the paper. Officers and men thought he was joking. Tobacco sent by the *Daily Sketch!* Why in the name of wonder should strangers send us a present?

Yet it was true. For each and every one there was a little tin of tobacco, two packets of cigarettes and two boxes of matches, "with compliments and good wishes." If only the donors could have seen the surprise, stupefaction almost, and the gratitude with which that present was received, how happy they would have been. We received many such parcels during the days to come, but the pleasure they gave was never dulled by repetition, and we never ceased to wonder at and appreciate warmly the generosity and kindly thought of good friends at home.

About that time we heard, again with no little astonishment, that both officers and men were to receive a regular government allowance of tobacco. There is no need at this stage to speak of the importance of tobacco to our fighting men. It is perhaps a libel on their powers of endurance to say that they could not get on without it, but the ration and supplies from home certainly make the whole world of difference.

Everyone smokes all day long, from the officers at G.H.Q. right down through the ranks. At first it was a pipe, although Thomas Atkins never has cared about pipe-smoking. But as the days wore on and the stress continued we all drifted almost unconsciously to the cigarette. A matter of nerves, the doctors will tell you, and I suppose that is what it was. It was no use trying to induce the men to stick to a pipe as being better for them. No, it must be cigarettes. Given a cigarette our lads will bear the most horrible wound torture with fortitude, and it is the first thing they ask for on recovering consciousness.

★★★★★★

So accustomed are we now to the perfect organisation of the Red Cross work, and the speedy removal of the wounded from the firing-line, that many will doubtless be surprised to learn that the Force had no motor ambulances available until about the third week in September. One need hardly remark how urgent was the need for this transport and how difficult it was to deal properly with the more serious cases. The wounded were got back as far as Braisne, a few miles south of the Aisne, and thence by rail. But it was a dreadful ordeal for the sufferers under the somewhat primitive arrangements which were the best available.

Some day it is to be hoped that there will be published a full appreciation of the magnificent work performed by the doctors and R.A.M.C. staff, especially during the first eight months. Everyone knows that our R.A.M.C. ranks second to none in the medical services of the nations, [1] but never have its unfailing skill and self-sacrificing devotion been more finely exhibited than under the ghastly conditions of this modern warfare.

We marvel, or should do if we were not so well accustomed to it, at the surgical skill displayed in modern hospitals under ideal conditions of working. Conceive, if you can, the work of the regimental doctors in the advanced firing-line trenches where they endure the same hail of shrapnel and bullets as their fighting comrades. There they wait, with their stretcher-bearers, ready at any moment to "go over the top "to tend and bring in the men who fall in the charge.

Imagine, too, the Advanced Dressing Station, which is nearly always within the fire zone, the remains of a cottage perhaps, or maybe a "dugout." Here the sufferers are tended rather more carefully than was possible in the actual firing-line: wounds are washed, given antiseptic treatment, and bandaged thoroughly before the patients are sent forward on the next stage. A sight, this, once experienced never to be forgotten. The rows of wounded men, the gasping moans, or heavy, stertorous breathing of drugged sleepers, with the doctors and order-

---

1. Due in largest measure to the wonderful foresight and untiring labour of Sir Alfred Keogh, Director-General of the A. M.S. Never may his name be forgotten, for he is one of the greatest of Englishmen.

lies moving swiftly from stretcher to stretcher, while overhead shells burst and bullets hum. It matters nothing to the staff that at any moment the Red Cross flag may attract the enemy's special attention, and a couple of well-placed shells end it for all, doctors and patients alike. The work goes on with never a break, day or night, the staff snatching food and sleep when and where they can.

Yes, I hope that book will soon be written; and written not by any member of the corps, but by someone of sympathy outside who will pay the fullest possible tribute to this noblest of all professions.

CHAPTER 11

Still at the Aisne

K. Hen. *For never two such kingdoms did contend*
Without much fall of blood; whose guiltless drops
Are every one a woe, a sore complaint,
'Gainst him whose wrongs give edge unto the swords
That make such waste in brief mortality.

With the close, on September 18, of that stern four days' battle for the heights commanding the Aisne we get the first hint of the change which was to come in the general character of the fighting. Two points should be noted, the one being a result of the other. Let me first recall to mind the position of the opposing lines.

You will remember that at Mons and through the Retreat the British Force held the post of honour on the extreme left of the Franco-British line. When the Allies turned at the Marne a new French Army was formed to the west of the Force, so that when we advanced to the Aisne we had about 200 odd miles of French troops on our right and about 50 miles of French on our left. This French line on our left followed the course of the Aisne to north of Compiègne and then made a sharp bend, almost a right angle, to the north on the road to Noyon. A glance at the picture map facing p. 1 will show the position.

Now, the first point was this. On September 18 General Joffre informed Sir John French that in order to put an end to this hold-up of the Allied advance he proposed to extend the French line on the left so as to try to get round the German right. It was the same strategy which he had attempted at the Marne battle.

The second point followed. To quote Sir John French:

It was now evident to me that the battle in which we had been engaged since the 12th inst. must last some days longer, until the effect of this new flank movement could be felt and a way opened to drive the enemy from his positions.

This meant that the British had to dig themselves in as strongly as possible and then hold on for all they were worth until the order came from the French commander-in-chief for a big attack. It also meant that we should have to start a proper system of reliefs for the men in the trenches, just as though they were on sentry duty. In this way, then, was begun that trench warfare which soon was to become so painfully familiar to our men and our people at home.

Right along the top of the northern ridge, and in German hands, there ran the famous highway known as the Ladies' Road. This has so often been described that there is no need to say more about it here. From the moment the British had crossed the Aisne this road was their objective. To win it meant that you commanded not only the river valley, but also the country to the north of the road. It was therefore a very important position, and the Force had confidently started in to capture it.

Mercifully the future was hidden from them. For three weary years, short of four months, did the Allies strive to take and hold that ridge. It was not until the first week in May, 1917, that the French, backed by overwhelming artillery, at last brilliantly carried it by assault.

The infantry, then, settled down to this most uncomfortable mode of fighting, and, as is the way with our army long since accustomed to campaigns under all conditions in every corner of the world, they very quickly adapted themselves to it. Some of the difficulties I have already suggested, and indeed when one recalls the lack of tools and necessary materials, and compares the later conditions in Flanders when trench warfare developed into a fine art, it seems astonishing how splendidly the men managed.

Barbed wire, for instance, which is of the first importance, was only to be obtained in small quantities. So neighbouring spinneys and farm lands were raided for wire rabbit netting and ordinary fence wire. It wasn't very much good, but it was better than nothing, and you did occasionally succeed in tying up the wily German into knots when he became too venturesome.

There were two special forms of discomfort which helped to make this trench life so trying. During the first fortnight or so it rained hard nearly every day, and as the men actually lived in chalk the state of their daily existence is more easily imagined than described. The trenches higher up the hill did get a certain amount of drainage, so it was only very wet chalk. Lower down the water stayed there, and you sat about or stood all day long in a kind of thick milky mixture. Good honest mud can be eaten with a rasher of bacon or added to a billy of tea, and you do not bother about it overmuch. But chalk is another matter. Chalk sticks and tastes gritty, and you cannot get rid of it. Then with the fine weather came the chalk dust, and that filled your eyes and ears and nose and lungs. Really there was little to choose between wet or dry.

The other discomfort was another new feature, at least in this form, and a horrible one it was. In many places our trenches were only 80 or 100 yards distant from those of the enemy, and—well, what happens to the men who fall, dead or wounded, in those great massed attacks of the Germans? It is one of those things which never seems to occur to the man in the street who supposes, if he ever thinks about it at all, that they "get buried somewhere." Nor can he realise the appalling slaughter when rank upon rank of closely packed men advance against modern quick-firing guns or British musketry. To read that 400 enemy dead was the result of an attack against one small section of trench means to him very little when his brain is overwhelmed by the enormous figures in which we count today.

Stand in a corner of one of the front line trenches for five minutes when a German attack develops, an attack in six closely packed ranks with reserves following. The first two ranks appear 200 yards away, and upon the instant every machine-gun and rifle opposite to them opens fire at top speed and with perfect accuracy. Before 20 yards have been covered more than half of the men in those two ranks are down. The gaps fill as more and more blue-grey figures crowd up. Now they are beginning to step over the bodies of their fallen comrades. The slaughter continues; with every ten yards covered it becomes more and more deadly. Great lanes are rent through the advancing mass, and now those behind have actually to clamber over their dead. Still they press on, but more slowly. The dead are heaped higher and higher, for those who climb are shot down and fall upon this writhing parapet. Thus the trench is reached, but the defenders can see nothing of the ground in front, for before the trench lies a new rampart—of dead; a rampart perhaps five feet high. Then follows the steel.

There the dead remain. And slowly the air becomes tainted with the heavy, musty smell of decay; the acid, fetid odour of rain-sodden bodies, blotched, bloated and hideous. It soaks in through every pore

MAJOR-GENERAL SIR E. H. ALLENBY

of the living men in the trench and saturates their very thoughts waking and sleeping with the loathing of it. And ever above the dead and dying hover the ghoulish carrion birds.

In due course, after several days, the enemy may find opportunity to remove the dead for cremation in the great kilns they are constructing, or to cart them back to the Corpse Factories which energetic commercial companies soon had in working order.[2] Let nothing be wasted of this "cannon fodder," which William Hohenzollern has so thoughtfully provided.

That is modern war. And it is well for the people to visualise it that they may swear a mighty oath to so work and work that never again shall the world know such a nightmare of horror.

★★★★★★

But our share in the Battle of the Aisne spreads over a wide expanse of ground. It was only up in the trenches on the hill-side that this cloud of death hung so heavily. Nor indeed did death always reign there. For one afternoon, when there was a lull in the firing from both sides, I saw two sleek brown cows wander slowly across the bullet-marked ground until they came to a trench and there gaze placidly down upon the strange earth-dwellers. It was a curious sight in the midst of all that carnage, and the men were perhaps even more surprised than the cows.

Here is a homing aeroplane. Let us take the observer's seat as the pilot wings slowly back to the aeropark on this warm, sunny afternoon of a St. Martin's summer and catch a glimpse of the rest of the battlefield.

The machine rises, and immediately beneath there spread out the thickly wooded lower slopes of the Aisne ridges. A little to the left (we are heading southwards) a glimpse of water suggests the canal, and hard by you will see the roofs of houses. That is the village of Bourg, where the 1st and 2nd Divisions have their H.Q. There is a warm welcome for a guest if you look in at the Officers' Mess, and mail day is quite a good time to select, for the chances are that a hamper of succulent dainties has just arrived from Fortnum & Mason's. Of course, a "Jack Johnson" may select that very moment to drop in too, but such little contretemps will only add zest to the meal.

---

2. It is understood that these factories were in operation quite two years before their existence was discovered by an omniscient section of the English Press, but, indeed, there is nothing very novel about the system—or, rather, the German application of it.

Now we are climbing higher. Take a glance behind and you will catch the white gleam of the chalk where the trenches and quarries scar the hill-side. Immediately beneath unwinds the ribbon of the Aisne, and far to the left you may trace the silver thread until in the hazy distance the twin towers of Rheims Cathedral stand out darkly against the mist of the encircling hills. To your right little villages nestle cosily all along the valley, half hidden amongst trees, but you will be able to pick them out by the positions of the river crossings, the pontoon bridges, or the wreckage of the old solid structures. There in the distance is Venizel, with its double bridge, pontoon and road; it marks the extreme west of the British position.

★★★★★★

If a brief digression be permitted, it was Venizel which inspired the first of the poems written on active service in this war by a soldier. You will find it published in the *Times* one day of October, 1914. It was the first of that great stream of poetry from our fighting men which has so astonished the world by its nobility of thought and utterance, and which, in creating anew for us this dear England of ours, has sent men to their death for Her with a happy smile upon their lips, and has, too, been an abiding comfort to their loved ones left bereaved.

And she is very small and very green,
And full of little lanes all dense with flowers,
That wind along and lose themselves between
Mossed farms, and parks, and fields of quiet sheep.
And in the hamlets, where her stalwarts sleep,
Low bells chime out from old elm-hidden towers. [3]

In nearly every one of the villages on the southern bank a division or a brigade has its H.Q. All are well within the fire zone and liable to be shelled at any moment if the enemy know them to be there. If you approach the house in a car you are requested to pull up some distance from the entrance, so that the position may not be marked down by a possible enemy airman. Otherwise, beyond a small flag by the door and the coming and going of a few officers and orderlies, there is nothing to show.

And indeed as you look down from your seat there is nothing to suggest that you are flying over a battlefield unless it is the puffs of smoke from bursting shells and the blurred reports from the guns. Of the infantry there is never a sign, and search as you may you will

---

3. From *England*, by Geoffrey Howard, Lieutenant, Royal Fusiliers.

hardly find one of our batteries. Battery commanders have learned a good many things in the last month, and the art of concealment is one of them.

Do you see those great fountains of earth being thrown up in that large open field down there? Those are shells from an enemy battery. They imagine that they are shelling one of our batteries, whereas the only living things in sight anywhere near are three women quietly working in the next field. We did have a howitzer battery near by two days ago, but as soon as the German airman had spotted the position the battery commander took his guns away. You will now find them 600 yards off on the far side of that wood. In the meanwhile the enemy shells come plumping methodically down eighteen a minute, at the same precise intervals of time and distance. The little piece of amusement has already cost them about £25,000 at a modest reckoning, and the net result is a strip of field rather badly cut up.

We are now flying low over a broad tract of flat countryside chequered with fields under steady cultivation and crossed here and there by yellow, dusty roads. Now and again you will catch a glimpse of a swift staff car or half a dozen motor ambulances, and you are disappointed, for there is no other sign of movement. But away to the east and west there are woods and tree-shaded roads. Peer through the leaves and you will see columns of transport, battalions on the march, batteries halted by the road-side awaiting orders, cavalry horses picketed out enjoying a few hours' grazing.

In the fields around the peasants go on with their work and children play the old, old games as unconcernedly as though there was never a soldier or gun within a hundred miles. And yet the shells come over in a never-ending stream. From here to Rheims and beyond are wide vineyards, and the harvest must be gathered that the good wine of France may not fail. There are fields which must be tilled that the earth may still bring forth her increase. But your French peasant and *madame* his wife are fatalists both, as are most of their countrymen and women, and so the work goes forward.

"But yes, *monsieur*," he will tell you, "it is indeed sad that men should so kill each other. For me, I remember the terrible 1870 and the accursed Boche of those days. He is no different, and I fought. But now I am too old, though I would gladly fire a gun for *la Patrie. Eh bien, qu'est ce que vous voulez que je fais, moi? Le bon Dieu* He gives to us the good earth. Shall we not thank Him for the gift by using it? It matters not that we die today or tomorrow. That does not concern us."

And so flying over this curiously deserted countryside which yet teems with life and movement, we are nearing the little market-town of Fère-en-Tardenois. Here is G.H.Q. whence a hundred threads of communication radiate to keep the commander-in-chief and his departments in touch with every part of the Force. And here, too, is railhead, the aeropark, and the end of our flight.

They say that if a man stands for long enough on the corner of Piccadilly Circus he will, sooner or later, meet all his acquaintances. The same remark might well apply to G.H.Q.; not, perhaps, so much in Aisne days, as later in Flanders, when there was a continual procession of somebodies and nobodies to worry a long-suffering Staff.

But even now at Fère you would constantly meet well-known faces from the London world, and wonder mightily what business took them there. War was then a stern business, and the latter-day self-conducted tours of "the front" had not then been inaugurated. So one day you would see the then First Lord of the Admiralty, a well-known K.C., a late War Minister, a famous Nonconformist minister, a prelate of the Roman Catholic Church, a minor royalty or two, and many another. Anyhow, they did not return home and write books upon the war "as I saw it," so all was well.

Apart from little incursions like these, G.H.Q. seemed to the officer visiting on duty to embrace a very happy little family, where everyone was on the best of terms with everyone else and all pulled together with fine efficiency. Nowadays G.H.Q. seems to share the duties of a huge Government department with the business side of a universal provider like Whiteley's, and the old bonhomie and intimacy have gone for ever.

★★★★★★

With half an hour off duty from G.H.Q. for an evening walk officers would stroll up to the flying-ground to see the aeroplanes come home and glean some news from "the front." Flying men have an extraordinary sixth sense which enables them to tell positively whose machine it is when the aeroplane is no more than a speck in the far distance. So, at the sunset hour, little groups gather on the flying-ground to watch anxiously for their comrades' return, telling over the aeroplanes as they appear.

Here there is no panoply of war, no hint of the grim slaughter which is being carried on a few miles northward; only a sheer ecstasy and pride in the grace and purity of this new creation of man's. The flight of a single aeroplane still has the magic to bring us all out with mouths agape to gaze at the wonder of it; but in the flight of a squadron there is something akin to the incomparable majesty of battle-cruisers steaming swiftly into line ahead; and the world can offer no more inspiring sight.

As the sun dips swiftly down, great beams of ruddy gold shoot forth and spread like the shafts of a fan across the faintest green of the west. At the high summit a belt of lightest, feathery cloud seems to hold and imprison the flood of light, and there burns and glows with the shimmering iridescence of mother-of-pearl.

But there is little thought just now for the glories of a sunset, and all eyes are strained to the north for the first sign of the returning airmen after a somewhat perilous day.

A sudden exclamation from a young flight lieutenant, and quickly he takes his field-glasses.

"It's Murdoch," he says with decision.

And now, if you have had an air or sea training, you may just distinguish, far away, against the dove-grey breast of the sky, a little moving speck. Indeed, it might be a mote dancing down a sunbeam; and yet this officer has seen it for a biplane and named the pilot.

A second speck hastens after the first. "There's Jimmie!" says someone else; "the old 'bus is doing fine." A third, a fourth, a fifth, and each is named down at the first moment and with more than a hint of relief.

Now the vanguard is well in sight, and still the specks climb from out the grey north into the palest blue of the heaven. Nearer still, and your landsman's ears have at last caught the whir of the propellers, and with the sound you at last see them as a flock of homing wild swans flying orderly in wedge fashion behind their leader. The last rays of the dying sun strike athwart the planes and tint them redly as the pilots "bank" slightly.

The position of the aeropark is an excellent one, wide and spacious; no need to manoeuvre carefully for a landing. Above, the air is brilliant with sound; seventeen aeroplanes have been counted, and comments run from mouth to mouth as the men below swiftly detect any mishaps. But there is an eighteenth yet to come, and no sign of her, near or far.

"Looks as though old Fleabag has been done in," says our flight lieutenant slowly. (P.S.—Fletcher-Bannister is rather too much of a mouthful to pronounce when you're in a hurry, and what more appropriate pet name could be found when a fond aunt has just sent him a most lordly, warm and woolly sleeping-valise for the cold nights? Incidentally, it is only very popular, or very obnoxious, officers who have pet-names, and as the R.F.C. doesn't carry any of the latter class we may presume that "Fleabag" was one of the former.)

By now the leading pilots have decided exactly where they will land. In ones and twos they spiral down and level; then, softly, their aeroplanes settle to earth and so lightly taxi forward to the expectant groups of officers and mechanics.

"Hullo, old son, any luck?—We've got a tophole pigeon-pie for dinner.—How's brother Boche today?—Did your tank leak after all?—You'll want a bit of patching up, young feller-my-lad." These, and half a hundred similar remarks. But most insistent of all, "Where's old Fleabag? They've not downed him, have they?"

"Don't know what happened to him," comes a reply. "Engine trouble, I think, and he had to go down. We were somewhere near Laon and brother Boche was potting away like the very devil."

So the groups break up for tea and cigarettes. But the flight lieutenant remains behind, still searching the gathering dusk with his glasses, and the flight commander joins him. There is always hope, and Fleabag is an exceptionally good man, though inclined for too many risks. Yet, after all, that is a flying man's job.

"He oughtn't to have taken that new machine without a good run through first," observes the commander; "he was asking for trouble. But we'll have the lights on," he adds, turning to give the necessary orders.

The darkness creeps on apace, and with the shadows a little puff of wind from the southeast suggests that a breeze is freshening up. Those prevailing winds from our rear have been a constant trouble to our airmen all through. In the far corner of the ground a searchlight fizzes angrily for a few moments before it decides to burn properly, and almost at the same instant the flight lieutenant detects a faint star of light in the northern sky.

His whoop of delight brings a rush of feet from near-by tents, and the men crowd out to see. "It's old Fleabag, you chaps," he cries, dancing round; "he's signalling for lights." And two or three race hard for the searchlights which are there to illuminate the landing-ground.

Now the sound of propellers is distantly heard, to be drowned for a moment by the mighty cheer which goes up. "Good old Fleabag!—By gum, he's done 'em after all!—Cheeroh, Fleabag! Are we downhearted?"—with the inevitable long-drawn response.

274

And Fleabag, just to show that he's glad to be home again, and that it's a jolly sort of little old world after all, and that there are a lot of jolly decent sort of chaps in it, and that brother Boche is really a harmless sort of blighter who can't help it, and that, with luck, there'll be a letter from her waiting for him, and that, again with luck, there'll be some pigeon-pie left if he hurries—in short, just to show that he's glad to be alive, he does a couple of fine looping stunts, slips down a giddy spiral, and makes a perfect landing without turning a hair.

And there we'll leave him, for it isn't the slightest good asking him about his enforced landing in the enemy lines, nor how he jumped his machine over the edge of a quarry to escape, nor any little details of that sort. But tomorrow morning at daybreak there will be an admirably drawn report lying on the commander-in-chief's desk. And a little later in the day, should you chance to be there, you may see old Fleabag, shivering in every limb, standing before the field-marshal, explaining a few more points and receiving in return just the kindly nod and the two words of appreciation which are worth infinitely more than all the M.C.'s and D.S.O.'s.

Yes, there's a good deal of the silent Senior Service about the R.F.C., and that alone is a good enough passport to the affections of the warm-hearted British public.

CHAPTER 12

The Move to Flanders

K. Hen. *Mark then abounding valour in our English,*
That, being dead, like to the bullet's grazing,
Breaks out into a second course of mischief,
Killing in relapse of mortality.

The battery was having an afternoon's stand easy, and Stanion, the senior subaltern, thought it a good opportunity to pay a visit to the section on detached duty and see how they were getting on under the command of our old friend Sergeant Smart. The two guns were in action, artfully concealed from aircraft about fifty yards beyond a ruined farm.

"Well, Sergeant Smart, going on all right?"

Sergeant Smart scrambled to his feet, saluted, and thought that they had nothing to complain about.

"How about getting home by Christmas," asked Stanion; "do you still think we shall do it?"

"Well, sir," said Smart, "I don't see how we can be stuck here much longer like this. 'Tisn't in human nature. And those Russians, they ought to be in Belgium by now. Shouldn't be surprised if we didn't get them on the run again any time now."

"Back over the Rhine, you think? "asked Stanion with the suspicion of a twinkle.

"Oh, yes, sir, we shan't stop this time. And then, I suppose, we shall go and give them 'Ome Rule same as we did the Boers. We're a funny lot," Smart added meditatively.

Stanion burst out laughing. "Well, Sergeant, you're not altogether wrong. I believe we're going to move—no, I don't know when, but we've just had a hint to be ready at a moment's notice."

"A proper move, sir? Pity if it wasn't, because we've made it very comfortable here, sir.

"Yes, a proper move this time," said Stanion. "Don't harness up, but see you're quite ready. By the way, heard the crown prince's latest?"

"Is that the man who stole the—"

"Yes," interrupted Stanion hastily. "He was holding forth to some of his friends. 'Gentlemen,' he said, 'it is all a lie that you read in the French and English papers about the English Army still fighting. The English Army no longer exists. I give you my word of honour as a gentleman that we have captured or destroyed it altogether.' Quaint sort of chap, isn't he? I wonder if he really believes it. Well, I'll just go round the horses."

★★★★★★

This particular "latest" was actually well authenticated, and the statement was made in all sincerity, if not by that remarkable individual certainly by one of his personal staff. Shakespeare's *Henry V.* supplies us with the usual apt commentary.

Already, by the last week in September, preparations were well forward for inaugurating the "second course of mischief," although scarcely so much as a hint of its nature was allowed to leak out. When everything was ready definite orders were issued for immediate action, and even then commanding officers were as much in the dark as they had been when leaving England six weeks before. It chanced that a week or so earlier a paper of "Instructions for Billeting Troops in Belgium" had been circulated. But this had been taken to mean that a straightforward advance was imminent; no one anticipated what actually happened.

There were several good reasons why the British Force should be moved if possible. One was that such excellent material would be more valuable in the difficult open fighting to the north than shut up in trenches which could be held by less experienced troops. A second, that by moving nearer to the coast we should have our sea bases more handy and so lighten the serious problem of transport. We should also come back to our old position on the left flank of the Allied line.

But perhaps the most serious consideration was the strong menace which the Germans were directing against Antwerp, the last remaining stronghold of the Belgians. Whether the higher command realised that the fall of the city could only be a question of a few days one cannot at present say, but it must have been recognised that the situation was very grave. If Antwerp fell it would mean the release of at least

277

300,000 fresh German troops to sweep down past Ghent and Ypres.

During the last half of September General Joffre had been carrying on his strategy of attempting to outflank the German right. More and more French armies had been pushed up until, by September 30, the French line extended northwards from Compiègne right up to Arras. (It is worth glancing at the picture-map to get the general idea.) You must imagine that line as a stream of water flowing along fast against the side of a steep bank. At some point that bank will surely come to an end, when the stream will curl round the corner and dash in.

But the stream flowed ever on and on, dashing against the bank, and nowhere was that gap reached. In fact, to abandon the metaphor, the French, instead of finding any weakening in the German line, were met by an ever-increasing resistance as they pushed northwards. And when it was found that the country was swarming with German cavalry it became evident that the enemy, too, had some big scheme in hand, and certainly had no intention of being taken unawares by an outflanking movement.

The German scheme was, in short, to seize the coast and ports of the Channel. "To Calais!" was now the cry of every good German, just as he had lately shrieked "To Paris!" and you will remember how they boasted of mounting great guns on the coast in order to bombard Dover.

Such, then, was the general idea at the end of September, and it will be seen at once that there was to be a race, the enemy trying to reach the seacoast, the Allies trying to prevent them—though how stern the race would be no one then guessed.

★★★★★★

There have been so many astonishing feats performed during this war that one has come to live in a language of superlatives. Taking it all round I suppose that the evacuation of the Gallipoli Peninsula was as remarkable as any, this and the incredible feats of arms in the Battle of the Landing on the Peninsula. But ruling out the Dardanelles Expedition, the three most striking achievements on the British side seem to me to have been the Battle of Le Cateau, the First Battle of Ypres (as it is called) which resulted in the saving of the Channel ports, and the evacuation of the Aisne position. Of course, in this last it was share and share alike between our good French Allies and ourselves, or it could not have been accomplished as it was.

And the remarkable thing about the move from the Aisne is that there is nothing to say about it. The organisation was so perfect that when the moment arrived there was never a hitch in the working. Thus people pass the achievement by with a little nod of appreciation, regarding it as all in the day's work. Yet consider for a moment what was done.

The British were holding a difficult front of twenty-six miles in length. Along this front, or in reserve immediately behind, we had approximately 70 battalions of infantry, 15 regiments of cavalry, and 84 batteries of artillery, horse, field and heavy. At least, that was about the strength on paper.

The German lines were, in many places, no more than 100 or 200 yards distant from the British trenches. In addition, the enemy dominated the situation with their big guns; but, despite the heaviest attacks, their infantry had nowhere been able to break through the British line.

The problem before the French and British commanders was to withdraw all the British troops and put French in their places without letting the enemy know.

At the Aisne, owing to the position of our lines, it was never a very easy task to take a company or battalion out of the firing-line for a few days' rest and replace it by a new one. When it is a matter of changing, say, a brigade, the staff work has to be most carefully thought out in every detail. It is as though you are placed in charge of a signal-box at a big railway junction and have to work the points and signals without the help of the interlocking system.

If you can imagine something of the difficulties where our own troops alone are concerned, you will guess how complicated the business becomes when the troops of another nation come into the picture. The orders must be so carefully worded that there may be no possibility of mistake or misunderstanding when translated; the time-tables must be most precise; the officers and guides must know every yard of the ground blindfold, because the changes have to be made at night, with no lights, and in complete silence—these and a score of other details for the infantry.

With the artillery there is the handing over of the gun positions, the interchange of maps and sketches showing ranges to various targets—all complicated by translation from English to French. Then there are the changes at all the H.Q.'s, the rearrangement of communications, telephones, etc. The detail of it all is endless. And it must all be done in secret.

I do not say that the move was so successfully carried out that the enemy had no inkling of what was going on. That was probably quite impossible in view of their elaborate system of secret agents. But at least the Germans made no sign during those few hazardous days, and the British were got away and the French moved in without any complications.

★★★★★★

It was on Saturday, October 3, that a start was made with the first units to be moved. Some of the cavalry and the rearmost columns of motor transport were the first to go. Everything combined to send the men off in the highest spirits. It was lovely autumnal weather—days of bright, warm sunshine, nights of soft, radiant moonlight. Everyone was thoroughly tired of the inaction of trench life, and now they were off again, once more into the unknown, with a prospect of real movement. No one knew for certain our destination save, vaguely, that it was Belgium. But Belgium was flat, and that meant congenial work for cavalry and guns. Oh, yes, all would go well now, and we should soon get round the German flank once we had brother Boche in the open. Then, Hey for England, Home and Beauty!

It took just about a week for a unit to complete the move. The Second Army Corps, for instance, was clear of its positions by October 5, and reached its new line in Flanders on the 11th. For most of the officers and men it was a week of picnic holiday despite the long marches. Certainly trains and roads and villages were rather too crowded for perfect comfort, but no one bothered much about that. Then it was rather jolly marching by moonlight. Nearly all the movements were made by night to escape air observers. And it was rather amusing having all the guns and vehicles covered with foliage and branches of trees. If a battery or column was doing a spell of daylight flitting and an enemy airman came over, you just halted and pretended to be a little wood. And the airman would fly home and tell how he had discovered a copse of trees which was not marked on his map, and please see that it's included in future editions—at least, that is what we hoped he would do.

It was rather like the fairies in Kensington Gardens who are in the middle of a delightful game when, suddenly, a grown-up mortal comes along. All the fairies have to do is to stand perfectly still and pretend to be flowers, when the poor ignorant mortal will just exclaim, "What a lovely bed of daffodils!" and go blindly on his way.

★★★★★★

Then, odd as it may seem, a great many of our men saw French troops for the first time. There were the typical French *poilus*, so well known from sketches and photographs. And everyone was struck by their astonishing marching powers. Here is an infantry regiment rambling along all across the road; no idea of marching in fours; no thought of keeping in step, and yet "getting there" with the best. And the men! Whether the type has altered I do not know; but I seem to see them now on the march, with their refined faces and beards which have never known a razor, looking (save for uniform and kit) as though they had stepped out from the canvas of some dim cathedral altarpiece of "The Last Supper."

Then there were the cavalry in their blue and red uniforms, with the baggy trousers and riding-boot *continuations* and the long plumes from their helmets. You have seen them so often in the first act of Carmen. Sometimes they would be wearing steel breast-plates and back-pieces, just as Meissonier painted them; and always the same wiry little horses of the obvious Arab strain which will carry their riders to the very last gasp.

Our men of the mounted regiments were quick to notice and criticise points about the horses of our Allies. Certainly with the draught horses of the guns and transport, the difference between English and French methods in the care of their animals was very marked. But then, we are a nation of horse-lovers, and therein lies the secret. When a battery has half an hour's halt, and there is a patch of grass handy, you may be certain that our drivers will take the bits out and let the horses get their heads down for a few mouthfuls. Nor will you see a mounted man trot along the hard road if there is the choice of a stretch of turf alongside. Trifles? Yes; but it is the never-failing attention to such trifles which has helped to make our Army draught horses the peerless animals they are. It is good to observe that this war has taught us to bestow similar care and attention upon the men.

Then one noticed the difference in equipment—belts, harness and so forth. Just as our equipment (like the commissariat) always astonished and delighted the French, so our men could never understand how the French harness and leatherwork held together. "*Mais si pratique*," your *poilu* would say, fingering an officer's Sam Browne belt. No, the French do not (or they did not) go in for practical articles, the ordinary, everyday necessaries as we understand them. I remember trying to buy a little air-pillow in cities like Rouen, Havre, and elsewhere. It was unobtainable. "Oh, yes," I was always told, "you have such practical articles in England; but in France—no."

But if we were ahead of the French in draught horses and equipment, our Allies had their revenge with their field-guns and the world-famous "*Soixante-Quinze.*"

So much has been written about this remarkable weapon that there is really nothing very much left to tell. The most striking characteristic about it is, I think, the perfect simplicity of the mechanism. It is so simple that the Germans have never been able to discover the secret. For the legend goes that if the gun be taken to pieces the secret vanishes into thin air. To place a ".75" side by side with one of our eighteen-pounder field-guns is like comparing the simple engines of a penny steamboat with the intricate mechanism on an Atlantic liner. Where our gunners have to tackle a maze of levers and bolts the French have about three to deal with, and it looks as though a boy of ten could learn it all thoroughly in a quarter of an hour.

And, of course, the French gunner is devoted to his ".75." With a sympathetic audience he is as happy and proud as a lover to tell of the charms of a beautiful mistress. He will show you how the first round fired fixes the gun so firmly in position that every succeeding shell can fall within a couple of yards of the first; and he can fire twenty rounds or more a minute with a good man to load. The German can manage eleven only. Then he will balance a glass of water or a halfpenny on the gun-wheel, and so clean is the discharge and recoil that the water will not be spilled. And he will tell how, within thirty or forty seconds of a demand through the telephone, his battery can lower such a curtain of shell fire as to render quite impassable a zone of ground perhaps twice the length of that occupied by his guns. Truly a remarkable weapon, as the enemy know to their cost; and, in the hands of French gunners, typical of the genius of the French nation.

★★★★★★

Some units went all the way by road, others partly by train and motor-bus. Those going by road found the journey most enjoyable, for the route lay through a beautiful countryside untouched, save in one or two places, by the ravages of war. Mareuil-sur-Ourcq, Senlis, Amiens to Abbeville was the road. Not very many were lucky enough to secure a day in Abbeville, but to those who were it seemed like a tiny glimpse of Paradise with the beautiful old buildings and fine shops and excellent restaurants.

Last, but certainly not least, were the baths. And, oh! the joy of a real big bath and unlimited hot water! The first real bath for nearly two months; and it had to last for another two months or so. For an extra 25 *centimes* you got a little muslin bag of lavender soap-powder. How one wallowed—the only word! Do you remember the lines in Kipling's *Back to the Army again?*

If you were to ask an officer who took that road what his most vivid impression had been he would probably reply—— Guess! No, I am sure you won't! Well, the number of girls' schools there were. Who the billeting officer was I do not know; but he certainly possessed a sense of humour. You would halt in the town or village where you were to stay for the few hours, and there would be the billeting officer, and interpreter waiting with a little sheaf of papers to allot the billets.

"Major Landale, Captain Richards and Second Lieutenant Wiley, I've got an excellent place for you in the girls' school down by the church," he would say gravely. "You will be very comfortable."

Can you not see Wiley, pulling his tie straight and flicking the dust from his boots as he starts off down the street in ever such a hurry in case that very accommodating billeting officer should change his mind? Then Richards suddenly remembers that he must find a job for his junior subaltern which will keep him busy for a spell. So off he starts in pursuit.

The major, being a dignified individual, as befits a commanding officer, follows more leisurely. But I should not be surprised if he, too, were not turning over in his mind a possible job for his captain.

Wiley and Richards made a dead heat of it. But how curious! Where is that cheerful sound of merry laughter and quaint giggles which one always associates with a well-conducted seminary for young ladies? The place is silent as the grave. Wiley tries so hard to look unconcerned as he rings the bell.

Steps down the passage and the door opens to reveal—oh, yes, there is no doubt about it—the somewhat hard-featured dame of un-certain age who yet beams benignly through her spectacles at her visitors—the guardian dragon.

"But enter, *messieurs*; I am very happy to receive you. And you will remain quite undisturbed, for my girls still make their holidays. *Tout va bien, n'est ce pas?*"

Our gallant officers are understood cordially to agree; but there will be wigs on the green the next time they come across that very accommodating and sympathetic billeting officer.

Coincidence or no, a girls' school was the selected billet at three out of the five halts. The climax came when a famous and popular general discovered that he had been given one for his H.Q. This time the girls were actually in residence, but they were promptly bundled off home by the dragon-in-charge, much to the disgust of the junior officers and—dare one add?—somewhat to the regret of the young ladies themselves.

★★★★★★

So, then, you picture the columns trekking hard northwards. Gone are the vineyards and lovely uplands of the Aisne country, the deep forest glades of Compiègne, and now, from a glimpse of the sea near Abbeville, guns, horse and foot are streaming into and across the dark manufacturing district, the Black Country of France. The vivid contrast strikes everyone, and it is not a little depressing. The weather turns stormy and colder, and there is a heavy presage in the air of the stern winter months which are to follow.

The Second Cavalry Division (General Gough) and Second Corps are the first to arrive, and they join on to the extreme north of the extended French line hard by La Bassée. A country this of railways, canals, and low-lying fields cut by pollard-fringed streams, of gaunt chimneys and curious, misshapen manufacturing plant, of dismal slag heaps and hillocks of slate and rubble.

Next follow the Third Corps coming round by St. Omer, in which town G.H.Q. were soon established; and, finally, came the First Corps, arriving on October 19. The last of the seven divisions had yet to appear.

The race for the seacoast was ended and won, but by the narrowest margin. The first few days quickly brought home to everyone that it was no longer a question of outflanking the enemy. It was to be a grim struggle to the death in which the British were once again to play their historic part. The thin line, stretched taut along a front of forty miles, must once more stand on the defensive and hold, if it may, the overwhelming massed attacks of an invading host.

Our country's frontiers are high-water mark on the enemy's coasts. With the Channel ports and coast in German hands the danger to England, despite the "sure shield" of the navy, would be very real. At home, while there was the hint of an awakening, the cry was "Business as Usual." A few score miles from London seven little divisions were mustering for the last, the greatest, of all the great fights of the old Regular Army. It was for England, and upon Her very frontiers. A worthy and a noble end!

CHAPTER 13

The First Days in Flanders

K. Hen. *Either our history shall with full mouth*
Speak freely of our acts, or else our grave,
Like Turkish mute, shall have a tongueless mouth,
Not worshipp'd with a waxen epitaph.

It is no purpose of this narrative to follow in detail the course of the operations—indeed that would be well-nigh impossible in a single volume. The stage is now set in an arena so vast, the drama goes forward in such a maze of action that you who sit imagined spectators of the scene can hope for no more than a series of dim impressions of the whole. And just as the spectator sitting at the edge of such a stage is apt to find his ideas most strongly coloured by the events which befall immediately in front of him, so the author hopes that he may by his illustrations of stray incidents truthfully suggest the character of the entire drama.

For each incident is but a part of the whole. Walk round the arena, and you will find it reproduced a hundred times in as many varying forms, and all with the single end in view. In capacity for self-sacrifice and heroism there is nothing to choose between the fighting men of the three Allies embattled in one long line against the invader.

Pause for a moment at the northern end to watch the gallant little remnant of the Belgian Army, war-worn and battered by two months of incredible hardship and fighting, thrust back foot by foot across their ravaged country-side, until at last they stand at bay in the last little corner which remains to them. Peer through the rolling waves of smoke and flame and you will see the kingly figure of their noble Leader as he walks to and fro along the ranks with words of praise, of hope and encouragement. And, at the last, when all is done that mortal man can do, behold him give the command to open the great dykes and flood the country, determining rather to restore to the sea his dearly loved land than yield it to the mercy of such an enemy.

And as our Belgian Allies held with us the road to the coast, you will not grudge the record of one act of gallantry taken from scores which the Belgians performed in those days.

A German company, with machine-guns, was holding a farm on the edge of the flooded country. Between them and the Belgian trenches there flowed a swift stream, too deep to ford, too broad for planking. But near at hand was a heavy wooden bridge which the country-folk worked to the stream by means of a great lever. Just now the Germans held it, raised on their own side.

The Belgians determined to clear the enemy out of the farm; but to do this the bridgehead must first be won and the bridge swung over. Volunteers were called for. It was a desperate, deadly task. The first man crept out from the trench; he was shot down before ever he reached the river bank. A second followed; he, too, fell, but a little nearer to the enemy.

A third crept out, a young lad of nineteen years. Throwing himself flat on the ground, he wriggled along to the bank. Just as he reached the water, two bullets took him in shoulder and hand. Into the river he plunged and swam steadily forward as the bullets rained down about him and churned the water to foam. His comrades, ready for the supreme moment, watched him anxiously, not daring to speak.

Steadily forward, and now he is half-way across. A bullet cuts through his scalp, another tears his ear, and he disappears under the water. A fourth volunteer prepares to follow, when suddenly the head of the swimmer appears again and near to the shelter of the farther bank. A hoarse cheer from his friends, and he nerves himself to his task.

Hand over hand he climbs up the bridge supports and grasps the lever. Almost exhausted, yet he throws his weight to it, and the bridge begins to sway and dip. The Germans hastily run for a machine-gun to place at a commanding window of the house, firing madly with their rifles the while.

Now the bridge begins to swing down, but, oh, so slowly to the anxious watchers on the far side. Lower still, and now it swings to its own weight, while ever the young Belgian clings to the lever. With a clash the bridge falls into place, and on the moment the Belgians are out of their trench and half-way across. The heaviest machine-gun fire cannot stop them, and with one mighty rush they carry the enemy position.

Gently his comrades loosen their young hero's arms from the lever, which he grips fast even in death. With a last salute they buried him close by the bridgehead which he won, and which, they tell me, the Belgians still hold to his memory.

A week or so before the Belgians opened the sluice gates to flood the country, and almost simultaneously with the arrival of the British from the Aisne, there appeared off the coast three or four strange ships newly commissioned in H.M. Navy. Monitors, they called them, and being heavily armed and protected and drawing but little water, they were able to come close in shore and shell the German right flank. The practical help thus given to the hard-pressed Belgians and French at the northern end of the line was very great, but possibly of even more value was the heartening moral effect produced by the appearance of ships belonging to the "all-powerful" British Navy. Our Allies felt that at last there was big support behind them with a promise of more to come.

I wish that I could tell, too, of other incidents in this northern area, of the invaluable help given by the French Marines and others, but the tale would be well-nigh endless. You must turn to other volumes.

★★★★★★

The British line, about thirty miles in length, ran from Bixschoote in the north to Givenchy in the south. Ypres, you will see from the map following, is just south of Bixschoote, where the line made a sweeping salient to the east, guarding Ypres and returning to the diagonal north and south by Messines. It should be noted that immediately to the north of the Second Corps came Conneau's French Cavalry Division, so that here, as at one or two other points, the British had a sprinkling of French troops to help them. It was a line for which there were no reserves available, and from October 11, when the Second Corps came into position, until nearly a month later when the first great Battle of Ypres had begun to die away, every man was in all day and every day.

It was a remarkably close thing, that race for the sea, and one cannot help thinking that had the Germans struck hard in the region of Ypres some time during the week following the arrival of the Second Corps they would have won through. The Allies were building up troops from the south, and there were already the Belgians in the north. But between these two forces there was still a gap, and the gate

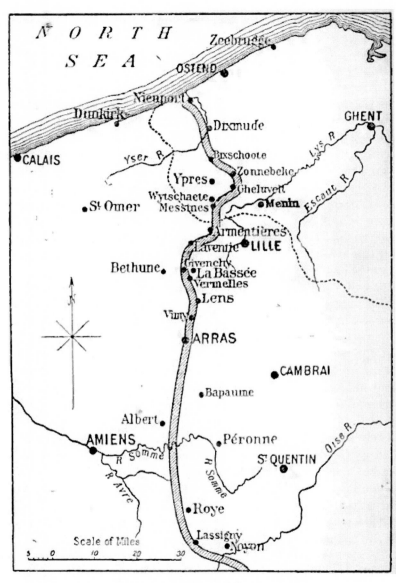

MAP OF THE ALLIED LINE FROM NOYON TO THE COAST

was not flung to and barred until October 19, when the First Corps arrived. For a few days this part of the line was being held by the Seventh Division and Third Cavalry Division. Of the mighty deeds of these Immortals something must be said later.

If it is so difficult for the spectator to follow clearly the course of the action in this great arena, it may be imagined how enormous is the task which falls to a commander-in-chief in the directing of it. Even with the most elaborate system of telegraph and telephone, the wholehearted aid of aircraft and the Intelligence system, and the most loyal of staff work, it would seem a physical impossibility for one man to keep a responsive touch upon the hundred pulses of a modern battle-line, his own and the enemy's. He must, one supposes, keep in mind a general plan drawn out upon broad lines, and leave the execution very much to the discretion of the subordinate commanders. Sometimes the chief knows that the work can be accomplished if the troops play up to him; sometimes the scheme is only one of two or three alternatives. If it fails, another will be tried.

This somewhat trite observation is made to remind the reader of the very great difficulties which existed at this time in Flanders, and of the impossibility (so one imagines) of gauging accurately the strength of the enemy and his possible plans. It is a proud thing that we should be thrilled by the unwavering heroism of our soldiers in the face of overwhelming odds, such as they were during the first year or so of this war, but there will come a time when our people will inquire why they always had to fight at such a disadvantage.

The Allied commanders, then, had two or three definite alternative plans in view when the British arrived in Flanders. Whether any of them would succeed no one could tell. At least, each one of them involved *attack* in some form. But again, as at Mons, a scheme of attack was doomed to failure. The British worked desperately at the several points assigned to them, but always as they advanced they found themselves battling against continually increasing numbers, and so were forced to the defensive. These were the opening stages of the fighting in Flanders; let me try to give you some idea of the general character of the work. Remember that it was not yet fully realised that it was to be a battle for the coast; it was hoped that we might be able to cut in to the enemy's right flank, or possibly to break his main line of communications.

At the close of the preceding chapter I gave a hint of the main features of this new countryside—a slice of industrial Yorkshire or the Potteries dropped into the flat water country of Essex, Norfolk, or the Fens. There was only one hill, and that quite a little one, in the district.

During the past six weeks our men had experienced a remarkable variety of fighting. Now another kind was added to the list—the close infighting of villages and many waterways, yet with the use of modern explosives. Londoners actually had an admirable illustration of it a few years ago in the extraordinary episode of the "Sidney Street Siege (Whitechapel)," when Peter the Painter held a company of the Guards at bay in a London street with an automatic pistol. It may be remembered that Mr. Winston Churchill proposed to send for a field-gun to shell the house, so difficult was the situation.

If you will imagine the difficulties of that little episode of a London street increased a hundredfold by barbed wire entanglements, sandbags, barricades, machine-guns, and all the other devilries of modern war, you will get some idea of what our troops had to tackle in capturing a village house by house. And the incredible thing was that in those days our guns had no high explosive shell with which to smash down the buildings. It was at the very end of October that the first tiny supply of H.E. was issued to batteries by way of an experiment and to see how it worked. This was through no fault of G.H.Q., for there was no H.E. at home.[1] As again and again one recalls facts like this and the disabilities under which our men so often worked, their achievement appears still more marvellous.

You see, then, in your little corner of the arena, the infantry of the Second Corps swinging out into an extended line on the dismal, misty morning of October 12. "Push ahead" is the order of the day. Behind them battery commanders are selecting positions for their guns, and cursing heartily because there are no pleasant little spots from which to "observe" the fire. In fact, it was difficult enough to find sensible gun positions with any open field of fire available; and when it was a case of advancing the battery generally found itself held up by some muggy, sluggish stream, or a coal pit, or a row of workmen's cottages.

The Middlesex began their day with a depressing experience. They were across one of the main roads, when down the road towards them came a black mass of people. Taking it for another German trick, the battery in support was rung up and told to be ready.

Nearer came the swarm, and the adjutant who was looking through

---

1. *Cf. The Retreat from Mons,* where it is recorded that during the Retreat a large percentage of our casualties was due to German H.E. shell.

his glasses paused to wipe the lenses, thinking that something had gone wrong with them. Right in front of the advance there plodded steadily a huge gipsy caravan covered all over with pots and pans, bird-cages, bedding, clocks and other odds and ends. The caravan seemed to be moving by some sort of machinery, but when it came nearer it was seen that there was a diminutive donkey between the shafts.

The appearance of the thing and the contrast was so comic that all the men burst out laughing. But the laughter was soon changed to murmurs of astonishment and pity. Close behind there followed rank upon rank of old men and women, young girls and children; per-ambulators filled with little household treasures, pitifully foolish they seemed; crazy carts, with decrepit ponies or panting dogs to pull them, jammed wheel to wheel with a fine Daimler motor-car crammed full with carcasses of sheep and chickens, or a brougham filled with fire-irons and a "grandfather" clock.

The Middlesex opened their ranks, and the stream poured through. The women and men looked neither to right nor left. On they trudged, with faces set stonily to the road before them. They had wept once, but now there were no tears left to give blessed relief. In dozens, in scores, in hundreds they passed, until the men of the Mid-dlesex grew dizzy with the black pageant of sorrow. The Germans were somewhere behind them, a young girl said over her shoulder as she shifted a baby from one arm to the other.

Such rations as they had the Middlesex handed out with a cheery word of would-be encouragement. There passed an old, old man in a tattered uniform, on which shone the cross of the *Légion d'Honneur*, he trailed his musket of 1870. Barefoot he trudged, his feet cut and bleeding with the pave road, and he leaned upon the arm of a girl, his granddaughter perhaps, who supported him tenderly. As they passed, the adjutant drew himself up and saluted. And the girl threw herself at the officer's feet, seizing his hand to kiss it, murmuring broken words.

So they all passed. Just a few hundreds out of the millions harried and hunted by the Hun-hounds. Where were they to go? What were they to do? God knows. "It is all a part of the great game of War; these do not matter," say the Hun-hounds. "Only wait until we land in Eng-land! Then shall you see our methods."

The Middlesex and other battalions pushed slowly forward in ex-tended lines. French cavalry, with ours, were out in advance. Scouting work in those days was a very ticklish business, as you may guess, for scattered parties of Germans would be found lurking in all sorts of places, expected and unexpected. And the byroads twisted and turned in such bewildering fashion that often our men would find themselves attacking an enemy outpost from the rear. A country like this where the Second Corps was working is much better adapted for defence than attack, just as is our own English countryside, with its many woods and hedgerows, its little fields and rambling lanes.

It was equally bewildering in the case of the villages, for you could never tell whether or no they would be occupied by the enemy. A cavalry squadron would advance, dismounted, crawling forward through the outskirts of a little town and expect to tumble across a nest of machine-guns at any moment. Instead, they might well find themselves greeted by a bevy of blithesome damsels bearing jugs of beer and other refreshment particularly grateful to hungry and thirsty warriors. There would follow a few minutes' interlude of the character generally associated with a meeting between cheery khaki-clad warriors and blithesome French *demoiselles* (I refrain from giving the name of the regiment in case some young ladies at home might have a word to say), and the squadron would be off and away to the next point.

And the very next village, although on the same line of front, might be barricaded and loop-holed and held strongly by the enemy in every house. And there was no way of telling until the men found themselves under sudden fire. The erstwhile inhabitants have formed a part of that mournful procession which has just passed.

There was one hamlet of a single straggling street which looked safe enough, and the patrol leader determined to take it at the gallop. Fifty yards off, with the place as silent as the grave, they clapped spurs to their horses and started. Round a bend in the road they came full tilt at an unexpected barrier across the street. The leader, with the first files hard upon his heels, cleared it in his stride and landed right on top of a dozen crouching Germans. At the same moment a couple of machine-guns began to bark from the windows of the houses opposite, and our men found themselves in a trap with a second barricade farther down the street. Four or five of the horses had refused the jump, and after a few minutes' stern hand-to-hand fighting the whole party was shot down with the exception of a couple of troopers who got back to warn the infantry behind.

The story was much the same with the infantry, faced by these awkward conditions. The contest was always too unequal, and our casualties were exceedingly heavy. There was nothing in the nature of a battle, but just an endless series of little fights in which our men always attacked prepared positions. The gunners, needless to say, backed up the infantry as well as they could, but they, too, were equally handicapped, for the average field-gun firing shrapnel is of little use against houses. In the first two days of this advance a couple of battalions had as many as 900 casualties amongst N.C.O.'s and rank and file, and I do not know how many amongst the officers.

The infantry fought their way forward hour after hour, with never a pause day or night for five days; just dropped down where they stood for odd snatches of sleep. You will get some idea of the way they were engaged from the fact that on October 13 and 14 the 18-pr. field guns of one single division (nine batteries) fired in support approximately 13,500 shells.

This may seem little enough against the tremendous expenditure of ammunition in later days, but in 1914 the organisation of ammunition supply, from the base to the railhead, from railhead *via* motor-lorries to the divisions and so on, was never intended to grapple with so heavy a demand. Yet somehow or another, as in every other department, the strain was met, and neither guns nor men went short until—but that shall be told later, in its place.

★★★★★★

There were many reverses during those misty October days, but there was one in particular which sent a little gasp of dismay from Corps H.Q. right through to the rear. Two famous County battalions especially were hard hit, but the day was a black one for the entire brigade.

It happened down near Givenchy. The enemy had been strongly reinforced, and they determined upon a counter-attack. It was finely carried out, and the Bedfords had to bear the brunt. The attack was too strong for them, and the Bedfords were gradually driven back, clinging hard to every point, as a man does when he is swept away by a strong current.

Unhappily, though, their retirement laid bare the flank of their neighbours, the Dorsets, as well as that of four guns which were in support. The enemy swung half left and took the West Countrymen on this exposed flank.

There was no need for an urgent message back to the guns, for the guns were caught in as heavy a storm as the infantry. The gunners ceased their fire for a minute to man the gun-wheels and trails and run the guns back a little to change the direction of fire. But half the detachments were down before they could do so. Still they worked to it, and with a big effort got one of the guns in action in the right direction without masking the fire of the others.

The Dorsets could do but little to protect themselves. To swing back their own flank only meant leaving the poor shelter of hastily dug trenches to fight in the open. They were caught; no supports were available; and whether they stayed or tried to retire they seemed doomed men. To stay meant annihilation; in retiring some might get through.

So they staggered out into the pitiless storm and started back in open order by short rushes.

"Where be they guns o' ours?" said a man to his next file during a moment's pause. "We've not a-yeard vrom 'em vor a spell."

"Hold yer clacker, carn't 'ee! They be hevin' as warm a time as we, I dessay," replied next file.

Alas! he was only too correct. The guns were not firing because there was no one left to serve them. Every man of the detachments, the officer and Nos. 1, all were down, dead or dying, where they had kneeled by their guns.

The lines of the Dorset men, pitifully thinned by now, were swept back. Still they dropped to fire a clip of cartridges, jumped to their feet, bending double, ramming home a new clip in time for their next turn. So they got back, back past the guns where each stood mute by its little pile of dead.

A subaltern of the Dorsets leaned for a moment against a gun-wheel, catching his breath in short, hard gasps. A thought struck him. Crouching to the ground he hastily examined the gun. Yes, it had been made useless, the breech block was all jammed and twisted. The next? Yes, that too. The third? An enemy shell had smashed that. The last? But a bullet caught the young officer in the side before he could reach it. Still, he dragged himself across the little space which yet seemed endless and got to the gun. It seemed intact.

He knew little enough about guns, but he guessed that if he got the breech-block out or smashed it this would be better than nothing. So he set to work with a spanner lying near and by good luck hit on the right bolt and pulled the block free. With a last conscious effort he hurled it away into the stream close at hand and collapsed across the gun-trail. There some of his men found him five minutes later, and within an hour or so he was in hospital in Bethune.

One gunner, at least, salutes in gratitude a very gallant gentleman of Dorset.

★★★★★★

But in the battalion that day the Dorsets lost some 400 men and many officers. A black list, indeed, and especially severely felt in any one of our County Regiments. For those regiments are as little families where the colonel commanding is indeed the father, and where the loss of a member is mourned as that of a brother. When the regiment is ordered on active service the men of an English County go forth to fight for their homes and their women folk, with a pride and hope in their hearts such as can never be known in a regiment recruited from all over the kingdom.

It is, I think, deeply to be regretted that our people are told so very little of the deeds of these splendid County Regiments of ours. The Old Army has shown that it works and fights as one magnificent unit, Horse, Guns and Foot, and its members, I know, resent the bestowal of special praise, however splendidly earned, upon what may be termed the more "popular" regiments while other regiments, equally deserving, seem to be passed over.

The County Regiments do their duty, and more than their duty, very quietly and without talking. They do not advertise. But it is the County Regiments which have made the British Army. Look back through the great wars of the past and note the names of the men who followed Marlborough and Wellington, aye, right back to the yeomen of Agincourt and Crécy.

The men from the West Country, the hillsmen and dalesmen of Yorkshire, the men of Kent, of Surrey, of Essex and Northumberland, of Worcester and Warwick, and a score more. These be your Englishmen who stand for England and the pageant of her fair Counties. Let Her people know this, and then let them humbly thank God that England can yet breed such men to stand for Her against the enemy and keep Her safely.

Chapter 14

"As We forgive Them"
(An Interlude)

K. Hen. *Upon the King! Let us our lives, our souls,*
Our debts, our careful wives,
Our children, and our sins, lay on the King!—
We must bear all.

Gaunt-set against the dreary, wasted fields of that still inviolate corner of Belgium there stood a wayside crucifix. The setting sun stabbed into the poisonous haze of bursting shells with bloody swords of light; and dimly through the choking fumes the Christ looked inscrutably down upon the skeleton rafters and battered walls of the little village.

A Belgian officer stood at the cross roads. For some minutes he had been listening intently to and identifying the reports of the distant enemy guns, making quick notes in a book. A heavy shell dropped and burst some twenty yards down the road and, almost unconsciously, he moved closer to the crucifix. As he did so a shaft of light pierced through the haze and fell clear upon the face, curving the lips (or so it seemed) into a tender smile.

The officer bent his head in a moment's silent prayer; then resumed his work of observation. The roar of the enemy guns redoubled in intensity, and a storm of shells poured over and through the torn roofs and walls. "Possibly there will still be left some living creatures, women, perhaps, and children, who need killing. This evening's 'hate' should finish them."

From the cellar of a house which stood apart outside the village a timid procession of some ten or twelve children came cautiously up into the twilight. School had lasted a little longer than usual, for the "hate" had begun half an hour earlier. Generally it was possible to be at home ere it started.

Close along the hedge they crept, holding one another fast by the hand. Pitifully nervous, pinched with starvation, shrunken little arms and legs shining dimly through rents in torn coats and skirts, so they came by the image of one who, many centuries ago, had beckoned little children to Him.

First of the line went Jeanne-Marie, always the dear leader. Only a close observer could have seen the terror which would spring to the calm grey eyes, for the dark curly head was held so bravely.

"Let us hasten," she said; "the good mother will be anxious."

The children clung more closely to each other and hurried on. A howitzer shell burst true in the middle of the road barely a stone's throw in front of Jeanne-Marie.

With a shrill scream of terror they turned to run back to shelter. "Help! Save us," they cried in their agony of fear.

Jeanne-Marie pressed her hands over her aching temples. "Bravely, little ones," she cried. "We should be brave. See, *le bon Dieu*; let us say our prayers."

And so at the foot of the Cross the children knelt meekly down. Twelve tiny heads bent reverently over the folded hands. The officer stood close behind as though he would guard them; while around and above a legion of devils shrieked and sported over their hellish toys.

"*Our Father,*" said Jeanne-Marie, lifting her poor wan face to meet the Eyes which gazed steadfastly down upon the little suppliants.

"*Which art in Heaven,*" the children echoed bravely after her. "*Hallowed be Thy Name. Thy Kingdom come.*" The officer took a step forward and knelt by little Pierre. The devils still laughed in derision.

"*Thy will be done on earth,*" prayed Jeanne-Marie. "*As it is in Heaven,*" the children and the officer followed her. And the heart of the world throbbed up to God in the petition from those tender lips.

There was a moaning crash as the remaining walls of one of the houses near by fell in an avalanche of masonry. A small yellow mongrel dog dragged itself painfully along the ground towards the children, its piteous howls drowned in the unholy din.

"*Give us this day our daily bread.*" And the officer hid his face in his hands, for he could not bear to look upon the poor pinched faces by his side.

"*And forgive us our trespasses,*" prayed Jeanne-Marie, "*as—*"

"*And forgive us our trespasses,*" murmured the children. But they could go no farther. The yellow mongrel had reached its tiny master and, with a choking sigh, fell dead across his knees.

Pierre buried his head in the shaggy coat. The other children looked hopelessly towards Jeanne-Marie and then towards their shattered homes. The clouds of smoke drifted blood-red over the ruins.

"*And forgive us our trespasses, as*——" they began once more.

But it was another voice which responded.

"*As we forgive them which trespass against us.*"

The officer had risen from his knees and now stood beneath the Cross, one hand resting upon the Sacred Feet. The children looked up and they recognised him at last.

For the officer was Albert, King of the Belgians.

CHAPTER 15

The Coming of the Indians

Exe. Your brother kings and monarchs of the earth
Do all expect that you should rouse yourself,
As did the former lions of your blood.
West. They know your grace hath cause and means and might;
So hath your highness—never King of England
Had nobles richer and more loyal subjects.

When the history of these times comes to be written there will be no more glowing pages in that great record of endeavour and achievement than those which tell of the rally to the flag by the Overseas Dominions and Dependencies. And wonderful beyond all will be the story of India, "the fairest jewel in the Crown."

In Germany's deep-laid plans for a "reckoning with her greatest enemy," as soon as France and Russia had been disposed of, there was one fact upon which she counted as absolutely certain, and that was the insurrection of native India. It is one of the many striking instances of Germany's ridiculous belief that other peoples must think and act as Germany would; and of her complete failure to appreciate the real meaning and purpose of Empire as viewed by England. For the British Empire is not based upon *materialism*, but upon *imagination*.

So when the call came India did indeed rise as one man—but to stand by the side of the British *raj*. The princes of her peoples did not wait to call for evidence nor to argue about the justness of the cause. They *knew* the cause must be a righteous one, and with one great heart and soul they offered themselves, their men, and their treasure to further it. And when they had offered all that they had to give they besought the king to issue his further commands.

As with the princes and nobles so it was with the people. In every corner of the Indian Empire the men of the mountains and the plains hastened to the banners of their chieftains. Men who three little months before were counted bitter political agitators were the first to call upon their countrymen to fight for the English *sahib*. And so they came flocking in. From far away Tibet, the dim, mysterious "Roof of the World," and the mountains of Kashmir to the uplands of Kandy; from the river jungles and swamps of Burma to the blinding sands of Baluchistan they rallied to the call.

And the women of India, what had they to give? Their husbands, sons and brothers? They gave them proudly. Their treasure, their little savings, their jewels and trinkets? Unfaltering they poured them into the common treasury. And when there was no more to give they could yet offer up hands of prayer for their loved ones and the success of their fighting.

Truly, as Mr. John Buchan remarks:

> The British soldiers and civilians who had found lonely graves between the Himalaya and Cape Comorin had not lived and died in vain when the result of their toil was this splendid and unfaltering loyalty.

In the roll of India's great princes who rode out to war with their men no name is more famous or more honoured than that of Major-General H.H. Sir Pratap Singh Bahadur. They say that long years ago he swore never to die in his bed. Now, when over seventy, he hoped that his oath might be fulfilled, and thus he came to France.

★★★★★★

It was during the last days of September that the Indian contingents began to arrive and disembark at Marseilles. First came the Lahore Division under Major-General Watkis, then the Meerut Division under Major-General Anderson, and later the Secunderabad Cavalry Brigade and the Jodhpur Lancers. General Sir James Willcocks was in command of the Corps.

The regiments included in the corps worthily represented all that is finest in the fighting strength of our Indian Army. Battalions of famous Sikh Regiments, Companies of the Sappers and Miners, Bhopal Infantry, Gurkha Rifles, Baluchis, the Scinde Rifles, the Jats, and Vaughan's Indian Rifles, while amongst the Cavalry were crack regiments like the Deccan and the Poona Horse. A brave array!

For most of the men it had been a great adventure that voyage from India, for it was the first time they had ever seen the sea. It required a deal of persuasion at Bombay on the part of their British officers to get many of the men on board at all. Eastern races are not troubled overmuch with nerves, and they are accustomed to take things as they come with philosophical resignation. But those great moving castles which rocked up and down upon this amazing new element—that was too much, and they feared the worst.

Nor was the worst long in coming. "Our hearts and entrails became as water and heaved within us," a stalwart Sikh was heard to remark afterwards when the bitterness of death had passed away and they were safely on shore once more. And it can hardly have been a merry voyage, with the men lying in rows upon the deck, tightly clasping their bodies lest their stomachs should melt utterly away, and in a dozen dialects calling Heaven to witness their piteous plight.

But the joyous welcome which they received in sunny Marseilles from the excited and impressionable French of the South made ample amends, and with life flowing again through their veins they counted the hours until they could play their part in the *sahibs'* war.

For a spell the men were kept in camp farther north in the hope that they might become a little acclimatised, but events were moving so rapidly, and the need of reinforcements was so urgent, that the Lahore Division was railed forward and brought up to Bethune on October 20.

They arrived in the nick of time for the Second Corps. For ten days and nights General Smith-Dorrien's troops had been fighting without rest as they had not had to fight since that great day at Le Cateau, and they were nearly at the end of their tether. Within a few days the Indian Division received its baptism in the fire of modern war. The enemy had taken the village of Neuve Chapelle, and the Indians, supported by British troops, were ordered to recapture it.

★★★★★★

And here, if you will, you must try to imagine in some measure how these first glimpses of modern war appeared to Indian troops. Our Indian Army, British and Native, is, you must know, kept always in the very pink of condition. Its training is carried on under conditions closely akin to those of active service, and such as are impossible to our Home Army. In fact, one might say that one part or another of the Indian Army is always on active service, at work somewhere on the frontiers of India.

The valour of the Gurkhas, Baluchis, Sikhs and other fighting peoples is a household word throughout our Empire, and we have come

301

to expect great things of them. But no army in the world could train adequately for modern war, because it was only possible to guess but vaguely and within definite limits what it would be like. No one, for instance, could really picture the devastating effect of big gun fire. (Remember the surprise and shock caused by those big German guns at the Aisne.) No one realised what trench warfare would be like, nor the appalling slaughter caused by machine-guns.

You must picture, then, these troops, the bravest of the brave in clear fighting, thrust into the murderous hell of suffocating high explosive shell and quick-firers. You must see them struggling hopelessly against an unseen enemy who rains down death upon them from guns five miles away.

"But, *sahib*, why did you not tell us?" said a Baluchi to his company commander; "why did you not teach us this warfare?"—and there was a whole world of pathos in the remark. For how could it be taught, save by bitter experience?

And the lesson, taught though it was at last by experience, was a long one ere it was learned. With the battle-ardour of those men, soldiers from their childhood, and with the blood of a hundred generations of soldiers in their veins, it was impossible to keep them under cover in the trenches. They would not stay down. The sight of those serried ranks of blue-grey uniforms drove them mad. At last there was the enemy they had come to fight!

"*Sahib, sahib*," they would cry, "we are not children and cowards to skulk behind earthworks."

And over the parapet they hurled themselves in a frenzy. There was no holding them.

Such was the tale when a battalion of Sikhs went into action for the first time. It was horrible. Barely a tenth of the number struggled back to shelter. The remainder—mown down before they had gone twenty-five yards.

But God help the Germans when the Sikhs or Gurkhas did get to close quarters with them! It may sound bloodthirsty, but one felt that just retribution was being taken for the thousand nameless atrocities, for the massacre of women and children. The sight of those great bearded men, the crimson turbans gleaming above their swarthy faces, the blood-lust in their eyes as they came crashing into a trench, seemed to fascinate and paralyse the Germans, striking them helpless.

★★★★★★

By the end of October the fighting at the southern end of our line had developed into a desperate defence. The casualties in the Second Corps had been very heavy. In a little over a fortnight they had lost 360 officers and 8,200 men. In one day alone 65 officers and 1,600 men were counted out; while the West Kents, one of the most famous of all the County Regiments, who had been clinging hard to a hopeless position for ten days and nights, fought on until they had but two officers (second lieutenants) and 150 men left. But never a yard of ground did the enemy wrest from them. It was a feat of iron courage and stern endurance which has rarely been equalled and never excelled in this war.

But the infantry had reached the limits of human endurance. They must be withdrawn, there was no other alternative. The Indian Corps, with its two divisions and cavalry now complete, were ready to replace them. So the exhausted troops were taken out of the line, the artillery still remaining, and the Indians stepped into the breach. It should be mentioned that in each Indian Infantry Brigade there is included a British battalion.

The good folk of the Pas-de-Calais will long tell the story of how India came to France and dwelt among them. For a few brief months this hard-featured, drab-tinted land of industry was "made glorious summer" by the glittering trappings of the sunny East. It was indeed a curious experience to turn from an old French town with its mediaeval church and homely market-square where voluble French housewives haggled over the price of carrots and potatoes and find yourself in a quarter which, apart from the houses, might have been the corner of an Indian bazaar which one knows so well.

Here down the street would pass lordly Sikh and lithe Pathan in unconscious dignity intent on the business of the moment. A quaint, ramshackle cart, with its heavily-spoked wheels and a mule between the cumbrous shafts, would rub axles with a staff motor-car. In a doorway lounge a group of British officers in the sun-helmets and tropical khaki uniforms of the East. Turn aside from the road into a small compound (the word is inevitable) and you sense at once the curious, parchment odour of the East mingled with the smoke of wood-fires, the faintly acrid smell of *ghee* bubbling in a pot, the cooking scents of strange spice-laden concoctions. Close against a tent two grey-headed veterans squat upon the ground impassively grinding at a quern, with never a glance at the terrified "baa" from a goat a dozen yards away being killed for dinner. Here and there crouch figures closely wrapped in blankets against the cold, nothing visible of them save a hawk-like nose and two glittering eyes.

It was a serious responsibility this bringing over of the Indian troops at such a time, and it has been much criticised. The cold, biting weather, the sleet and icy slush of Flanders, the rain-soaked fogs combined to play havoc with the health and moral of these children of the sun. And yet it is difficult to see what else could have been done without giving offence and damping the noble ardour of the Princes of India. The Indian Government knew full well the conditions of a northern winter, and they must have represented the facts to the Indian leaders. But apart from the righting value of such splendid material, it must have been recognised that the moral effect of their presence in France would prove a tremendous asset—as indeed it did. Doubtless the original idea was to give the men more time to become accustomed to the new conditions before bringing them into the firing-line, but, as I have remarked, the position became so serious that reinforcements had to be brought in at any cost.

And yet it was very sad to the splendid Indian Cavalry to be used for the dismounted, rough-and-tumble work of the trenches. It had to be, and right loyally they responded to every summons. But one could not help recalling their record, proudly inherited from sires who warred against Alexander of Macedon, as horsemen second to none in the world. There is, however, little room for sentiment in war.

One incident, in which a Sikh figured, was typical of many others, and well shows what these men do when they get a real chance at close quarters.

It was in a fight for a village, and a Sikh, finding that the enemy were firing from a first-floor window, entered the house and ran upstairs. Bursting open the door of the front room he found just a dozen Germans inside. Silently he set to work with the steel.

After he had killed eight of the twelve he marshalled the remaining four, barely able to stand from terror, marched them downstairs and back to his commanding officer, and very simply told his story.

"Why did you not kill all of them? "said the officer jokingly.

"I began to feel tired," the Sikh replied. "But," stretching out his sword-arm, "I am rested now. I will finish."

The Germans bolted off hard down the road with their hands up, and did not stop running till they could throw themselves on the ground before the first British soldier they came across.

When at the Aisne the news came round that the Indian Corps was on its way to France everyone at once exclaimed, "What a hell of a time they'll give the Germans in night work! "For we all felt instinctively that that was their real job. Those of us who knew the Far East could well foresee the trouble there would be with native races in face of the German shells and machine-guns, and how reckless they would be in attack. But the creeping out at night and slipping into the German trenches with the kukri, and so keeping the Boche's nerves continually on edge—that was the very thing, and we waited impatiently for the fun to begin.

On most nights there were attacks of a kind, generally trifling affairs, little expeditions to cut wire, to clear up an awkward corner and so forth. But I well remember the first real night attack in which Indians were engaged, for it chanced to have happened on the same evening as a birthday celebration of mine, in which four of us had done justice to a tiny plum-pudding sent out from home. "*And all merry*," as Pepys would say.

★★★★★★

It was close upon midnight when the curtain was rung up upon the first act. The scene is the long, low-raftered kitchen of a farmhouse not far distant from the well-known "railway triangle" in the Bethune district. By the light of a few smoky oil-lamps half a dozen officers of the Black Watch are poring over a large-scale map spread upon the table. Close against the hearth Stewart, the last joined subaltern, sits carefully cleaning his revolver; opposite him another officer is cramming a few sandwiches and some chocolate into his pockets.

To them enter a couple more officers. The new-comers wear the light khaki uniform of the tropics and bear the badges of a famous Gurkha regiment.

"Evening, Major; sorry we couldn't get here before," the taller of the two remarks. "Had a rare job to find the house. One of your chaps at the end of the lane put us right, after trying to run me through with that beastly bayonet of his. Took us for German spies or something."

"Sorry, Johnston," the major apologised, "but you won't get out of that nasty habit of creeping about at night. I don't wonder he tried to stick you. How are your 'children' tonight?" he added. "Pretty fit?"

"Fit!" said Johnston; then, with mock politeness, "the officers, N.C.O.'s and men of the Eenteenth Gurkhas return thanks for kind enquiries, and beg to state that despite the cold snap they are in the very best of health. Fit? They're simply sitting up on their hind legs and asking for it. I've never seen 'em like it. Seriously, Major," he went on, "if you haven't fixed up a top-hole scheme for tonight I believe

305

HON. MAJOR-GENERAL H.H. SIR PRATAP SINGH

there'll be a mutiny."

The major laughed again. "I think we shall be able to satisfy even your bloodthirsty 'little people' tonight," he said. "Look here—" and he pulled the map round.

Then followed a close recital of instructions with a short discussion afterwards. At 12.25 precisely the Major took his watch from the table and closed it with a snap.

"In twenty minutes, gentlemen," he said. Then, "Orderly! Where's that whisky that came today?"'

The whisky was promptly forthcoming, and mugs were filled.

"Here's luck!" and the mugs clinked together over the table.

The major shook hands all round and left the room. The remaining officers turned quickly to buckle on belts, revolvers and kit and followed him. Stewart remained for a moment to blow out the lamps.

Just before he puffs at the last one he pauses, glances over his shoulder and stealthily draws from his pocket a tiny morocco case.

"Wish me luck," he whispers, "it may be the last time."

And the fair young face within beams up at him, a world of loving thought in the deep hazel eyes.

With a little sigh and a little laugh he presses it to his lips. *Puff!* The last lamp is out. The door closes silently, and the room is empty save for the firelight shadows which flicker in mocking dance across the walls.

★★★★★★

The second act is a short one, and the scene is the small *place* of the little village which the two battalions have made their rendezvous. The men are a little way out on a field. It has been a lovely autumnal day of brilliant sunshine succeeded by an evening of radiant moonlight so bright that it was possible to read a printed page. But fortunately for the venture, big clouds have crept up, and by midnight it is pitch dark. In a corner of the place the major has grouped in front of him the officers and N.C.O.'s.

In a few brief sentences he sketches the plans for the attack. The objective is simple—three parallel trenches, with their communications, which lie between the ruins of a village on our right and a shattered farmhouse on our left. There is to be no firing until the men have won the third trench (bombs had not then come into fashion with us). The Gurkhas take the left, the Scots the right of the line. The guns will be ready to stop enemy reinforcements upon a rocket signal: they have been cutting the wire entanglements during the day, but there is certain to be a fair amount left. Everything to be done in dead silence. These and a few other necessary orders.

"Fall in now, please," concludes the major, "and I will give you five minutes or so to tell your men. Good luck to you!"

Ten minutes quickly passed and the order was given to start. The men marched off, the Indian battalion leading, in perfect silence with broken step. A mile or so forward the Gurkhas turned off down a branch lane. Everything was timed to the minute. The Scots halted just short of the village which the Wessex had won that afternoon; the first-line enemy trench was 150 yards away on the far side The Gurkhas were to have the principal share in the attack, for they could work more silently; the Scots could hardly hope to reach the first trench unperceived even if all the wire was cut. If they attracted the enemy's fire it would not greatly matter, for the real attack was to come from the left.

★★★★★★

And so to Act 3. The major is standing at the head of the column, watch in hand. Two minutes to the time and all well so far. There is no firing from the left, so the Indians must have got to their position without mishap, and that was perhaps the most important part of the work. The rest should be easy.

Again the watch is closed with a snap. "'A' Company," whispers the Major.

The Scots file through a big gap in the hedge and vanish like ghosts.

Now to follow the Indians.

A man from each of the six companies of the battalion has been chosen, and these six men draw lots for the post of honour. The six go forward, the lucky man leading. They are given five minutes' start, and the battalion follows by half companies as far as the ruined farm-house. If you had been standing within ten yards of them you would not have heard a sound, and they have to clamber over a great pile of dead bodies and horses.

The Six creep on in single file so swiftly, so silently that they might have been some weird night-beetles. Each can just catch the faint glimmer of steel from the man in front. There has been left by accident a lucky gap in the wire about five yards wide; that gap has sealed the fate of the trench-dwellers.

The leader raises his arm and the others drop flat on the ground. He creeps forward two more yards and then lies still. A head with a flat-topped cap on it appears for a moment above the parapet and looks round. Evidently satisfied it gives a little yawn and disappears.

The Gurkha heaves himself over the parapet and drops like a cat into the trench. But one foot stumbles over an unseen German lying asleep at the bottom.

"Keep your feet out of my—" a guttural voice begins to mutter when the sentence is cut short by a little choking gasp. The *kukri* has taken its first victim that night.

The sentry, some seven paces away, turns at the sound. All is silent again. He leans back against the trench-wall, eyes half closed.

For thirty seconds the Gurkha stands motionless. Then he begins to steal along under the dark edge of the parapet. Five yards, four, three—a quick spring, a gleam of steel, and without a moan a second body lies at the bottom of the trench.

The Gurkha seizes the dead man's rifle, puts his cap on the bayonet, and waves it twice over the top. The faint hoot of an owl answers the signal. The Five drop quietly over the parapet with the first half company not far behind them.

Then the deadly work begins. The Indians are thirty yards along the trench before the first rifle-shot rings out. But by that time fully thirty Germans are lying in curious, huddled attitudes to show where they have passed. The surprise has been complete.

Now the second half of the company and the third are pouring over the lip of the trench. It is becoming a ghastly massacre, for the whole of the northern end of the first trench is won almost without a struggle.

Almost simultaneously with the first shot a second is heard from the southern end where the Scottish battalion is attacking. There has been no attempt to kill the sentry, but the first line of the Scots, in open order, has got to within fifteen yards of the parapet, and there the wire has held them. It was the fling back of a cut strand which drew the sentry's fire. *Snip, snip* go the cutters, and the Scots begin to tear madly at the wire with bleeding fingers.

A wavering line of fire breaks out from the trench, but the Scots, with perfect discipline, carry on with their task. A star-light shoots into the air, hangs a second in a brilliant flare, and falls. A hoarse murmur and muffled shouting comes down the wind from the north.

"Aye, they'll be needing all the breath they've got the nicht," a Scot remarks grimly in an undertone.

The firing grows stronger, and some of the Scots are beginning to drop. The captain of this company takes a bullet in the shoulder as, bending low, he cuts swiftly at the wire. Now they have nearly got it underfoot. No possibility of further concealment, but the second line is close behind.

With two short whistle-blasts the captain calls to his men, and he is over the edge with a sergeant and three others close upon his heels. Crash goes his fist with the wire-cutters full in the face of a stout German, and the man goes down as the officer tugs out his revolver.

Now the Scots are coming fast over the parapet. Many of the second line clear the trench and make straight for the communication. More stars gleam into the air, and a searchlight, away on the right, begins to fizz into a beam. It sweeps round and faintly reveals a swarm of dark forms to the north, where the Gurkhas climb across the space to the second-line trench.

At the junction of the trenches there is the maddest confusion. Where there is barely room for two men to pass each other the floor becomes blocked with bodies, friend and foe. Men clamber over each other, thrusting and tearing and stabbing. Some from the rear trenches run up the communications to support their comrades only to become jammed fast by others running back. And through it all Scottish bayonet and Gurkha *kukri* work steadily on until the trenches and cuttings become a horrible, dripping shambles.

Even now the enemy to the rear cannot grasp what is happening, for the firing seems to have died down. Only there grows that curious noise of stifled shouting and hissing.

At last an enemy battery opens fire and the shells plump down into the broken village and the Wessex lines well behind the attacking battalions. This should mean prompt retaliation from our own guns, but the battery-commander guesses what is going on, and so he sits patiently waiting for the rocket signal. He has got his guns ready, carefully laid upon the area to the rear of that third trench, and the single word "Fire! "down the telephone will set his clockwork machinery in motion.

The Scots climbing into the second trench join hands with the Gurkhas, so perfect has been the timing of the attack and its execution; and the whole affair, since the first sentry was killed, has lasted eight or ten minutes—perhaps not so long.

The capture of the second line is not quite so simple a task, but it is quickly accomplished. For speed is everything now if they are to win the third. The attacking waves pour on, leaving supports to settle with the remaining defenders. The enemy guns have got some hint of the serious menace, and gradually drop the range, searching back.

Lieutenant Stewart, with the supports, had charge of the rocket signal, and now that the second line is passed he decides that the moment has come. Crouching into a corner of the trench he carefully places the rocket-stick, strikes a match, and lights the fuse. Is it odd that amid all this welter of killing his thoughts should fly back to that last evening at Henley Regatta, the hundred Chinese lanterns on punts and houseboats mirrored in the dark, peaceful Thames; the glitter of fireworks over Temple Island? Four little months ago!

With a fizz and a splutter the rocket soars aloft and breaks into a shower of purple stars. Before the last glowing ball has broken the guns of the battery crash off in "two rounds gun fire," followed by the steady, regular concussions from "battery fire, five seconds." Telephone wires are being trailed out to the rear as the attack develops, and a gunner officer comes plodding along with his two operators trying hard to weather the storm of enemy fire.

Nothing heartens the infantry more than the knowledge that their own guns are backing them up, and the first burst of shrapnel one hundred yards in front of them brings a hearty cheer from the Scots.

"Yon's verra excellent practice, I'm thinking," said one of them breathlessly as he jabbed his bayonet home. "Just a wee bit mountain mist to damp the de'ils."

But the shout told the enemy at last what was up against them. There was no mistaking a Scottish cheer. And from the other flank there came such a series of blood-curdling yells as must have sounded to the panic-stricken Germans like a pack of fiends loosed from hell. The trench leaped into flame from rifles and machine-guns. But it was too late. The Scots and Gurkhas hurled themselves straight for German throats, while behind the enemy the bursting shells told that more guns had come into play to cut off supports.

The third line trench was won, and the Scots set feverishly to work to consolidate their new position against the counter-attack which was certain to follow. But there we will leave them happily in possession, and hope for the best in the beating off of the attack which did indeed develop at dawn.

"Weel, Johnny," said a Scot to a black brother-in-arms, "ye'll have had a good nicht the noo!"

"Johnny" grinned broadly.

CHAPTER 16

The Eve of St. Crispin

O now, who will behold
The royal captain of this ruin'd band
Walking from watch to watch, from tent to tent!
For forth he goes and visits all his host,
Bids them good morrow with a modest smile,
And calls them brothers, friends, and countrymen.
Upon his royal face there is no note
How dread an army hath encirded him.

"Tomorrow is Saint Crispian" Just five hundred years before, and almost upon this very ground, had Harry of England met and broken, in fair shock of battle, the chivalry of France.

"What is this castle call'd that stands hard by?" says Shakespeare's Henry.

"They call it Agincourt," replied the French herald.

Then call we this the field of Agincourt,
Fought on the day of Crispin Crispianus.

On Crispin's Day, 1914, was England once again embattled against an enemy. Once again, with "lank-lean cheeks and war-worn coats," her sons faced overwhelming numbers. How would the issue fall?

The fighting all along the line had been gaining in intensity, and the Allies stood hard upon the defensive. A week earlier the Seventh Division and the Third Cavalry Division had come down from Ostend and were thrown forward to hold the approaches to Ypres until the First Corps could come to their support. On October 21 Sir John French, realising the increasing numbers of the enemy and that the original plans for an advance could no longer hold good, pointed out to his corps commanders that the utmost to be done "was to maintain our present very extended front and to hold fast our positions until French reinforcements could arrive from the south." On October 25 the violence of the German attack began steadily to set towards a climax.

So on this Crispin's Eve it is not unfitting that we too turn our backs for a short spell upon the firing line and see how the rest of the host fares at this tremendous crisis of history.

Here, then, are the H.Q. of a corps. They are housed in an imposing *château* standing in the midst of a beautiful park which marches with the ugly industrial land. It is a corps which has had to bear some of the hardest knocks of the war, and during the last few days it has been fighting for its very existence. We stand barely out of earshot of the guns; and yet you might very reasonably doubt whether there is a war on at all.

Turn in at a door labelled "Signals." In the hall are a couple of motor-bicycles being cleaned, and in some cane-bottomed chairs lounge three or four dispatch-riders scanning the pages of the *Tatler* and *Sketch*. A little farther on, through another door, you enter a room where a couple of officers lean over a big map covered with tiny flags and pinned to the dining-room table. Here you may find the position of every single unit in the corps, and from the clock on the mantelpiece you may take "Signals" time.

In the next room, obviously the salon of the house, are four typists clicking away at their machines. In one corner the A.Q.M.G. is giving some instructions to the O.C. of an ammunition park; in another a French officer is explaining something to the head of the A.G.'s department. You want to see the provost-marshal about some court-martial case? Certainly. Everyone is readily accessible if it is business, and as no one is there who is not on business you very quickly get through with your mission. I have no doubt the commander-in-chief would see you in a moment if you once dared to send your name in.

But the remarkable fact about it all is that there is never a suspicion of hurry or worry. You may see far more bustle in a solicitor's office in Birmingham. The only time I ever saw Corps H.Q. begin to get a little excited was on the day when General von Kluck was captured, together with four of his staff.

What? Didn't you know we captured von Kluck? Oh, you ought to hear about that—it is really rather amusing.

It began (so far as I was concerned) when my "batman" called me

313

in the early morning. Whenever my boots were dropped with a crash I knew something had happened: it was his method of drawing my attention to the fact that he was bursting with importance.

"Have you heard the news, sir?" he started. (Morgan was really a Welshman, but I never could reproduce Welsh.) I lay expectant.

"We've captured old von Kluck," said he triumphantly.

"What?" said I, really aroused this time. "One of our men?"

"Oh, no, sir. Some sentry out by Dickybush."

"Oh!" said I. "How did he do it?"

"Well, sir, the general was coming along in his big car with three other officers. He seems to have taken the wrong road and didn't know he was in our lines. He stopped to ask the sentry the way."

"Yes," I said, "go on." This was getting exciting.

"The sentry, sir, spotted at once they must be big bugs of Germans, pushed his bayonet in at the window and yelled 'hands up' loud enough to fetch out the N.C.O. of the guard. So old von Kluck was taken proper."

We were getting used to rumours by this time so I was rather sceptical about this one. But, sitting down to breakfast, in burst our impressionable junior subaltern.

"I say, you chaps; heard about von Kluck?"

Yes, we had heard something.

"They've got him," said Tiny Tim (he was six foot tall), dancing round the room; "captured him by Wipers. Old Kluck and a whole brigade of foot-sloggers" (*i.e.* infantry).

Two hours later a battalion of the Warwicks came along.

"Morning, Simpson!" I hailed the adjutant. "What's all this about von Kluck?"

"G'morning," replied Simpson. "Yes, it's quite true. One of our patrols rounded up the general and a brigade of the Prussian Guard."

This sounded genuine enough, though it seemed too good to be true. But Corps H.Q. would know. I had to call there in the afternoon, and it was at once obvious from the air of suppressed excitement that something had happened.

"Heard about von Kluck?" remarked a young signal officer.

"I've heard something," said I. "What's happened?"

"It seems that he and an escort of about half a dozen troopers rode straight into one of our patrols. Our chaps charged and old Kluck got knocked off his horse. The cavalry chaps say they stood round him in a ring to listen to his language. He must have been sick." That was

314

Signals' version and quite the most entertaining.

"I hear they've taken von Kluck prisoner," said I in tentative fashion to the D.A.Q.M.G.

"So they say," replied the D.A.Q.M.G. "I don't know much about it yet, as the news only came through this afternoon. I believe some sentry held him up in a motorcar with four of his staff."

That was Morgan's version, and it seemed the most likely.

The next day we heard that there wasn't a shred of truth in any one of the versions. Nor was it ever discovered how the rumour originated.

They say that the clubs at home are hotbeds for rumours, but they cannot hold a candle to "the front." The number of times the *Kaiser* had been assassinated, or had been bombed by our airmen! And the number of times the crown prince had been buried! Each fresh occasion would add a little zest to life, and we lived in hope until the rumour was discredited.

★★★★★★

It must have been about this time that Herr Lissauer, and the German public generally, provided the British Army in the field with perhaps the greatest joke a British Army has ever known—"The Hymn of Hate" and "*Gott strafe England*." And when dear old *Punch* published the portraits of a German family, with dog and sausage attachment, indulging in its morning "hate" the whole army rocked with laughter. German prisoners were invariably asked to "oblige" with the famous anthem, and if they did it nicely and snarled properly over the "hate" part of it, they were suitably rewarded with cigarettes. Yes, at least we owe Germany our gratitude for initiating that "Hate" campaign, for humour was a very precious thing in those days of stress.

À propos of German prisoners (of whom, naturally enough, we did not take a very large number at that period), it is interesting to notice that in two characteristics at least they were similar to prisoners taken two and a half years later. At a time when the British were fighting for their lives against vastly superior numbers both of men and guns, the Germans captured were generally either raw recruits or middle-aged men. They always used to hint broadly that the German moral was getting badly broken; that they were half-starved and sick of the war; that they recognised the hopelessness of their massed attacks; that the leadership by their regimental officers was bad; that the English gunnery was devilish and that their losses were terrible. These and other like facts. Of course, these yarns, with copies of captured letters and diaries, were faithfully reproduced in our home Press, and must, too, have had a certain deceiving effect upon our Intelligence Department. They certainly heartened our own men.

But if you compare these features with the condition of prisoners taken during the Allied offensive in 1917 you will find that they are almost identical. The moral is obvious. Then, as at any time during the succeeding three years, the enemy constantly created the impression that they were coming to the end of their manpower. They would put into the line recruits of eight weeks' training, or men drawn from their last reserves. One incident will illustrate this.

A certain eminent K.C., whose name at the outbreak of war was a household word (we will call him Robinson), was given a job on the lines of communication. A party of 100 German prisoners was brought down under a very small escort, and Robinson offered to take charge.

Taking over, he was marching the men along when a voice from the crowd hailed him by name. Robinson took no notice, and the voice hailed him again. Finally he turned towards the speaker, whom he seemed vaguely to remember.

"Yes," said Robinson, "what's the matter?"

"Don't you remember me?" asked the German.

"I'm sorry. I can't say I do," replied Robinson.

"Surely you remember last June the case of —— v. —— in the High Court?" And the German named a *cause célèbre* between two big firms which had once aroused much interest.

"I was the defendant," added the German, "and you were my counsel."

"Of course," said Robinson. "But what on earth are you doing here?"

The German, who was actually a leading Berlin banker, then told how he had returned to Berlin towards the end of July and had gone on with his ordinary business.

"Three days ago," said he, "I was at home with my wife when I received an order to join the next draft to my regiment. They gave me two hours' notice. We were sent straight up to the front line, and— well, here I am, and jolly glad too."

In face of incidents like that it is hardly to be wondered that our people imagined that Germany was feeling her losses. What would German G.H.Q. have thought had they taken prisoner a well-known London man who, four days before, was sitting in the manager's chair of the City branch of the London and Westminster Bank?

One is happy to pay tribute whenever possible to the courage in battle even of an enemy like Germany, and it should be recorded that those youngsters of 18 and 19 advanced to the attack almost always with the disciplined courage of veterans. There was at least one occasion when a company or more of those lads—part of an officers' training corps, I believe—attacked one of our trenches with such gallantry and *élan* that they thoroughly broke our defence and captured the trench.

And here is another interesting fact which arouses many conflicting thoughts. Over and over again half-written letters to their home folks have been found on German and Austrian soldiers, officers and men, couched in such terms as an educated Frenchman or Englishman might have used from the battlefield—and indeed often has used. Expressions about "fighting for the cause of liberty," "freeing the world from the oppressor," and so on.

One boy wrote to his mother:

> Do not grieve for me should I die, but rather be proud that I have fallen in so glorious a cause, to protect you and Bertha and to help free our Fatherland from the terror of the invader.

It is difficult to reconcile such thoughts with the knowledge that from childhood German men and women have been taught to believe in the omnipotence of Germany as the future Over-Lord of the nations: that any means to that end are legitimate.

A well-known German author in 1897 wrote:[1]

> We are indubitably the most martial nation in the world. We are the most gifted of nations in all the domains of science and art. We are the best colonists, the best sailors, and even the best traders. And yet we have not up to now secured our due share in the heritage of the world. . . . That the German Empire is not the end but the beginning of our national development is an obvious truth.

But a digression on the subject hardly falls within the scheme of this volume, so we will not pursue it. One may, however, suggest that when Germany prates about the war being one of pure defence for her she probably desires to convey that any war for her would be defensive. For Germany asserts that she is ringed round by enemies, and,

---

1. *Die Weltstellung des Deutchtums*, by Fritz Bley.

confident that her country will be attacked, that it is quite legitimate that she should get in the first blow. But then, all Germany's statements form such a maze of lies and contradictions that one really cannot bother about them.

★★★★★★

There are so many features of interest "at the back of the front" that it is rather difficult to decide at which to pause. Many of these features have long since become familiar to the people at home through books and pictures, but at that time they were all novelties to us out there and a constant source of surprise and, one may add, generally of gratification.

There were, for instance, the hot baths and "wash and brush up" arrangements for men coming out of the trenches. Very primitive they were at first, but the system was quickly improved and extended. Then there were the weird goat-skins by way of winter coats. The smell was somewhat penetrating, but they were very useful, and the men came to regard it as a kind of fancy-dress ball. Amateur George Robeys appeared in every unit, and you constantly met a counterpart of that mirth-provoker waving a great club and performing the "Prehistoric Man" act, wherein He of the Knotted-Knees breaks bread with She of the Auburn Locks and is slain for his temerity by He of the Fearsome Face.

The motto which G.H.Q. set themselves to follow was this. "*If a unit wants anything, and money can buy it and transport can bring it, then it shall be procured.*" And this actually meant *anything*, whether wargear or articles for increased comfort. I do not say that these things were procured at once, for that was well-nigh impossible. You at home will recall the stress of that first winter when the home organisation must have been topsy-turvy. But G.H.Q. recognised the need of doing every imaginable thing which could contribute to the health and well-being of the men, and set to work with that end in view.

Others more worthily have paid tribute to this work of the commander-in-chief and his quartermaster-general, but if "twenty years a soldier" may add his little tribute I can only say that the care and solicitude evinced by them, and the apparent miracles which they wrought, seemed to the old stagers like some wonderful dream. It was a ghastly winter that first one at the front, but the men stuck it in the knowledge that everything that could be done for their comfort was being done.

And generous friends at home can never, never guess what their loving parcels of comforts meant to officers and men. A little tin of chocolate or peppermints, with half a dozen penny packets of cigarettes, *and* a tiny note enclosed—you were at once a king among men.

Upon one occasion only did I hear an expression of doubtful gratitude from the recipient of a parcel. And as it was the only occasion you shall hear how it came about, for there is a little moral attached.

Private Smithson rejoiced in the gift of two pairs of beautiful thick, soft, woolly socks. They formed part of a parcel from some unknown lady, and had been distributed by the C.O. There was just time to put on a pair before parade. From parade the battalion went off on a route march by way of exercise.

Before a quarter of a mile had been covered Smithson felt something irritating and uncomfortable in his boot. As the march went on his discomfort increased and his foot began to throb and ache. But he stuck to it like a Trojan.

At last, after several hours, Smithson got back to billets. He tore off his boot. No, it was the sock. Off came the sock, revealing a great blister on his toe. In the sock was something hard. He put his hand in and drew out a piece of crumpled paper. Smoothing it out he read the words, "With love from Amy."

You'll remember, Amy, next time to pin your little message outside, won't you? Then it will be all right.

★★★★★★

The question of recreation for the men in the form of entertainments, games and such like had hardly then been seriously considered. A little later the subject was recognised as being of the very first importance. In every way possible the men must be relieved from the terrific strain when not actually in the firing-line; their spirits must be kept up and so their health maintained.

In an earlier chapter mention was made of Captain Eldridge and his little concert at the Marne. During the winter this officer was most energetic in giving these entertainments whenever chance offered, and since he was the pioneer and most popular with the men, any record of this feature of life "at the front" would be incomplete without some mention of his work. Here is an extract from one of his letters which appeared in the *Times*:

> Last Saturday I had a specially large and attentive audience for my weekly *causerie* to the men. I had only a smallish barn available,

and about 60 or 70 men could not get anywhere near. I gave, first, a general synopsis of events by land and sea, with some account of the Russian Army, the difference in temperament, etc., between their men and the enemy. Then a couple of *Punch* articles, which were much enjoyed; lastly, an attempted forecast of the future, the spirit of youth, and of the nation, and wound up by reciting the 'St. Crispin' speech from *Henry V*. I give another chat tonight— probably the last possible for some little time. I hope to give some recitals of Dickens's *Christmas Carol* just before Christmas—if the enemy will graciously permit.

It may be added that Eldridge was able to give a few recitals of the *Carol* that Christmas, and that they were very deeply appreciated.

À propos of concerts and music, a word on "Tipperary" is not out of place. One is always loath to destroy a popular superstition, but that now world-famous tune was not nearly so much sung in France in those early days as people seem to imagine. Personally, it was not until the middle of December that I heard the song at all, and for the first time. Of course, it was sung a good deal, but so were several others, and there was not much to choose between them in popularity, although "Tipperary" was undoubtedly the best tune.

But since then, mainly through popular sentiment, "Tipperary" came to be recognised as the marching song of the "Contemptibles." It never was that, but it has become something else. It seems now almost on a par with the National Anthems of the Allies. For it is often sung at the end of a concert with "God Save the King," and very frequently the men rise to their feet for the singing of it. Several times I have seen it noted in the Press that "Tipperary" is dead. That is incorrect. It has become canonised, if one may use the term, by reason of its association with the men of the Old Army, and so is sung on special occasions only.

★★★★★★

At that time I do not think that the activities of the Y.M.C.A. had yet reached "the front." I seem to remember the first of their tents or huts arriving about the end of December. Where a volume might well be devoted to praise of this organisation's work it is impossible to convey in a few lines how inestimable a boon to the men this work has been. One may say, I think, that the Y.M.C.A. has proved itself to be one of the most valuable allies a British Army in the field has ever had.

For many years I have seen something of the activities of the

Y.M.C.A. in all parts of the world, but it is the war which has brought the Society to the fulfilment of the best ideals. In September, 1914, the Y.M.C.A. found itself. At the beginning there was more than a hint of the missionary and text element, but this was speedily cut out, and the men soon came to realise that here indeed was a splendid friend. All welcome and no questions asked! A social club with unlimited membership, no entrance fee nor subscription, and with premises wherever they are wanted. The only visitors to whom the Y.M.C.A. very regretfully cannot refuse admittance are German shells. Here's wishing them (the Y.M.C.A., not the shells) all the best!

★★★★★★

And what of the officers? They needed recreation if anyone did, and there was very little for them outside an occasional game of soccer with the men. As a matter of fact, officers are never off duty; at least, they never were during the first winter. But when you have British troops on active service you may be certain that the officers will find something in the way of sport. Did not the Iron Duke have a pack of hounds with him out in Spain? An admirable precedent!

Some cheery souls went out partridge shooting near Hazebrouck. Birds were fairly plentiful and a good many brace found their way to officers' messes. But more than one officer complained that it was rather dull when he couldn't hear the report of his own gun owing to the heavy firing going on.

By the way, it is curious how little affected is bird life in and about the front lines. One would have imagined the little creatures scared to death by the detonations. And yet, in the spring and early summer, infantry advancing over "No man's land" or through woods would often disturb nesting birds. Or perhaps from beneath their very feet a skylark would soar aloft carolling her eternal song of hope.

In a singularly beautiful poem called *The Rainbow* one of our soldier poets [2] has recorded an impression of this. I venture to reproduce the *stanza*:

From death that hurtles by
I crouch in the trench day-long,
But up to a cloudless sky
From the ground where our dead men lie

---

2. Leslie Coulson, a sergeant in the 2nd London Regt. Royal Fusiliers. He was killed in action at Lesboeufs, October, 1916. A sweet and gentle spirit, totally unfitted for war, but a man whose lion-hearted courage and pride of race carried him through. A little volume of his poems is published by Erskine Macdonald.

A brown lark soars in song.
Through the tortured air,
Rent by the shrapnel's flare,
Over the troubleless dead he carols his fill,
And I thank the gods that the birds are beautiful still.

To return to the officers and recreation. There was one famous occasion (this was in 1915) when a big field turned out for a cross-country paper-chase after the *Kaiser*. At least it wasn't really the *Kaiser*, but an officer made up and dressed to look like him. It was a great day when veteran general officers and junior subalterns, mounted on all sorts and conditions of hacks and hunters, careered in mad pursuit after the All-Highest. The "War Lord" laughed so much that he rolled off his horse and so was captured; but the chase had been long and stern before that auspicious ending had been reached. But it was the Seventh Division which hit upon the most exciting and the most productive kind of sport. This was in Belgium on their way down to Ypres.

A certain number of armoured motor-cars were available, and parties were made up to go Hun hunting. A "book" would invariably be made upon the possibilities of the day's "bag," and the parties would sally forth armed to the teeth in these forerunners of the famous "Tanks." Different routes were selected, and the cars were headed straight for the German lines. The game usually consisted of adventurous Uhlans, cavalry patrols on outlying pickets, and it was a very poor day when the cars would not return with German helmets, lances and rifles dangling all over them like scalps to a Red Indian's girdle. The Belgians also were particularly clever at the sport.

There are so many other features behind the lines about which it would be pleasant to chat. But there is sterner work in hand and we must hasten to it. You should, then, picture the British troops on this Eve of St. Crispian troubling but little about the so dread army which would enround them. They are weary, very weary, but calm and confident. There is little or no hint at the various H.Q.'s of the stress of the fighting, and the services of organisation are working admirably in keeping up the supply of food, clothing and ammunition.

But the storm hour by hour grows in intensity, and the line of khaki is being worn very thin. And even the commander-in-chief, hardened though he is, looks towards the south and hopes French relief may not be too late.

The Roll of the Third Cavalry and Seventh Infantry Divisions

General Officer Commanding—Maj.-Gen. Sir H. Rawlinson.

THIRD CAVALRY DIVISION

General Officer Commanding—Maj.-Gen. the Hon. Julian Byng.

6TH BRIGADE

Brigade Commander—Brigadier-General E. Makins.

3rd Dragoon Guards [1]   1st Dragoons (The Royals)

10th Hussars

7TH BRIGADE

Brigade Commander—Brig.-General C. T. McM. Kavanagh.

1st Life Guards   2nd Life Guards

Royal Horse Guards (The Blues)

Royal Horse Artillery

Batteries "C" and "K"

Royal Engineers

3rd Field Squadron

SEVENTH INFANTRY DIVISION

General Officer Commanding—Major-General T. Capper.

20TH INFANTRY BRIGADE

Brigade Commander—Brig.-General H. G. Ruggles-Brise.

1st Batt. Grenadier Guards   2nd Batt. the Border Regt.

2nd Batt. Scots Guards   2nd Batt. Gordon Highlanders

21ST INFANTRY BRIGADE

Brigade Commander—Brigadier-General H. E. Watts.

2nd Batt. Bedfordshire Regt.   2nd Batt. Royal Scots Fusiliers

2nd Batt. Yorkshire Regt.   2nd Batt. Wiltshire Regt.

22ND INFANTRY BRIGADE

---

1. Joined division early in November.

323

Brigade Commander—Brigadier-General S. T. B. Lawford.

2nd Batt. The Queen's   1st Batt. R. Welsh Fusiliers

2nd Batt. Warwickshire Regt. 1st Batt. South Staffordshire
Regt

Cavalry (attached)

The Northumberland Yeomanry (Hussars)

Royal Artillery

R. H. A.—Batteries "F" and "T."

R.F.A.—Batteries 104, 105, 106 (XXII. Brigade), 12, 35, 58 (XXXV. Brigade).

R.G.A.—Heavy Batteries 111, 112.

Royal Engineers

54th and 55th Field Companies.

CHAPTER 17

The Holding of the Gate

West. *O that we now had here*
But one ten thousand of those men in England
That do no work today!
K. Hen. *What's he that wishes so?*
My cousin Westmoreland?—No, my fair cousin:
If we are mark'd to die, we are enow
To do our country loss; and if to live,
The fewer men the greater share of honour.

It has been said that no single infantry division of the British Army has ever been composed of a more splendid fighting personnel than was the Seventh when it landed in Belgium.

For the benefit of the uninitiated I may here explain that when a British battalion of the Line is mobilised from its peace footing to war strength a considerable number of reservists are recalled to the colours to make it up to that strength. For certain reasons, partly because the battalions had been drawn from duty abroad, it was necessary or it was difficult to add these reservists to the strength of the Seventh Division. Thus the division took the field with comparatively few additions to its ordinary strength.

To emphasise the importance of this (although there was possibly a slight diminution from full war strength) I cannot do better than quote a remark once made to me by a distinguished military authority.

The average British Line Regiment (or Battalion), has, on its Peace establishment, no superior in the world as a righting force. When you add its Reserve and bring it to War strength you detract perhaps 25 *per cent*, or more from its value.

It may, perhaps, be compared to a crack polo team. The players, both individually and in combination, work up to a fine point of perfection, and any alteration in the team by putting in another man as a substitute is bound to affect that combination. The analogy is not very sound, but it may suggest the meaning of that remark.

If, then, we accept this *dictum*—and the facts certainly upheld it in this case—it is a little easier to understand how it came about that this division should have added so imperishable a lustre to British Arms.

The 7th Infantry Division and the 3rd Cavalry Division landed in Belgium on October 7. On the previous day the Belgian Army had begun to withdraw from Antwerp, and with it was that Naval Division of ours which had been hurriedly equipped and sent over to try to save the city. On October 9 Antwerp lay open to the Germans. It became the task of the division to act as rearguard and cover the retirement of the Belgians.

Once again, then, just as at Mons, a British force disembarked, and within three or four days found itself involved in a general retirement before overwhelming numbers. At Mons the British had to go because the French did; at Antwerp they had to save the Belgians.

The first three or four days of such conditions are always difficult for the men; they have to get acclimatised, as it were. So at the very beginning discipline was put to the test by continuous marching and counter-marching, for which the men could see no object. Backwards and forwards they went between Bruges and Ostend, and the pave roads caused considerable suffering. No one really knew what was happening, and, naturally enough, there was a certain amount of "grousing."

The confusion after Mons was sufficiently trying, but it was nothing to the chaos which reigned after the fall of Antwerp. If you can picture Liverpool suddenly abandoned of all its great population, the people crowding into the shipping in the harbour or streaming out across the countryside with such few possessions as they could carry; if you then mingle with these folk a tired, battered Belgian Army of all arms, you will get some idea of the scenes which the 7th Division witnessed. Upon less seasoned troops the effect might well have been dispiriting.

The Belgians gave our men that generous welcome which we have come to know so well, and heaped such little gifts upon them as they could. There were the usual amusing comments from the bystanders as the troops swung down the roads. The Gordon Highlanders, for instance, were seriously pointed out as "the wives of the English soldiers," and the wrath of the Jocks when they heard it was well worth seeing—from a respectful distance.

With the fall of Antwerp and the retirement of the Belgian Army through Ghent towards the coast the orders for the 7th Division were to conform to the movements of the 3rd Corps, which was to the south of Ypres. At this time there was hardly any idea that the enemy were developing an attack upon that city.

The seven days which elapsed between the landing and the arrival at Ypres were most exhausting ones. There was not a great deal of fighting, but it was sufficient to react upon the nerves of men who were marching night and day without proper rest. In fact, towards the end of the week the infantry were in much the same condition as their comrades had been after Le Cateau in August. [1] And oh, those *pavé* roads!

If you look at the map shown earlier you will see a little town called Menin about 12 miles east of Ypres. This formed a useful tactical point for the enemy, and Sir John French decided that a big effort should be made to occupy it. The 7th Division and cavalry were accordingly ordered to advance through Ypres and make the attempt upon the morning of the 18th October.

Extending out into a line of some twenty miles or more, which ran in a curve from Langemarck on the north to Zandvoorde on the south, the infantry and cavalry advanced straight towards an enemy some seven times their own strength.

The cavalry pushed ahead out on the left flank, and soon after 9.0 a.m. their outposts encountered the first skirmishing patrols of the enemy. As usual our men took the initiative and charged home. But this time the odds were too heavy, even with our main bodies coming up in support, and the order was given to retire.

In those days there was still something left of the glamour of war; still a little of the pomp and circumstance remaining to the mounted troops. And in all mounted work I doubt whether there is any movement which is more thrilling, more inspiring, than when a horse battery comes into action in the open. Most people, I suppose, would give the palm to a *pukka* cavalry charge, with men and horses going "all out." And certainly such a charge must always swing the excitement of the onlooker up to fever heat. But ask a cavalry man what he thinks about the work of a Horse Gunner Troop on an occasion like

1. *The Retreat from Mons.*

that of Moorslede or Ledeghem on this morning of October 18.

You picture the cavalry gradually falling back fighting a series of little rearguard actions against ever-increasing numbers of enemy cavalry. You see here a troop dismounted lining a hedgerow, there a squadron dashing out from cover of some farm buildings to cut off a too adventurous enemy patrol. Always retiring but contesting, and with fine effect, every yard of the ground. [2]

It was "K" Battery which helped to hold the ground near Moorslede, and "C" Battery which helped the 6th Cavalry Brigade to capture Ledeghem. As the designating letters have already been given we will allow them to stand here, otherwise one purposely refrains, so far as possible, from distinguishing units where all did such wonderful work.

The battery was not so spick and span in appearance as it had been ten days before. The mud and rain of Flanders do not tend to improve the look of steel and leatherwork, nor were the horses any the better for the ceaseless trekking about the country. But the rust remained on the surface (if you take my meaning); it certainly had not penetrated into the machinery.

From an early hour that morning the battery had been manoeuvring over the very unpleasant countryside, and as breakfast had been a very trivial meal no one was in the best of tempers. Now there was a brief halt under cover, with the men dismounted, while the battery commander was out half a mile ahead discussing details with the officer commanding the brigade.

Events move very swiftly where cavalry are concerned, and the brigade commander, with a map spread out across his knees, had barely indicated the spot whence the latest report had reached him when one of his staff cantered up.

"They're pushing us back rather fast, sir," he said, "and there's only Captain ———'s squadron on the line by Zeeden farm."

The brigade commander made a rapid calculation and gave a curt order to the staff officer. Then, turning to the battery commander:

"We shall want you in a few minutes, Cranshawe," he said. "There's your direction, will you select your position, please?"

---

2. "Considering the amount of opposition encountered against largely superior numbers," so wrote the G.O.C. of the 3rd Cavalry Division, "our casualties were small, whilst there is no doubt that the enemy suffered very severely at our hands. This smallness was largely due to the skilful manner in which each brigade was withdrawn."

"Right, sir." The battery commander saluted, waved a signal to his sergeant-major and horse-holder and galloped off.

There is nothing in military tactics which calls for swifter and surer decision than the manoeuvre and "action" of a horse battery. (Don't forget that a horse battery is really a cavalry unit.) In this respect it is not unlike the work of a T.B.D. commander in a "general action" at sea.

The battery commander took a rapid survey of the line of enemy approach, noted the points where his own cavalry were ready to work in support and attack, and quickly made up his mind on the best position for his guns. The sergeant-major had by this time got back to the battery and reported to the officer left in command.

"Get mounted!" the command rang out.

The men heaved themselves into their saddles, and the Nos. 1 moved sharply round their teams and vehicles to see that all was in order. The officer acting as battery leader cantered ahead towards the major.

"All right, Matheson, I'll take the battery," said the major, without lowering his field-glasses. "Are you ready?"

"Yes, sir. Battery column, head towards the road," replied the subaltern.

"Right. You can get back," said the major. "We're going to support ——'s squadron directly they quit that farm," he added, indicating some scattered buildings about three-quarters of a mile away.

With a salute the subaltern wheeled his horse and started back. For another couple of minutes the major remained, carefully noting the movements of the enemy cavalry concentrating towards the farm. Then a glance toward his battery, and a swift calculation how many minutes it would take to bring it into action; then another look at the farm, and, slipping his glasses back into the case, he was off after his subaltern.

A couple of signals and the battery was on the move at the trot. Another, and the head of the column changed direction. As it did so there came just that little touch of comedy which often means so much to men in the field; something to spin the current of thought into another direction.

Alongside the battery came racing one of the farm dogs with a great piece of meat in his jaws; close at his heels snapped a friend of his, and labouring heavily behind there floundered an old woman brandishing a pitchfork and screaming out horrid oaths.

It was the merest trifle of comedy, but the contrast between that episode and the stern business in hand was certainly very ludicrous. It sent the spirits of the men up a hundred *per cent.*

Now the battery commander has his battery moving fast, exactly parallel to the position he is going to take up, and happily sheltered from enemy observation by a slight rise in the ground. A couple more signals and the sections swing into line at the canter.

Into line they swing, intervals and alignment as perfect as at a review in the Long Valley. Away up the incline and the canter is really a gallop. *Bump, crash, bump* over the ragged ground thunder the guns. No whip to the teams—*they* know well what is expected of them—but here and there a tap on the shoulder of the off horse to steady him and keep the direction exact.

Up the rise they thunder. Now they are at the top, the level. Perfect line, perfect intervals as always, yet every team is stretched out in mad career. How will they ever pull up! you exclaim. Steady! steady all! Watch the battery commander galloping ahead.

He has timed the movement to a quarter of a minute. The enemy cavalry converging is close upon the farm which our squadron (what is left of it) is holding. Over his left shoulder he catches just a glimpse of a relieving troop or so of ours already on the move.

Steady! All eyes on the battery commander. Ah! there it is. Just the little tightening of the bit rein, the least check of the gallop. Almost imperceptible, but every man has noted it.

Just three seconds later. A short, shrill whistle: arm straight above head: arm straight down to ground.

Halt! Action front!

A matter of seconds again, and every man (save the drivers) is off his horse. There is no "halt:" it seems, indeed, no more than a check of the pace. Yet every man is down. The battery commander has in some miraculous way got to the flank of the battery. The gun-trails are somehow got clear of the limbers. Away to the rear race the gun-teams, round swing the guns, and the first two ranging shells are bursting this side and that of the German cavalry before ever you have counted to twenty.

★★★★★★

The orders for the cavalry division on that morning of the 18th were to cover the left flank of the 7th Division in its projected attack against Menin. The enemy strength was too great, and thus both infantry and cavalry were thrown upon the defensive. It was a repetition of what was happening to the Second Corps down by La Bassée.

On the 19th the First Corps had finished detraining at St. Omer and was being brought forward as rapidly as possible. But in the meantime the 7th Division and the cavalry had to hold the ground. On the 21st these two divisions found themselves facing an overwhelming attack.

Before Sir Douglas Haig's Corps comes up let me suggest very briefly the conditions under which the 7th Division was working.

First of all, remember it was a new division which did not possess the experience won from the Aisne defences: they did not yet know the paralysing effect of the German artillery nor what German massed infantry attacks were like.

It was open country, almost entirely flat, but broken by odd houses, hamlets and woods. The "gate" to be held had no natural advantages to help the defenders. The entrenchments were of the most hurried character, shallow gutters cut in the soil and the earth banked up.

In guns as in men our artillery was hopelessly outclassed, not indeed in personnel, but in numbers and weight of metal. You will have noted from the Roll shown that the division had not a single 4.5 (howitzer) battery. Nor was there any H.E. shell.

And of that little Force a full third was not infantry but cavalry; men who in training have nothing to do with trench work. And such trench work! But at Ypres they were all in the line, every man of them: 1st and 2nd Life Guards, the Royal Horse Guards (the Blues)—how often have you seen them as Sovereign's Escort clattering down Whitehall, watched the Guard changed at 11 o'clock? Fine stay-at-home soldiers you thought them, perhaps; and yet on the Regimental Colour you will find emblazoned "Dettingen," "Waterloo," "Peninsula," "Tel-el-Kebir." Yes, they were all there in those blood-soaked trenches round Ypres, holding grimly on with their comrades of the Foot Guards. With them, too, fought the Northumberland Yeomanry, the first Territorial regiment to go into action; and those two batteries of the Horse Gunners.

Such was the line. What was it?—one man to every seven yards? It cannot have been more. And in places where there was no difference between front and rear each alternate man had to face about to fire. Supports and reserves there were none.

"Hold on for all you are worth!" came the message from Sir John French when they turned at bay. "Hold on!"

They held on.

★★★★★★

331

Upon the arrival of the First Corps there rested with Sir John French a grave decision. Should he strengthen his long thin line already well-nigh breaking, or should he try to stem the new German advance which was developing to the north of the 7th Division?

With fine courage he made his decision and sent the First Corps to prolong the line to the north; to share equally with their comrades of the 7th Division the undying glory of that tremendous struggle against and victory over such mighty odds—odds of perhaps six or seven to one.

How can one tell the tale! A little impression sketched in with wavering lines is all that one may expect to give. And yet one dares to hope that even so crude a picture may contain elements to stir the blood and awaken a passionate gratitude to the men who stood for England's bulwark through those drear October days and nights.

It seemed that the men might almost as well have been lying in the open for all the cover the trenches afforded. It was the deadly German gunnery with the H.E. shell which worked the havoc. To describe it is impossible. Hour after hour and day after day without a pause the shells poured down with perfect accuracy, straight into the trenches, in front of them and behind them. On the first day one battalion of the 7th alone lost 10 officers and 200 men. How a single man of it remained alive is a mystery. And so exhausted were officers and men at the very beginning of that awful period that some would sleep through the hideous din as calmly as though they were at home. To awaken and grasp once again with almost nerveless fingers the rifle which still lay against the shoulder, or to pass unconsciously into the last quiet sleep of all.

"Hold on!" And something of a cheer ran down the line as the message was passed. Men glanced hopefully over their shoulders; then with a little sigh turned once more to their work.

Again and again the Germans broke into the defence. Sometimes they would capture a trench; often they would hesitate on the very edge and fall back.

On the 24th (one takes incidents at random) the Wiltshires were cut off and surrounded. For three hours and more they went on fighting. Some were captured, many more fell where they stood. Ringed round, ammunition nearly gone, they charged into the enemy and back again with bayonet and clubbed rifle. And almost at their last gasp a handful of the Worcester and Highland Light Infantry got to them and cut them out.

Another Homeric fight was that of the Royal Scots Fusiliers. Like the other battalions, they had gone into action more than 1,000 strong, and, with them, the numbers had gradually ebbed lower and lower. The end came when this remnant too was cut off. Message after message was sent to them to retire, but the message never arrived. No relief was near; nothing could be done for them. They just fought on and died. A fight to the finish. And when at last the enemy wave curled sullenly back and the battalion roll was called, seventy men and a second lieutenant answered to their names.

Now and again the German gunners lifted their range a trifle, and hard behind the shells came a blue-grey mass of infantry. Steadily is on parade they advanced shoulder to shoulder, rank upon rank. Then once more British musketry would take its toll and German dead would pile up before the trench which might be reached but not won.

In front of one County battalion ran a cutting considerably wider than the average trench and some hundred yards long. Time after time the German infantry advanced over this until soon the cutting was filled level to the ground with dead, so that the enemy could march straight over their fallen comrades.

There was a subaltern of the Scots Fusiliers who was told off to stop a flank attack. He took twenty men and posted them at intervals through a wood. With this he suddenly discovered that he was quite close to a couple of German machine-guns. So he took his rifle and, ensconcing himself behind a tree, set to work upon the gun detachments. In a minute or so he had picked off every man. More men were sent up, and these, too, he picked off. And so it went on until the officer, firing 150 rounds, had shot no fewer than 70 Germans. I believe this subaltern received the D.S.O. for his exploit.

But all this time, if the German losses were heavy, our own casualties were mounting up. Hardly one of the original trenches remained, and the men took what shelter they could in the great holes dug by the German shells. Steadily, as the hours passed, were our numbers brought lower and lower; and still the little remnant stuck to it.

Here is a battalion of the Royal Welsh Fusiliers; 1,000 odd strong they went into action. Within three days they had lost 24 officers and over 700 men. And still they fought on and held the line. And so it was with nearly every unit.

"Hold on like hell!" Again and again came the message. But the hours passed and exhausted troops ceased to care what happened. It became a joke—a grim, ghastly joke.

And yet General Joffre to the south was working hard for his Allies. On the 24th, so he had told our commander-in-chief, the 9th French Corps would be thrown into the fight to the north of Sir Douglas Haig's command. And true to promise the French arrived. But that was to the north, and the British had still to bear the brunt of the offensive upon Ypres.

★★★★★★

Once again one must needs record with regret the methods of the Hun soldiery. Ask the Worcesters if they recall that day when they came across some score of our wounded lying on the ground all with their throats cut. Ask the Royal Fusiliers if they remember retaking a certain trench and finding in it another score of our lads who had been wounded and who also had had their throats cut through. Ask other battalions if they remember October 29 and a certain German attack, when the Huns advanced, stabbing with the bayonet our wounded men as they lay before them on the ground. Oh, yes, the Germans are courageous enough with the bayonet at moments like that!

A small patrol of ours went out one day. They did their job, and, incidentally, took one German prisoner.

"Hallo!" said the company officer on their return; "did you only get one Boche?"

"Yes, sir," said the N.C.O.; "and we had the very devil of a job to get *him* past the Blankshires."

The Blankshires, you see, are another regiment which will remember.

Down on the right flank the enemy have burst through. Supports? There is some cavalry of ours up on the left flank. That is all that can be done. So the cavalry brigades trek down south from their hard-held position to throw themselves into the gap. And ever the ranks are thinned, while the casualty clearing stations in Ypres and the villages near, where the R.A.M.C. work, splashed with blood from head to foot, look like horrible slaughter-houses.

How supplies of food and ammunition were got up to the firing line one cannot tell, for night brought no respite from the pitiless hail of shell. It was a drink of water when you could get it, and some chocolate and biscuit if you were lucky.

But the line still held.

★★★★★★

It is well that stories of individual deeds of gallantry should be recorded when possible that they may serve for an inspiration to the men who come after, although where every man wrought so famously one hesitates to mention names. Yet no one, I think, will grudge a "mention" to E. J. Kennedy, a *padre* who was army chaplain to the 20th Brigade of the 7th Division. The Bishop of Winchester has spoken of him as "simple, manly, open-hearted towards man and devout towards God. His commanding stature and fine physical manhood gave him advantages which his fine character and genial nature used, by God's grace, to the best effect." He was universally loved, and died in harness a year later through overstrain of war work.

The situation near Zandvoorde, where the cavalry were, became one day more critical than ever. Kennedy had just reached the village and was eating some breakfast when the O.C. the brigade came along.

"Hallo, *padre*, good morning! The very man I want if you will help us," said the C.O.

"Yes," said Kennedy. "What is it?"

"We're in an awful hole out there," the C.O. went on, "and the Germans may break through at any moment. We must let Divisional H.Q. know how things are and so divert the ambulances coming out from Ypres. The wires are all cut. Will you volunteer? It's a risky job, but I've no one else to send."

"Write your message," said Kennedy, "and give me a minute or two to get these big boots off or I shall get hooked up in the stirrups."

Kennedy dived into his pack and sat down on a doorstep to change. A shell dropped in the street seven yards away, burst, and spattered the doorway with shrapnel bullets. By a miracle Kennedy was untouched.

"If that's a specimen I'm in for a lively time," laughed Kennedy as he swung into the saddle. A grip of the hand and he was off.

The road lay over the now famous Hill 60. Three miles of it, and under heavy fire nearly all the way. Kennedy bent low to the pommel and galloped. Shells were falling in every direction, but his splendid animal carried him along gamely, heedless of the bursts save for a momentary quiver of the flanks.

On they galloped through the storm—one mile—two miles—and the nerve-racking ordeal began to tell on horse and rider. Three miles! In amongst a crowd of panic-stricken refugees—so they staggered into Ypres and collapsed at the very door of H.Q.

"And all I remember is, friends flocking round As I sat with his head 'twixt my knees on the ground."

The message was delivered and the situation was saved. The *padre* they carried into the house, where he dropped into a heavy sleep, awaking fit and well six hours later.

★★★★★★

And now this awful work was nearing the climax, for the enemy had still to make their supreme effort. Yet, in God's name, what more was there that they could do?

More than half of the 7th Division had been wiped out already. The First Corps were in little better plight. One man to every seven yards of front, was it not? That was less than a week ago. Now it was one man to every twenty yards, at least down part of the line. There they lay in their pitiful cover, naked to the storm, rifles still to shoulder, blinded and deafened, in a stupor of utter exhaustion. Officers, staggering along the line, tried to awaken them. It seemed useless. A Force mightier than the Germans had supervened.

But the cavalry and infantry still held on.

CHAPTER 18

The Last Stand of the Old Army

K. Hen. *O God of battles! steel my soldiers' hearts;*
Possess them not with fear; take from them now
The sense of reckoning, if the opposed numbers
Pluck their hearts from them!

On this day of St. Crispin (October 25) the salient directly to the east of Ypres was held by the First Corps, the 7th Division and the Cavalry Division. To the south came Allenby's cavalry and then the Third Corps. To the north of Ypres was the Ninth French Corps and then French Territorials and Belgians up to the coast.

From the previous chapter you have, I hope, gained some impression of the condition of the British Force. All that I have said about the heavy losses of the 7th Division came gradually to apply to Sir Douglas Haig's corps. For the week following upon their arrival from the Aisne they, too, had to suffer as their comrades had done. And when, at last, the climax was reached on October 31st, the First Corps found itself fighting in a condition no whit better than that of the 7th Division.

Whatever may be said of the heroism of the French and Belgians to the north—and that fine Ypres salient that the Germans directed their mightiest efforts.

And now at the very moment when Germany was about to hurl the flower of her army against the meagre British line, when the enemy purposed to turn every available gun of an overwhelming strength upon the handful of men who dared to oppose his will, there happened an event as dramatic and momentous, surely, as any in the war.

To realise the significance of it you must first bear carefully in mind all that your imagination can picture of this desperate battle against odds; and then understand that a field battery of six guns, firing on an average 700 shells per day, was even then firing all too little for the needs of the moment.

Then learn that on this day the order was issued that every field gun in the Force must be placed on a *daily allowance of ten shells only!* In other words, a battery was allowed each day 60 shells to fire when 700 was not sufficient.

What the gunners said and what the infantry thought I leave you to guess. But I would also have you think of the high moral courage of the commander-in-chief who, upon the urgent representation of the Q.M.G. (Sir William Robertson), dared to issue such an order at one of the most critical moments of the world's history.

To put the matter very briefly, there were no more shells for the howitzers and eighteen-pounders in France, and the reserve at home was practically exhausted. It is probably no exaggeration to say that had we gone on firing at the old rate for another fortnight we should have had to "cease fire" altogether.

The courage of Sir John French's decision (if I may venture the comment) seems on a par with the one already noted when he dared to extend his line still farther north instead of supporting the battered 7th Division. By issuing the order about the shells he was able to build up at least something of a reserve to be used when any battery was faced with some supreme crisis. Though the price was very, very heavy, the situation was saved. Had he not dared to pay the price and to place once again his perfect trust in his indomitable infantry and cavalry, who shall say what the end might have been?

And it is well that the world should hear of this, for surely it throws another and a still stronger light upon the heroism of the first Seven Divisions during those fateful days. And will the German Staff ever dare to tell the German people how their armies could not break through even then? I think not.

On Wednesday, the 28th, there were but few attacks made, and the enemy's guns were almost idle. It was, however, but that solemn, deathly silence which seems to brood over an Eastern sea before the breaking of the typhoon. You may picture German G.H.Q., where William Hohenzollern is present in person, sending out through their admirable organisation the final orders for the great assault. You can see the officers and men of every unit making their last preparations, nerving themselves for a fight the issue of which cannot to them have been a moment in doubt.

Would you compare the two armies? Turn, then, to Shakespeare's *Henry V.* and read once again the fourth act, from the prologue to the closing scene. There shall you find it all set down in matchless verse. Here I can add nothing to that picture of genius.

★★★★★★

At daybreak on the 29th the storm burst. Heralded by a whirlwind of shells of every size, the German infantry charged down upon the devoted remnants of the First Corps, the 7th Division, and the cavalry.

And just as the tidal wave tears from the rocks the seaweed and limpet clinging fast, so was the 1st Division torn from its trenches and hurled back, gasping and blinded.

A moment's pause, the battalions turned, and, with the 2nd Division, crashed back again in a counter-attack.

A second time were the British forced back; a second time they recovered their ground. And so the fight swayed backwards and forwards. "Blinded, bloody and torn they reeled," but ever they won back again. And the enemy drew off, swearing that their spies had played them false, that there were two army corps facing them where they had thought it to be a division only.

"Another gap," they cried. "Take the break to the south where the cavalry are."

So another corps threw themselves at the men of the 7th Division. And the British cavalry, shattered remnants of two brigades, stood to it. Such was the weight of the enemy's gunnery that one troop of them was buried alive. The rest, o'erborne like the 1st Division, were thrust slowly back, struggling with impotent arms against the wave of Germans.

Back they went, clinging fast to every point of vantage—rallying, charging, and back again. An infantry battalion, close by, sees their plight and dashes straight at the Germans in a counter-charge. One skeleton of a battalion against eight German battalions! And that little one beat them, routed them; two score prisoners it took, ten score dead the Germans left behind.

Again and again the Germans charged; and the day passed into night—a night of blood-red flame and smoke. And still the British held the line. And ever the Germans drew back with their dying and their shame.

The blood-red night melted into a cold, grey dawn, and with the first hint of daylight the German gunners were at work again.

339

Now the British battalions are but little companies. The line which they have held is no more a line; but here and there are little groups of ghosts.

The Bavarians *must* capture Ypres. The "War Lord" is with them, and he commands. Therefore it must be.

And the ghosts of men who have said "No" through the last ten days of hell say "No" once again. It shall not be.

So the Bavarians came on and the British Infantry and the British Cavalry met them as they came.

In fair shock of battle they met. And they fought together as men have never fought before. Never at such odds have men fought. And the daylight drifted into darkness again.

All down the line the battle swayed this way and that. Here is a general in command of two companies of infantry; here a corporal acting as a battery commander—a battery of two guns. There is a junior subaltern leading his battalion in a desperate charge—a battalion of a hundred men. Every man is in. Here are cooks, grooms, officers' servants from a gunner battery lining up with picks and shovels, branches of trees, or bare fists. Why, in Heaven's name? To hold up and repulse half an advancing brigade.

"God of battles, was ever a battle like this in the world before?"

So wide was one of the gaps in the British line that a German corps had actually succeeded in marching through and taking up a position immediately to the flanks and rear of some half dozen of the skeleton battalions.

Then it was that these devoted regiments suddenly found themselves assailed, as it seemed, by their own comrades, for who save British should be behind them? Through the fog-laden, rain-soddened air the deadly streams of machinegun bullets tore through their ranks. And as the British crouched low and tried to peer into the mist to see how they should reply a Field Battery of ours poured its shells into the melee, unfortunately striking down several of our own men.

Who can tell the delirium of the hours that followed! The enemy to the front, to the rear, to the flank. A German Reserve Corps against the remnants of six British battalions, the men worn to a shadow by exposure, want of sleep, want of food. And yet they fought on. Now one battalion is gone, destroyed. A second has 150 men left out of 650, four officers out of sixteen. A third no officers and but a handful of junior N.C.O.'s to lead. And yet they fought on.

The slaughter of it all seems to pass human understanding. You hear of one single British company so surrounded by the enemy that the Germans did not even know it was there in the midst of them. And you hear of those few men within five minutes annihilating a German battalion, accounting for more than 800 of the strength. And still the enemy pour their masses into the battle.

You hear of the last remaining gun of a battery being brought into action on a road and fighting a duel at 500 yards range with a German field gun, knocking it out at last by a direct hit. Of a lance-corporal sitting in a shell-hole with a machine-gun firing methodically for an hour or more into the enemy ranks before they discover him—so mad is the confusion.

★★★★★★

And how do they fare in Ypres and Hooge, where the Divisional and Corps H.Q. are? Of what are the army chiefs thinking? Within three or four miles of the battle, sharing, too, in the storm of shell, there is never a hint of disaster. The staff go about their work as though the operations were fifty miles away.

The next evening there sped out of Ypres a dispatch-rider. One of those cheery souls he was who had come over with his motor-bicycle straight from a public school, all for the "fun of the thing." And what a record of gallantry, endurance and cheeriness under all hardships have those youngsters created.

"Carrying dispatches and messages at all hours of the day and night in every kind of weather, and often traversing bad roads blocked with transport, they have been conspicuously successful in maintaining an extraordinary degree of efficiency in the service of communications." That is the tribute of the commander-in-chief.

So Stanmore rode up and delivered his message.

"How are things going?" said I. "And how are you getting on?"

"Having a simply ripping time," said Stanmore, chuckling all over. "You never saw such fun as it was yesterday."

(This was some of the fighting I have just been telling about.)

"Oh," said I, "what was it?"

Stanmore sat down on a bench and nearly choked with laughing at his recollections.

"Had to get a message through to 1st Corps H.Q. at Hooge. Wipers! You ought to have seen Wipers.[1] It was too funny. Not a soul in the streets, every other house in the place burning like mad, and

---

1. I think Stanmore was mistaken in the name of the place. Ypres was not in this condition at the time.—Author.

shell pouring in all over the shop. I had to get off and wheel the bike because there wasn't any road left. Great shell-holes you could bury a 'bus in, and all the rest broken bricks and glass. It was a mess. One place I actually *had to pull up* because one of those Black Marias came along, took away the whole of a front of a house, went clean through and smashed into the house opposite. (Fits of laughter.) It was too silly to see all the floors and furniture just like a doll's-house. Dead horses and dogs and cats flying about. Two cats just missed me as they fell off a roof. A harlequinade wasn't in it. I simply rolled into a doorway and laughed till I could hardly see. Of course, H. Q. had been shelled out long ago, so no wonder I couldn't find the blessed place. Ran 'em to earth a bit later. Had the devil of a job getting back climbing over the ruins, and just as I was getting out of the town—oh, lord, you would have laughed—a big shell plumped down about 100 yards in front, and right out of the dust and smoke came one of our chaps wheeling his bike. The silly blighter had been and got a puncture." (Complete collapse of Stanmore.)

What German Army, I ask you, is going to contend against a spirit like that?

But it was a few days later that Stanmore brought the most delicious piece of news. Several of the staff of the 2nd Corps, being apparently bored with life and inaction (think of it!) had actually gone off to London on 48 hours' leave!

Leave, in the middle of all that fighting! It was really too gorgeous. And how mad the Germans would have been had they known.

Of course, one did not know then that the greater part of the 2nd Corps, being absolutely exhausted, had been withdrawn from the firing-line. Nor could one foresee that officers and men on active service were going to be given occasional home leave. At that time such an idea was incredible. In fact, when, about Christmas, a certain number of officers were told they might go back to England for 96 hours, several declined the leave, saying that they preferred to stay and see the business through. So convinced was everyone that two or three months at most would bring the end of the war. And of the officers who took the leave one at least returned before the 96 hours were up, being unable to bear the seeming apathy and ignorance of those at home.

★★★★★★

The third day of the great battle for Ypres had dawned. The 7th Division no longer existed as a command, and the heroic remnant had been placed under the orders of Sir Douglas Haig. Yet there could be no withdrawal of the men, for there was none to replace them. The line must still be held. Or if it can no longer be held, the Germans shall advance only over the English dead.

Once more came the whirlwind of shells; once more the blue-grey masses of the Germans swept down upon the defenders. At every point of the defence they struck. To the north where the 1st Division clung on grimly; at the 2nd Division, the 7th, the cavalry, and to the south at Messines, and where Pulteney's 3rd Corps fought.

Once again the 1st Division was swept back. And now as the very heavens seemed to rend apart with sheeted flame and pour down their deluge of thunderbolts, as the ground beneath rocked and heaved to the mighty concussion, so it seemed that exhausted nature at last snapped and broke and men went mad with the shock and horror of it.

The British were swept back, but some remained, remained to be clubbed down or trampled underfoot by the storming wave. The discipline which they had learned kept them there to the last, crouching in the pitted ground, but the brain of them had gone and left them helpless and unconscious, gibbering with unholy laughter.

"At all costs the line must be held," cried Sir Douglas Haig. And with the inspiration of their leader the division rallied. Once again the enemy advance was checked.

All down the salient and far to the south one British group of men after another (we cannot say battalions or companies) was hurled back; to rally and counter-charge, check and repulse the enemy. But, ah, the terrible price which must be paid for it!

Hour after hour passed and the issue still swung in the balance. Shortly after noon German shells crashed into the Headquarters of the 1st and 2nd Divisions, the brain centres of the corps. The general officers commanding the divisions were both put out of action, General Lomax wounded, General Monro unconscious; three staff officers of the 1st and three of the 2nd were all killed.

Within half an hour Sir John French was on the spot with Sir Douglas Haig. But nothing more could be done. The issue was in the hands of God.

From two to three o'clock the suspense was unbearable. It was the most critical moment in the whole battle, indeed since Mons, Sir John French has said.

You may picture those two men, the field-marshal and the general standing quietly by the great map spread on the table of the battered *château*: you see the staff going quietly about their work; and if the strain is telling you must needs look close into the eyes to detect it. There is nothing more to be done. Not even may any unit be withdrawn and thrust into another corner of the line. If the breach is made there can be no repairing. The seacoast and ports will be lost to us.

★★★★★★

Slowly the minutes pass. A quarter past two.—Twenty past.—Half-past. Are they holding still?

Suddenly over the wires comes the message, "The 1st and 2nd Divisions are *attacking* the German right."

General Landon, who, at a moment's notice, has taken over the command of General Lomax, is making the supreme effort.

The minutes pass.

Then, "German right being pushed back fast." Then, "Gheluvelt retaken—bayonet charge."

Is the tide turning? Can they do it?

Swiftly now come the messages. The left of the 7th Division is *attacking*. The 7th Division! Do you hear that? And they are *attacking*.

This retaking of Gheluvelt sets free some of the cavalry, the 6th Brigade, which has shared throughout in the glory of the 7th Division. Sir Douglas Haig seizes the chance on the moment, and the order is at once flashed to the brigade commander.

The squadron leaders (what matter the names of the regiments—they are of the 7th Division!) rub their eyes in astonishment. "Boot and saddle"? Horses? They must be crazy at H.Q.! But there is the order. "Get to it, lads!"

The lads get at their horses where they can, and the horses are as amazed as their masters. "This is a joke. Another ruddy route-march! ' But even a route-march is better than nothing.

"And where on earth have you been all these years?" say the horses, as they nuzzle for carrots.

"Sorry, old lady," says Trooper Tomkins. "Couldn't help it. Another job on. And a pretty —— one, too. But we're for it now. *Get up!*" And in goes the bit, on goes the saddle.

"Hurry up, boys," sing out squadron commanders; "not a moment to lose."

Squadrons fall in, some mounted, some on foot. And off they go hell-for-leather straight into the torn and tattered woods where the Germans lurk.

What a round up! "In at them, boys: get to it!" Horses crash and cannon off broken tree trunks in the headlong race; men on foot come smashing through the undergrowth, firing wildly from hip or shoulder as the Germans bolt from cover to cover. Clean through the wood they go; nothing can stop the amazing charge. Through the woods and out into the open again. On, on!

"It's Berlin this time, anyhow," gasps Trooper Tomkins.

At last they pull up as they throw themselves into a gap in the infantry line.

"Cheer-oh," says Private Williams as Tomkins drops down by his side. "'Ad a bit of a beano, 'aven't you?"

"Not 'alf," says Tomkins.

★★★★★★

By the late afternoon the British had won back almost all of their original positions, and before midnight; "the line as held in the morning had practically been reoccupied."

Just after the tide had turned, at 5.0 p.m., a French Cavalry Brigade got up to Hooge and pushed forward, dismounted, to the help of the Life Guards and Horse Guards.

And now turn to this little paragraph from Sir John French's dispatch:

> During the night touch was restored between the right of the 7th Division and left of the 2nd Brigade, and the cavalry were withdrawn into reserve, *the services of the French cavalry being dispensed with.*

Who can resist a thrill of ineffable pride in reading that last sentence? Hard set themselves, our gallant Allies had done all they could to send in time the needed support. Everywhere possible—a regiment here, a squadron there—they had given through those days of crisis; but the strong, solid reinforcement which would have meant so much was beyond their power until later.

No, it had been a square fight between British and German, and the British commander-in-chief was determined that once the tide had turned the day should be to his men alone. So I read it.

★★★★★★

The day was won, the crisis was safely passed. But the cost of it in human lives and suffering had been a terrible one. The flower of England's chivalry, her knights and yeomen had perished. The Old Regular Army had fought its last fight—the last, the greatest of all.

And it was in the noblest cause for which England has ever sent forth her sons.

Of the 7th Division, less than one month before there had sailed from England 400 officers. Forty-four returned. Their men had numbered 12,000. There were left 2,336.

"We thought," said a German officer, "that you had four army corps against us there."

In every division the tale was almost as heavy. The 1st Division and the 2nd Division lost nearly three-fourths of their strength. The 1st and 2nd Cavalry Divisions each lost a half.

Forty thousand men is the loss which they say the British suffered. Of the Germans there fell perhaps 250,000.

That it was a victory, and a decisive victory for our arms there can surely be no doubt. The Germans set out to achieve a definite object: they failed. The British determined to defeat that scheme: they succeeded. How the enemy failed, though massing against the defenders such overwhelming strength, we cannot say. And yet may we not cry in all reverence—

> *O God, Thy arm was here;*
> *And not to us, but to Thy arm alone,*
> *Ascribe we all!—When, without stratagem,*
> *But in plain shock and even play of battle,*
> *Was ever known so great and little loss*
> *On one part and on the other?—Take it, God,*
> *For it is none but Thine!*

And England never knew.

★★★★★★

There I leave the narrative. Much more might be told of the days that followed; of the stern fight waged unceasingly through November and December; of the attacks by the Prussian Guard; of the misery of that first awful winter in the trenches, when men lived and fought waist-deep in icy water and freezing mud; of the incredible cheerfulness, the unconquerable gaiety which met and overcame every hardship.

But the Last Stand of the Old Army is a fitting end. From now onwards the magnificent fighting qualities of the Territorial and New Army units were thrown into the scale, and the remnant of the Old Army, with the splendour of its traditions and the inspiration of its record, became the heart centre of the Army of a People.

There is in England today not a family which does not mourn the irretrievable loss of its own manhood—a son, it may be, the last of the line; a husband; a brother; a lover; a dear friend.

Many there are whose loved ones fought and died during those first four months of this great War of Liberation. They have, perhaps, no trinket of ribboned cross or order to show, to hold out and exclaim with tears of pride: "This my beloved won on such and such a day."

And yet, did they but understand, theirs is a treasure far more precious than any ribboned trinket, any so-called "honour." It is the treasure of a memory that he was ready to serve England when England called; ready to give all that he had to give at Her demand. Had it not been so his name would not now be emblazoned upon the Scroll of Honour amongst those of the men who fought at Mons, at the Aisne, at Ypres.

Whatever his motive—a love of adventure, an impatience with the trivial things of everyday life, a desire, perhaps, to wipe out some past misdeed—whatever it may have been, he was ready. And so to him there befell the proudest lot which a man may know—to die on the field of honour. Nay, more than this: to die in the company of such men as those who faced the fearful odds of the opening months of this war.

For what prouder thing can a woman say to-day than: "My husband, my son, was one of those who held the Ypres gate with the Old Army," or "He was one of the old 'Contemptibles'"?

There, indeed, is the honour. And the memory of it, though locked deep in the heart that no man may see, is dearer far than any decoration that the sovereign may bestow. For all who so fought are worthy of the bestowal.

★★★★★★

And, oh! may England never, never forget the debt she owes to those of her sons who fought for her then! For with the passing years the memory grows dim, and in times that are gone our people have sometimes forgotten.

But today it is the *Nation* which fights, and it is the *People* who shall see that justice is done. Justice and generosity to the living; justice and generosity to the dead and to their loved ones who once leaned upon them.

The great fight for *Freedom* is not yet won. For weary months—for years, perhaps—the bloody shadow of war may darken the world. But the end, and triumph, is certain if England and her Allies will, with all their heart and soul, but dedicate themselves to the unfinished work which their honoured dead "have thus far so nobly advanced."

And when at last the morning of a new life has dawned upon the world; when the day is set for the kings and captains of the people humbly to kneel with the nation before the throne of the Great Protector of the Universe and there to offer up their prayers of Thanksgiving—then, too, let England remember.

For in that mighty concourse shall a place be set apart—a place of the highest honour that all men may see, and seeing may remember—"That few, that happy few, that band of brothers."

So to a deathly silence shall the cheering die away. And through the silence, with dim, phantasmal tread, there shall pass the muster of the men who died. But first of that great army of Shadows to pass to the place of honour set for them shall march the immortal souls of those who, in 1914, saved England, who saved the world from the bondage of Hell.

Who shall sing the Song of them,
The wonder and the strength of them,
The gaiety and tenderness
They bore across the sea?
In every heart's the Song of them,
The debt that England owes to them,
The chivalry and fearlessness
That strove—and won Her free.

Authors Note

WITH SOME OBSERVATIONS UPON A SUBJECT OF IMPORTANCE

Seeing that comparatively few persons trouble to read any "preface" which a book may carry I am placing this particular one at the end of the volume instead of at the beginning so as not to interfere with a direct plunge into the narrative. Yet a preface may upon occasion serve a useful purpose, even though it be written for the satisfaction of the author rather than for the enlightenment of the reader. This one will, I hope, serve both ends.

Firstly, then, it seems well to explain that the design of this book differs, deliberately, from that of the former volume, *The Retreat from Mons*. This for two reasons. When *The Retreat* was written no account of that episode, embracing an outline of the military operations with an estimate of the more human side of the achievement, had been published. So the story was told upon those lines. And as it was an episode definite in itself, possessing also a clear-cut, artistic unity, the story was not a difficult one to tell.

But when the tide turned and one came to deal with an enormous battle-front and ever-increasing numbers the artistic unity vanished. Also it became impossible to combine a clear survey of the operations with the story of human endeavour—the spirit of the enterprise. The British public cares little enough about the former, but does wish to hear of the latter. And as my war work is, for the most part, concerned with the great majority rather than with the small minority, my choice of theme was at once decided. Besides, two or three admirable accounts of the military operations have been published, and there will be more to follow.

My idea, then, was to try to supplement these histories by a personal suggestion of what those months of September and October, 1914, looked like to the men of the Old Army. To set down a series of impressions gleaned from the very heart of those big happenings; impressions of events which stand out in one's mind like trees upon a skyline. The titles to the chapters will show how I went to work.

That was my original idea, and having little more than that in mind I was strongly averse from the compiling of such a book. It would lack, I felt, the great essential of every artwork. However, upon certain urgent representations, I began the writing. And, as I wrote, the form and purpose of the work became more clear. If I have succeeded in the task the nature of that purpose will be apparent: if I have failed the purpose matters not.

I should like it that this volume may be read as a companion to the previous one. Partly because it is a continuation of the narrative, although in a different form, but more particularly because several of the descriptions in *The Retreat* apply to similar situations in this volume: the German massed attacks, for instance.

One other point. It will be found that the chapters, or "Impressions" as I should prefer to call them, are as nearly as possible in order of time, keeping to the sequence of the military operations.

There is very little in this book, so far as incidents are concerned, which has not been a matter of personal observation or deduction. But there are some acknowledgments not already made in the text which I must make here.

To the genius of William Shakespeare I owe perhaps the greatest debt of all. His nobly patriotic and prophetic play, *Henry V.*, has not only helped to inspire my narrative, but from this play alone I have once again collected the little gems of thought and expression which I have threaded upon my story like pearls upon a cord.

In Chapter 6 I have quoted from two poems by Miss C. A. Renshaw, taken from her recently published volume, *England's Boys* (Erskine Macdonald). Of contemporary authors of military works I am indebted for occasional reference and verification of facts to Sir Arthur Conan Doyle (*The British Campaign in France and Flanders*), and to Lieut.-Colonel John Buchan (*Nelson's History of the War*). Through the courtesy of Lady Helen Forbes I am indebted to Major Ian Forbes, Royal Scots Fusiliers, for the outlines of one or two incidents included in Chapters XVII and XVIII: while Lieut.-General Sir David Henderson very kindly gave me some of the details which I have included in Chapter 6. Apart from the above, and one or two official publications, I have, of necessity, been compelled to write away from any library of reference. Nor have I any collection of "personal narrative" from which to draw.

I owe a special debt of gratitude to Lieut. Colonel Brindsley Fitzgerald for the care with which he has read my narrative in order to ensure its accuracy, and for making several suggestions, all of which I have adopted.

I must also express my thanks to Captain C. T. Atkinson, who has once again helped me with the Roll of Honour; and to Mr. J. H. Hartley, for embodying my suggestions in his spirited picture cover, (first edition).

Of the hideous and brutal side of the war I have tried to write with as much reticence as possible. Similarly on the subject of German Atrocities. No description, however vivid the writing may be, no pictures no photographs can ever bring the facts home to people who have not actually suffered. And yet I am interested to find that no passage in the earlier volume has been more widely quoted in the Allied and neutral countries than the one which described the mutilation of a little child. I only hope that the incidents described in this volume under the heading "*Kultur*" (Chapter 3) may become as widely known.

"There should be no false, vapid sentiment in refusing to think about these things." If I may be allowed to repeat myself: "There should not be a home in the British Empire where the facts of German atrocities are not known, and where, in realising them, hearts are not nerved to yield their last drop of blood in stamping out from the world of men the hideous Thing which has done them."

And there is no human brain that can conceive the nameless things which those monsters of infamy would do to English women and children if opportunity once served. Yet, today in England there are very many towns and villages where soldiers in training are regarded as interlopers, as interfering with business or disturbing the fair peace of the countryside. Or if not as interlopers then as fit subjects for robbery and extortion on the part of tradesmen, lodging-house keepers and others. This is a shameful thing, so that one conies to exclaim, "Is it for such men and women as these that our sailors and soldiers are fighting?"

★★★★★★

The root of this and similar ignorance is, of course, the lack of education, of enlightenment in war facts and ideas. The public generally are kept in ignorance of the course of events, or are misled by false optimism on the part of their responsible advisers, or are unable to appraise events at their real value. With the existence of a properly co-ordinated system of enlightenment these failings would be minimised.

A case in point was that of the first announcement of the Battle of Jutland Bank. On the Saturday when the first official intimation was published (a tale of disaster, it will be remembered) it chanced that I was in a great industrial city of the Midlands. It did not need five minutes to realise that the real truth was being withheld, and that the report would have the most mischievous effect on the public. There was little I could do to counteract it, but that little I did, and it proved effective so far as that district was concerned. I at once telephoned to the managers of the theatres and music-halls of the city and obtained a very cordial assent to address their audiences for ten minutes at each performance. Thus I was enabled to get directly at several thousand people of a big centre, to suggest to them the real facts, and to revive in them a faith which the morning's announcement had badly shaken.

M. Sarraut, Minister of Public Instruction in France, has put the case for enlightenment in a few admirable words:

"Education is a special personal means of seconding the efforts of our armies. Its role is, indeed, so to act that the entire Country shall know why it is fighting—for what past, for what future, for what facts, for what ideas; and thus, by informing national opinion with this knowledge, to maintain and strengthen the Country. in its unshakable confidence in, and its desire for complete victory."

In a scheme such as this one has to hammer for a long time at the doors of an unimaginative officialdom before they are opened. And the reference to personal work in this direction will, I trust, be forgiven, for it is only made to indicate what might be done. For two years now, since July, 1915, I have been hammering at those doors. At that time a comprehensive scheme was submitted to each individual member of the then government, and it was backed up with cordiality by every responsible journal (save one) in the kingdom. You will find the scheme outlined in the *English Review* of November, 1915. Some measure of success has been won, but this is infinitesimal compared with what might be done.

Take the work of the navy, for instance. It is the one subject above all else which appeals to our nation. They have the tang of the sea, the centuries-old tradition of an island race in their very blood. They love to hear what their sailors are doing and how the Grand Fleet does its work. The ignorance upon the most elementary facts is simply astounding. It is an ignorance which militates seriously against national effort. If one man, working unofficially and in his spare time, can give in a winter season seventy-six "popular" recitals on the work of the Navy and so bring the facts home to thousands of the general public and the troops, what might not be done under a carefully organised scheme?

Besides, apart from other considerations, the public ought to know. It is their right. Our navy, like our army, is not a race apart. It is *us*, our flesh and blood, a part of one big family. We are all working together to one common end. We cannot work together with the whole-hearted enthusiasm which the *cause* demands if one half of us is kept in ignorance of what the other half is doing. And, be it noted, the ignorant half is the one which supplies the "sinews of war."

I would particularly emphasise the need for a comprehensive organisation, because it is a project which necessarily demands such detailed and thorough methods and a man endowed with a practical imagination to direct them. To attempt a "muddling through" policy is futile.

As I write there has just been constituted a "War Aims Committee," designed to keep before the public the ideals for which we are fighting. The idea, so far as it goes, is excellent, and the committee, with its staff of helpers, will, I am sure, do excellent work. But it is only one more example of our traditional method of tinkering at a job by fits and starts instead of tackling the real project as a whole, visualising it in its entirety and getting a grip on to it. Incidentally, the work of this Committee will everywhere be recognised as being of an "official" nature. Any propaganda which bears such a mark can only be moderately successful.

Now here is another example of the practical effect of propaganda work. A well-known Member of Parliament, but a man of the people, and incidentally an admirable "popular" lecturer, went down to a great engineering works to lecture on "Trawlers and Mine-Sweeping." For this he received a trifling fee. A week later the managing director wrote to him to this effect:

"If we had paid you a fee five times as large we should still regard it as the finest investment we have ever made. Since your talk to our employees the *quality and output of their work have gone up twenty-five per cent.*"

No one, of course, would have anything revealed the knowledge of which might help the enemy. (All this has been said so often.) But while our people are remarkably patient, they have long since come to view with suspicion the official statement that such and such a fact has not been published because it would give the enemy information. On the other hand, when the First Lord of the Admiralty, in response to the strong popular demand for information upon the number of German submarines sunk, very frankly stated the precise reasons why the figures could not be given everybody immediately understood, and there was an end of the matter. The public must be told the facts; or if the facts may not be told the reason why must be plainly stated. That is the long and short of it. This is a war of peoples and principles, not of professional armies.

It is to me so incredible that after three years of war, during which the nation has risen to such splendid heights of self-denial, sacrifice and calmness under adversity, the people should not be considered worthy of confidence and trust. I can as readily understand the curious mentality of the German rulers. It is not merely wrong, it is worse—it is foolish.

It is foolish because every hour we are drawing nearer to a crisis when the people are going to speak, and with no uncertain voice. And unless the facts are perfectly clear in their minds there may follow disaster.

The public comments and demands consequent upon the humiliating air-raid over London on July 7, 1917, indicated very forcibly how public agitation might develop. It will be remembered, too, that that raid followed directly upon the revelations of the Mesopotamian debacle. Public confidence in the government was shaken to its depths. The people, in their magnificent loyalty, must be trusted. If there is a feeling that that loyalty is misplaced they will certainly demand a complete reconstruction—and they will secure it.

Keep the people informed and you keep them inspired. It is the one factor most needed to ensure that the national effort shall be kept tuned up to concert pitch.

Sir William Robertson has said:

"There comes a time in every war when the strain is heavier every day, is almost intolerable, and when a little extra effort will suffice to turn the scale. That time is coming now; and in this war, as in all others, victory will incline to that side which can best preserve the cohesion and courage and endurance of the nation."

Nor is it the mere publication of facts which is in question. There is also the necessity for presenting them to the public so that those who read may understand; the need for intelligent criticism and comment on the part of the Press. We have always been proud of the freedom which our Press has enjoyed in the past, and to it we can trace the working of many a reform. But if this freedom of discussion is denied or stifled the people immediately find themselves living in a world of suspicion and rumour. Not only are the public shackled, but the government also. For it is upon the Press that the government depends in great measure for a faithful reflection of public opinion.

There is also a very large section of the community which seldom reads a newspaper; men and women whose estimate of public affairs is generally derived from headlines and catch phrases. These, too, must be adequately catered for—and they were provided for in the scheme.

With one or two notable exceptions publicity schemes during the past have failed because (so it seems to me) they have been too academic. There has been no real attempt to force an entrance into the heart and mind of the big public. It has been like sending a University Extension lecturer to talk to the huge popular audience which nightly crowds to see a Lyceum melodrama. Apart from such a man as the present Premier, Lloyd George, those who have proved the most successful in propaganda work, recruiting and the like during the past three years, have been men like Horatio Bottomley, George Robey and Harry Lauder. Neither Robey nor Lauder is an orator, as one understands the term, but they do know how to grip a popular audience from the first moment of their appearance on the platform, and they know, from long experience, exactly what tells with such an audience.

If you want to get the facts and ideas of this War of Liberation home to the British public you must be ready to compete with the cheap novel, the music-hall and picture-palace, and to beat them on their own ground.

Emphatically you do not require politicians for such work. Propaganda, as I have suggested, is most effective when it is carefully disguised. The man in the street shies violently at the mere suggestion of education. But administer your dose like the powder in a spoonful of jam, and it will readily be swallowed. Here is an instance of one piece of propaganda work which has proved particularly effective.

In November, 1916, a certain well-known composer published a spirited and simple musical setting of a stirring ballad on *The Battle of Jutland Bank*. He did so in order that the general public might learn the facts of that naval victory of ours. It was placed on the market at two-pence a copy, all profits going to Naval War Charities. Today that song, taken up by the L.C.C. and other Educational Authorities, is being sung in schools throughout the Empire; it has won to popularity in the fleet and in the army, especially amongst the overseas troops; and it will undoubtedly in the future find a place of honour amongst those songs of the sea which we all love so well. Thus the song is helping to inspire the younger generation; and thousands of men and women are learning for the first time of the gallantry and work of our sailors in that particular battle.

The above is but a trifling incident, but it will perhaps suggest other useful methods in an organised scheme; also my meaning in advocating that a man of practical imagination, with broad human sympathies and a general knowledge in catering for popular entertainment, is the right kind of man to direct the organisation.

Take, for instance, the most obvious medium of enlightenment—"popular" lectures. There are very few men and women in the country—twenty, thirty, shall we say?—who can do such entertaining work on war topics with success. But no attempt has yet been made to utilise the services even of these persons, w r hen a trifling subsidy of a guinea per lecture would have secured them. Further, the man who for years past has directed the only Lecture Agency in the country, and who knows more about such work than any man in the kingdom, has never been invited to help the Government. Oh, yes, his name has been brought to official notice at least twice.

On the other hand, propaganda in Allied and neutral countries is really being conducted with success. But for propaganda at home—where it is most needed—there is no money and no real organisation. "We couldn't think of such a thing," says officialdom; "there is no precedent for it."

Then there is the drama, another admirable medium; sketches in the music-halls; telling films for the cinema houses; the issue of broadsheets by county newspapers to keep their readers informed of the deeds of the local regiments; the effective distribution in pamphlet form of "popular" war stories and articles by competent authors—but all these points were urged two years ago, and we still go on in the same old way, discouraging individual effort and refusing to allow an organised one. "There is no precedent!"

There is a strong feeling, which is growing in intensity, especially in the business and industrial circles of the Midlands and the North, that we are fast becoming lost in a maze of ideals without formulating any lear-cut policy of practical effort by which such ideals may be realised. After three years of appalling slaughter of human beings, and of colossal material destruction, we are still talking vaguely about the rights of democracy and the new life which is coming. But your hard-headed business man does not bother much about ideals, save indirectly. He wants to know where he stands. He wants a straight proposition at which he may work. Given that, he is ready to go on for another ten years if necessary.

We know in broad outline why we are fighting, and to what end. We have read the speeches of Mr. Asquith and President Wilson and half a score other leaders. We turn over on our tongues the sonorous phrases about "never sheathing the sword," or "the principles of civilisation and the liberties of Europe," and we are justly proud that such ideals should be ours. But there is a feeling abroad that the time has come when these ideals should be translated into the language of practical business.

"We intend to win this war," says, in effect, our old friend the man in the street, "but we want the job over at the earliest possible moment. How many aeroplanes do you want? 20,000? Certainly, you shall have them. Anything else?"

That is the attitude of the nation. They have given a blank cheque to be filled in to any sum. But this "nation of shopkeepers" possesses business instincts, and it is not content to go on indefinitely under existing conditions.

Nor should this policy of enlightenment be concerned only with current war facts and ideas. There are the details attending the conclusion of peace, together with the system of demobilisation; and there are the projects to be taken in hand after the war. One may perhaps summarise the three under the words inspiration, realisation, reconstruction. Under each heading a definite policy is demanded—so far as experience and human foresight can provide them. Each policy must be a national one, discussed and framed by the newly chosen representatives of the people. To this end a comprehensive scheme of education is obviously essential in order that the facts may be clear for such discussion and decision. Under neither of the two last headings have any concrete proposals been published, and that is why I suggest that we are still groping in the fog of ideals.

Surely by now the Allied Governments have formulated, at least in outline, the terms of peace which they intend to dictate. I use the word *dictate* because in certain quarters there seems to be some idea that the Allies propose to "discuss" peace terms with the enemy. That, of course, is impossible. Let the terms be as just, as wise and as moderate as may be, but there will be no discussion save only amongst the governments who will dictate them.

Again, under that same heading of Realisation, the people must be prepared for the process of demobilisation—of the armies, of the workers at home. It is surprising (and yet is it surprising?) how few persons realise what an intricate business that is going to be. An affair of years, perhaps.

Presumably some scheme is already in hand, with the actual details being gradually filled in. But the general public knows nothing about it, and if peace were to come suddenly (as it probably will) there would be chaos unless the public knew what to expect.

Under the third heading, the process which has come to be known as reconstruction, the points for discussion are endless. Agriculture, town planning, emigration, work or provision for the war-disabled, and a hundred other themes. These quite apart from the determined attempt which must be made to secure a lasting World Peace and an end for ever of the hideous slaughter of modern war. This generation will but initiate many of the schemes, but it is for us to see that the foundations are well and truly laid.

How and by whom is it all going to be done? Certainly not by men who are neither in touch with nor representative of the nation. The women, by the way, the leaders of their sex in this country, are just now far more closely in touch with the people than are the men.

But, so far as this country is concerned, it will be done by men and women who are of the people and elected under a newly devised and equitable franchise. And that they may be worthily elected it is necessary that there should be a widespread knowledge and appreciation of the issues at stake. An appreciation, too, that England is but one nation in a great Brotherhood of Nations. For it is in this knowledge, and the use to which we put it, that our future lies. This, and this only, so I believe, is the security which we can build up, and upon which we can wholly rely, against the havoc of another such war of hate and aggression.

If we fail in that dissemination of knowledge, if we stumble blindly upon victory, then all that we have suffered, all the lessons taught by this newly revealed brotherhood, all our individual sacrifices may have been in vain. England will not win this war with honour to herself unless she wins as a nation. The national service we demand can never be given until the people see with eyes of understanding.

Let England, Great Britain if you will, look to herself as her comrade nations of Canada, Australia, South Africa and the others will look to themselves. Then, in the fullness of time, with enhanced right and pride, will she take her predestined place in that great Federation of Parliaments which we all look to as the aftermath of this glorious rally to our *standard*, and of the *victory* which that rally ensures.

A. Corbett-Smith.

London,
September, 1917

LEONAUR

ALSO FROM LEONAUR
AVAILABLE IN SOFTCOVER OR HARDCOVER WITH DUST JACKET

THE RELUCTANT REBEL *by William G. Stevenson*—A young Kentuckian's experiences in the Confederate Infantry & Cavalry during the American Civil War..

BOOTS AND SADDLES *by Elizabeth B. Custer*—The experiences of General Custer's Wife on the Western Plains.

FANNIE BEERS' CIVIL WAR *by Fannie A. Beers*—A Confederate Lady's Experiences of Nursing During the Campaigns & Battles of the American Civil War.

LADY SALE'S AFGHANISTAN *by Florentia Sale*—An Indomitable Victorian Lady's Account of the Retreat from Kabul During the First Afghan War.

THE TWO WARS OF MRS DUBERLY *by Frances Isabella Duberly*—An Intrepid Victorian Lady's Experience of the Crimea and Indian Mutiny.

THE REBELLIOUS DUCHESS *by Paul F. S. Dermoncourt*—The Adventures of the Duchess of Berri and Her Attempt to Overthrow French Monarchy.

LADIES OF WATERLOO *by Charlotte A. Eaton, Magdalene de Lancey & Juana Smith*—The Experiences of Three Women During the Campaign of 1815: Waterloo Days by Charlotte A. Eaton, A Week at Waterloo by Magdalene de Lancey & Juana's Story by Juana Smith.

TWO YEARS BEFORE THE MAST *by Richard Henry Dana. Jr.*—The account of one young man's experiences serving on board a sailing brig—the Penelope—bound for California, between the years1834-36.

A SAILOR OF KING GEORGE *by Frederick Hoffman*—From Midshipman to Captain—Recollections of War at Sea in the Napoleonic Age 1793-1815.

LORDS OF THE SEA *by A. T. Mahan*—Great Captains of the Royal Navy During the Age of Sail.

COGGESHALL'S VOYAGES: VOLUME 1 *by George Coggeshall*—The Recollections of an American Schooner Captain.

COGGESHALL'S VOYAGES: VOLUME 2 *by George Coggeshall*—The Recollections of an American Schooner Captain.

TWILIGHT OF EMPIRE *by Sir Thomas Ussher & Sir George Cockburn*—Two accounts of Napoleon's Journeys in Exile to Elba and St. Helena: Narrative of Events by Sir Thomas Ussher & Napoleon's Last Voyage: Extract of a diary by Sir George Cockburn.

LEONAUR

ALSO FROM LEONAUR
AVAILABLE IN SOFTCOVER OR HARDCOVER WITH DUST JACKET

ESCAPE FROM THE FRENCH *by Edward Boys*—A Young Royal Navy Midshipman's Adventures During the Napoleonic War.

THE VOYAGE OF H.M.S. PANDORA *by Edward Edwards R. N. & George Hamilton, edited by Basil Thomson*—In Pursuit of the Mutineers of the Bounty in the South Seas—1790-1791.

MEDUSA *by J. B. Henry Savigny and Alexander Correard and Charlotte-Adélaïde Dard* —Narrative of a Voyage to Senegal in 1816 & The Sufferings of the Picard Family After the Shipwreck of the Medusa.

THE SEA WAR OF 1812 VOLUME 1 *by A. T. Mahan*—A History of the Maritime Conflict.

THE SEA WAR OF 1812 VOLUME 2 *by A. T. Mahan*—A History of the Maritime Conflict.

WETHERELL OF H. M. S. HUSSAR *by John Wetherell*—The Recollections of an Ordinary Seaman of the Royal Navy During the Napoleonic Wars.

THE NAVAL BRIGADE IN NATAL *by C. R. N. Burne*—With the Guns of H. M. S. Terrible & H. M. S. Tartar during the Boer War 1899-1900.

THE VOYAGE OF H. M. S. BOUNTY *by William Bligh*—The True Story of an 18th Century Voyage of Exploration and Mutiny.

SHIPWRECK! *by William Gilly*—The Royal Navy's Disasters at Sea 1793-1849.

KING'S CUTTERS AND SMUGGLERS: 1700-1855 *by E. Keble Chatterton*—A unique period of maritime history-from the beginning of the eighteenth to the middle of the nineteenth century when British seamen risked all to smuggle valuable goods from wool to tea and spirits from and to the Continent.

CONFEDERATE BLOCKADE RUNNER *by John Wilkinson*—The Personal Recollections of an Officer of the Confederate Navy.

NAVAL BATTLES OF THE NAPOLEONIC WARS *by W. H. Fitchett*—Cape St. Vincent, the Nile, Cadiz, Copenhagen, Trafalgar & Others.

PRISONERS OF THE RED DESERT *by R. S. Gwatkin-Williams*—The Adventures of the Crew of the Tara During the First World War.

U-BOAT WAR 1914-1918 *by James B. Connolly/Karl von Schenk*—Two Contrasting Accounts from Both Sides of the Conflict at Sea During the Great War.

LEONAUR

ALSO FROM LEONAUR

AVAILABLE IN SOFTCOVER OR HARDCOVER WITH DUST JACKET

THE 9TH—THE KING'S (LIVERPOOL REGIMENT) IN THE GREAT WAR 1914 - 1918 *by Enos H. G. Roberts*—Mersey to mud—war and Liverpool men.

THE GAMBARDIER *by Mark Severn*—The experiences of a battery of Heavy artillery on the Western Front during the First World War.

FROM MESSINES TO THIRD YPRES *by Thomas Floyd*—A personal account of the First World War on the Western front by a 2/5th Lancashire Fusilier.

THE IRISH GUARDS IN THE GREAT WAR - VOLUME 1 *by Rudyard Kipling*—Edited and Compiled from Their Diaries and Papers—The First Battalion.

THE IRISH GUARDS IN THE GREAT WAR - VOLUME 1 *by Rudyard Kipling*—Edited and Compiled from Their Diaries and Papers—The Second Battalion.

ARMOURED CARS IN EDEN *by K. Roosevelt*—An American President's son serving in Rolls Royce armoured cars with the British in Mesopatamia & with the American Artillery in France during the First World War.

CHASSEUR OF 1914 *by Marcel Dupont*—Experiences of the twilight of the French Light Cavalry by a young officer during the early battles of the great war in Europe.

TROOP HORSE & TRENCH *by R.A. Lloyd*—The experiences of a British Lifeguardsman of the household cavalry fighting on the western front during the First World War 1914-18.

THE EAST AFRICAN MOUNTED RIFLES *by C.J. Wilson*—Experiences of the campaign in the East African bush during the First World War.

THE LONG PATROL *by George Berrie*—A Novel of Light Horsemen from Gallipoli to the Palestine campaign of the First World War.

THE FIGHTING CAMELIERS *by Frank Reid*—The exploits of the Imperial Camel Corps in the desert and Palestine campaigns of the First World War.

STEEL CHARIOTS IN THE DESERT *by S. C. Rolls*—The first world war experiences of a Rolls Royce armoured car driver with the Duke of Westminster in Libya and in Arabia with T.E. Lawrence.

WITH THE IMPERIAL CAMEL CORPS IN THE GREAT WAR *by Geoffrey Inchbald*—The story of a serving officer with the British 2nd battalion against the Senussi and during the Palestine campaign.